THE CASCADES

TITLE PAGE PHOTOGRAPH Skiing at Mount Baker, on Artists' Point. (Photo by Bob & Ira Spring)

CONTENTS

ILLUSTRATIONS

ACKNOWLEDGMENTS: Photographs number 1, 4, 6, 10, 13, 16, 17, 25, 27, 28, 29, 30, and 31 are printed by courtesy of Ira & Bob Spring; numbers 2, 14, and 15, by courtesy of Al Monner; numbers 3, 5, 12, 24, and 26, courtesy of Ray Atkeson; numbers 8 and 9, courtesy of K S Brown; numbers 11 and 21, courtesy of William L Dawson from the National Audubon Society; number 23, courtesy Edward F. Dana from the National Audubon Society, number 18, courtesy Alfred M Bailey from the National Audubon Society; number 22, courtesy W. E. Shore from the National Audubon Society; number 20, courtesy Gayle Pickwell from the National Audubon Society; number 19, courtesy Ruth and H. D. Wheeler from the National Audubon Society; number 7, courtesy of the Art Commercial Studios.

INTRODUCTION

by Roderick Peattie

The Cascades are the last frontier of our mountains. They are essentially a wilderness. Even in places frequented by the casual tourist, as Timberline Lodge on Mount Hood or Paradise Inn on Mount Rainier or a visit to Crater Lake, one has upon oneself a sense of the wilderness immediately at hand and calling to be explored. So real and ever-present is this calling that it has brought together adventurous souls into groups because of their skill in mountaineering or their knowledge of secret trails. No range has so many mountain clubs, and each has a sense of ownership of the Cascades. There is a greater number of people of Portland, Seattle, and Tacoma who belong to such organizations, I suspect, than of any of the piedmont cities of the world. The byways and lonely paths, so little known to the public, are not secrets to them, or the trails among the trees of this greatest of American forests, the wild streams that are unbelievably exciting to fish, or the way to some distant peak unmarked by a trail. As a group, the people of the Northwest have a tremendous pride in the ownership.

So on summer week ends there is a steady stream of men, women, and children, each with the informal dress of the camper or hiker, from the cities and every town on the flanks of the mountains, going to very special places which are known only to them. Even in winter evenings they are busy planning their equipment for alpine climbs, their parapher- nalia for camping, lovingly putting their fishing gear in or- der, fixing a new carryall for their camera, or studying their flower or bird guide. Then comes summer and high enthusi- asm; with knapsacks on their backs or the trunk of the car packed to the limit, they start on their adventures. But win- ter is not confined to planners of summer trips. In winter there are the skiers, dressed in gay clothes, each headed for a loved destination. Indeed, the skiers find joy even in the summertime in the higher altitudes. There are not only ski tows and special runs for the beginner or the professional, but there are the almost unlimited miles of lonely slopes to be explored by the more daring. I know of no mountain area more completely, pridefully, and possessively claimed by a people than the mountains of the Pacific Northwest.

The Cascades lie principally in Washington and Oregon just east of Puget Sound lowland and the Willamette Val- ley. They run the entire depth of the states and include a little of California. They are divided in the middle by the Columbia River, forming a southern and a northern range. Moreover, the southern and northern parts have a somewhat different character because of the differing geology. The southern section is the more volcanic half and counts at least 120 volcanic peaks. Lassen Peak of California, 10,453 feet in altitude, was active from 1914 to 1921. Mount Shasta is one of the most prominent cones in America, reaching an elevation of 14,161 feet above sea level and more than two miles above the surroundings. It bears the Whitney Glacier, with a length of almost two miles. North of this in Oregon comes Crater Lake, and, last, Mount Hood, a peak much beloved by all in search of sport.

In the northern Cascades, Mount Rainier raises its splendid head to an elevation of 14,408 feet, and the foot of the mountain lies almost at sea level. On it are glaciers which descend in places to about 4,000 feet. One hundred miles north is Glacier Peak, from the top of which fifty glaciers are in sight. And, lastly, near the Canadian border, rises Mount Baker. This volcano was last active in 1870 and emitted smoke in 1903. In between the volcanic peaks are a confusion of low mountains, with few passes and literally hundreds of small glaciers, intensely glaciated valleys, and lakes. One lake is made by the damming up of a glaciated gorge by a moraine. This is Lake Chelan, a splendid sheet of water 88 miles in length. Its surface is 1,079 feet in elevation, and yet it is 1,419 feet deep, making its bottom 340 feet below sea level. The latitude of these mountains is far enough to the north to permit a relatively low altitude for a snow line, and the depth of snow increases mightily as one goes upward, until an average of 430 inches annually is achieved. Accounting for such heavy snowfall, the winters have a good deal of overcast sky, but the summers are high in sunshine. The western slope receives great snowfalls whereas the east has decidedly less, as would be expected in a belt of westerly winds.

There are so many who feel themselves authorities on this phase or that of Cascade mountain life that it was difficult to choose among them. Moreover, there are people who hold that the southern Cascades are particularly the mountains that they love, while, on the other hand, there are those who worship the northern Cascades and them alone.

The writers chosen have a nice impartiality and a fine knowledge of the whole of the mountain range. To Seattle and Portland I turned for most of them, but I have even gone to the towns on the east side to complete the list, and as far afield as Arizona. I offer them with distinct pride.

There are relatively few people living with the mountains, and of the few Margaret Bundy Callahan has been chosen to write their story. She is the one woman on the list of writers, and yet it is her task to write the story of their hardy life. She has been a newspaper and magazine writer in the Northwest for some years, but she began trips into the Cascades during her girlhood. After her marriage to Kenneth Callahan, a distinguished painter, she began a life work of exploring the peaks and hidden valleys of the mountains. For the last ten years they and their son have spent summers and every possible week end in the Mount Pilchuck region on their 160-acre tree farm which they call "Hemlock Heaven." I tell this story in detail not because it is so unusual but because it is so typical of lovers of the Cascades.

Grant McConnell was a find. He lives in Stehekin, Washington, on the east side of the mountains. He began education in Reed College and then went to Harvard and later to Oxford as a Rhodes scholar. He then settled down to write, and has written much upon the geography and history of the Cascades. He distinctly is one of those with whom the cult of the mountains is a prime matter. His is the task of presenting a general picture of the range and later the startling tale of mountaineering.

Weldon F. Heald lives on the side of a 9,500-foot mountain at Hereford, Arizona, and there he owns the Flying H

Ranch of 8,000 acres. Professionally he is a writer on mountains of the West. He contributed to *The Sierra Nevada* of this American Mountains Series, and he was one of three men who made the volume *The Inverted Mountains* a reality. He is author of innumerable articles and is writing a complete scenic guide to California. He is a vice-president of the American Alpine Club, a director of the Sierra Club, and a member of the Explorers' Club of New York. During the war he worked for the U.S. Army, helping to plan equipment to be used by soldiers the world over. He began his mountain experience in Switzerland at the age of eight During the first years of his college days he summered in the Cascades, and many times since has climbed, hiked, and explored them. He certainly is equipped to write on summer trails.

Walter McCulloch was picked to do the trees of the Cascades because he was a professor of forestry at the Oregon State College at Corvallis. But in him I discovered another writer for whom the Cascades were a cult. To quote him:

> "With me the Cascades are a religion. The Santiam country just east of us finds my wheel tracks at every season of the year. Only Tuesday I made a sashay over the Santiam Pass and back again in an afternoon, to restore my faith in the mountains. No man can be mean in the presence of those great white peaks, and their cool presence does things for me."

For thirty-six years he ranged the forests of British Columbia. He worked in the eastern forests of the Central States, only to return to the West and the Cascades. He writes as one who knows the forests of those mountains from first-hand experience. His mother came West by covered wagon, and his father was a pioneer in western river steam boating and in early-day railroad construction.

James Stevens is a most prolific writer and will be especially well known to the people of the Pacific Northwest. He is the author of some eight books, principally of the life in the lumbering camps and of our friend Paul Bunyan. *Big Jim Turner* is his latest novel. As a poet, he has contributed to a large number of anthologies. As a magazine writer, his stories and articles are many. He writes here the story of lumbering, and in his dramatization of the tale you will recognize him as a creative writer, for he weaves among the facts a dramatization.

I take great pride in discovering Harry W. Hagen. He is not by profession a botanist but a mailman. I love him because he is a layman who has discovered the flowers of the mountains and as a layman has studied the flora and has become an authority on the matter. I love him because he writes a story that shows how you a layman can come to have a knowledge of the wonderful flowers of the Cascades. It all began with his honeymoon, a planned climbing trip. But clouds defeated their climb, and on the way down he and his bride collected flowers. Challenged by their ignorance of the wild flowers, they returned to the mountains armed with books, and gradually they became flower enthusiasts. Today they have three children, and, packing them into the car, they go off to the mountains. The trip to their Bit of Paradise is a beautiful one, full of wonders of flowers, a bit of Shangri-La. It has no exact location, but each reader who climbs in the Cascades will be sure he has been there.

Ellsworth D. Lumley is a teacher at Roosevelt High School in Seattle. He has lived in the shadow of the Cascades all his life. For seven years he was a ranger-naturalist. For four years he has been president of the Seattle Audubon Society and is at present the National Bird Chairman of the National Council of State Garden Clubs. All this being true, I have asked him to write the chapter on birds of the Cascades. His story of the chickadee who perched on his hat, looking over the brim and answering his whistle, in itself makes his contribution worthwhile.

Herbert Lundy is a newspaperman and for a considerable time has been an editorial writer on the *Oregonian* of Portland. Lundy is now forty-three years of age. Since the age of four he has fished the rivers from the Rogue to the Skagit, and now he is instilling in his children the same enthusiasm. He writes, "I was raised on wet flies, salmon flies, spinners, and crawfish tails to the age of eighteen, when I discovered that the 'dry fly' was not just book talk. But I do not place the method before the results. I have caught a cutthroat on a red huckleberry. I like to catch fish." It is most generous of Lundy to let us in on his secrets of where and how to fish. As an editorial writer he shows his abhorrence of industrialization, stupidity, and greed polluting the streams and killing the fish. For this he is loved by the people of the Northwest.

When the manuscript for the book was received by the editor, Charles D. Hessey, Jr. was under nine feet of snow at Naches, sixty-eight miles from Yakima and two miles from transportation except on ski. One wonders how I discovered him. Hessey knows the Cascades as a skier of long experience. His experience is wider than the Cascades, for he has also skied in the Colorado Rockies. But in the Cascades he returned to do hundreds of miles on ski and to break new trails. He is a free-lance writer with a love of mountain climbing, of trout fishing, but, more especially, he is a lover of skiing.

These contributors are all people who believe the Cascades teach a way of life, and we hope that you will get something of their enthusiasm by reading this volume.

R. P.

THE LAST FRONTIER

by Margaret Bundy Callahan

The Cascade mountains will give you what you look for. If you seek relaxation, release of tensions, they will flood you with somnolence; if you demand challenge, physical or mental, they will be your stimulant; if indeed you search for the very spirit of Pan they will not disappoint you.

Julien Green, writing in his *Journal* some years ago, mentioned a nostalgia he had long harbored for a mountain range in western America named "the Cascades." He had never seen these mountains, but the name held a magic for him, and he yearned sometime to visit them. Had he followed his impulse he would have found the attraction of the name not at all illusory.

I wonder whether there is another mountain chain having such a variety of wonderland. Eleven major peaks thrust their snowy heads above the 10,000-foot elevation; from this height the hundreds of lesser peaks are like crests of waves on a stormy sea. Each peak has its own personality, is rich in its own intimate landscapes. The vast, impressive vistas of the ice-capped summits have their breath-taking splendor; but endlessly inviting are the miniature pools and meadows, rock-slide gardens, waterfalls, and rills of mountains in the 4,000- to 7,000-foot class.

There are the great rain forests with their dense, jungle-like undergrowth on the misty gray Pacific side, and the dry pine lands to the east—the sunny red bark of the trees rising from a carpet of brown, fragrant duff, quite free from the entangling brush you find on the western flanks.

Actually the Cascades have never been man-settled. They haven't even finished settling themselves. They are among the world's newest mountains and they are restless with the restlessness of youth. They break off in hunks and slide down canyons; they toss off their mantles of trees and sling them down roaring rivers into the Sound; they slide rain water and melting snow down their steep sides so rapidly that they swell their streams to flood stage in a few hours, wiping out bridges, inundating pastures, and swamping cabins that perch too close. It is as though the hundreds of peaks in the Cascade chain remembered the exciting period only a few million years ago when they first boiled up out of the retching earth and threw themselves against the northwest skies.

The coast lands to the west of the Cascades are settled—by truck and dairy farmers and by port cities; and the plains to the east of the Cascades are settled—by fruit growers, sheep ranchers, and townspeople. There are even a few intrepid folk living in the farthest reaches of valleys that are little more than cliffs in the great peaks, but scarcely enough to give the mountains a settled quality. The Cascades are largely wilderness, with vast areas still unexplored, inaccessible.

As is true in all formidable, rugged mountain areas, the

character of the Cascades has molded the lives of the people who live among them; as yet man has made little imprint of his personality on the mountains. Nature here is dominant, aggressive, in contrast to older ranges which have become relatively stationary, more quiet in mood.

The Cascades, constantly moving, may literally change before your very eyes. Each year during the thaw season gigantic slides send rumbling echoes like claps of thunder among the cliffs; sandbanks like those at Gold Basin on the Stillaguamish are alive with moving grains of brown sand, like a great hourglass that never runs out. On the eastern side of the mountains, lakes dry up; fertile areas become barren. A road, a mountain town will be in use for a short period, and then within a few years become hardly decipherable—overgrown with brush alders and fast-growing conifers, with a few rotting timbers, strewn cedar shakes, silvered and brittle, and scattered pieces of rusted mining or logging machinery to tell the story; or on the high plains east of the Cascades, blown drifts of sand, sagging frame buildings, and broken farm equipment.

Farm land becomes grazing land; mining areas become logging sites; mining camps and towns become mill or ghost towns. The lives of the people who have chosen to live in the Cascades are governed by this unstable quality of the land; they accept change in their own lives and circumstances as a matter of course and they develop a strong basic philosophy.

There is Wirt Robe, now in his middle 80's, who traveled west with his parents and brothers after remaining in Ohio long enough to cast his first ballot (for McKinley). He homesteaded in a rugged valley between Mount Pilchuck and Green Mountain, worked as a surveyor, trail maker, trapper, logger, shingle weaver, did a little farming, emerged from the hills to work in the Seattle shipyards during the first World War, weathered the depression harvesting pulp wood from his second-growth hemlock, and until very recently, when medical care became necessary, lived a bachelor's old age, a contented and alert recluse in a tiny one-room cabin. A big wood-burning range, a narrow cot, an oversize black leather chair leaking its horsehair stuffing, a battered table, pipe, worn deck of cards, a guitar, magazines, cross-word puzzles, a bowl of margarine, jar of peanut butter, loaf of bread, coffee, canned milk, and some candy bars—these the worldly goods. Thoughts and memories—these the riches.

Ask Wirt Robe about his health and he'll answer, "I'm like the friend who said he almost always noticed that if he lived through the first day of the New Year he'd live the rest of the year out." He has consciously passed up numerous opportunities in his lifetime to become wealthy because he "can't see much use in a lot of money. Just causes worries."

There is Nels Bruseth, who for the last four decades has combed nearly every alpine meadow and rocky crag of the Washington Cascades, who helped build the famous Cascade Crest Trail which connects the border of Canada with the high Sierras and thence with the Mexican border. During his thirty-five years with the U.S. Forest Service he has seen the mountain village of Darrington grow from a few mining shacks to a flourishing town, has seen the Indians moved back into the farther recesses of the river valleys, has made friends with them, learned their legends, has served as intermediary in troubles among the quick-tempered Appalachian mountaineers, many families of whom have moved into certain sections of the Washington Cascades over a period starting about 1910.

There isn't anything Nels Bruseth can't tell you about his region; he knows and loves both the people and the land. He is an amateur botanist, with an extensive collection of pressed specimens and color slides of every type of native flora; a student of geology, an historian, landscape painter, anthropologist, sportsman. He is the truly civilized man. His most concentrated desire is to have others learn to know and love the high mountain areas.

There is Fred Fuller, ex-sailor in the British navy, who arrived years ago at a Puget Sound port, traveled upriver in an Indian canoe, and has lived in the Cascades ever since. Small of stature, blue eyed, rosy cheeked, Fuller lives entirely by the craft of his hands in our machine age. He built his own sawmill, with which he sawed all the lumber from the trees he cut from his own forest to build his comfortable house and outbuildings. He grows his own grain, grinds his own flour, bakes his own bread. From his garden and orchard crops he cans enough food to last through the winters. His radio is a one-tube crystal set he constructed himself decades ago, the first radio receiving set, he boasts, in the whole county. He wears earphones and can get any program on the coast. He is surrounded by photographs and mementos of his past life; and as companions he has two enormous oak trees grown from acorns which he brought from England many years ago.

These are a characteristic few of the colorful individuals who live on the west side of the Cascades, people who live there because they love the land, whose most fervent wish is that they may be allowed by a kindly Providence to remain until the close of their lives in the homes they have built.

The mists from the Pacific which temper the character of the western Cascade country break forces on the flanks of the mountains, so that once you are over the summit you find entirely different conditions on the eastern side. Hot dry plains winds in the summer, and cold, clear air with occasional snows and blizzards in winter characterize the climate, bring about more severe extremes in temperature, far less rainfall, and more definite division of seasons.

Here, snuggling as far into the foothills as the soil permits, extend great orchards; apples such as grow nowhere else in the world, apricots, peaches, cherries, flourishing in valleys made fertile by gigantic irrigation projects. As you travel over the mountain passes the last glimpses you see of the orchards are from behind the dark flanks of the pine forests. These foothill orchards are a rare sight in blossom time, making a gay, lacy pattern of delicate color in dramatic contrast to the rich dark hues of the higher hills.

The Wenatchee Apple Blossom Festival is an annual event, occasioned no doubt partly by a spontaneous desire to share appreciation of the flowering trees, partly also by more commercial motives. All the distinguishing landmarks of every similar American festival are in evidence: the beauty queen, the smiling court maids, the bunting-decked floats, the booster speeches, the banquets, balls, infiltration of tourists. But you can walk off by yourself into the acres of blossoms on a fragrant May evening, with the foothills black beyond the luminous expanse of petals, and you will not forget the experience.

Thousands of acres of grazing lands exist in the eastern Cascade areas. The typical cow hand and the typical logger are as different in temperament as though they lived at opposite poles rather than on different sides of the same mountain range. The ranchman, accustomed to the open, dry, range country, hates the wet, closed-in, brushy forests of the western valleys; and the logger, after a spell of sagebrush, begins to feel dehydrated and his web feet itch for the green, rain-soaked sod of the coast.

The physiognomy of the eastern Cascade land changes also. To the Fort Rock Valley in 1902 came an enthusiastic young man. His name was Harry Crampton and he had traveled west from his parents' home at Dunnville, Wisconsin. He had seen in eastern Washington the great golden fields of wheat, had talked with the ranchers who had grown wealthy from a few years of bumper crops. The Fort Rock Valley in central Oregon, a high (4,600 feet altitude) flat tableland, accented by abrupt, dark, lava-rock buttes, looked to him like potential wheat-growing country and he staked out a homestead. A neighboring homesteader was a golden-haired school teacher from Portland, Stella Macauley, who had come west with her father some years previously. The Macauleys, it seemed, had come from a neighboring town in Wisconsin. The thrill of "folks from home" in that new country was warming.

Plans for the wheat ranch began to include plans for a wedding. The wedding materialized, but the wheat ranch did not. What Harry Crampton had failed to consider was the severe effect of Fort Rock's altitude on farming. Possibilities for grazing were good, however, and the Cramptons went into sheep and cattle ranching. This high Oregon plateau country was neglected by the first Oregon settlers, who were bent on the more fertile lowlands. It was consequently one of the last areas to be reached by railroad, and in the days before automobiles it was served entirely by stagecoach and by freight wagons drawn by six- to ten-horse teams. Travel was rugged, as indeed was everything else about ranch life, but the Cramptons loved it.

Winter temperatures frequently reached 30 degrees below zero; summers were hot and dry. Days throughout the year were packed with work from five in the morning until sundown. It was not, however, until the character of the land began to change that the Cramptons became apprehensive. There was no doubt about it, the ranchers all agreed, the Fort Rock Valley was becoming consistently more dry; the grazing land was losing its fertility, becoming desert. Gradually the settlers began to move out.

The Cramptons enlarged their home by moving a few of the abandoned cabins and attaching them to their original building. They grazed their stock on abandoned acreage. Work became more grueling, returns smaller. But they fought against leaving the valley they had come to love as home. Life still had its compensations. There was the precious social life centering about the little church; there were picnics and arrowhead hunting expeditions after the March winds had blown and shifted the desert sands; there were trips to the ice caves on hot summer days, where, just below the parched, sizzling earth you could carve from the cavern walls a chunk of ice big enough to take home for the refrigerator.

Most important, there were friendships with one's neighboring ranchers: the two young sisters with the red Irish hair and wind-burned cheeks who, with their mother, ran their own ranch, performing all their own chores; the erratic, prophetic, Bible-quoting old Russian bachelor, living alone on his small run-down farm. There was the day-by-day comradeship with the ranch hands: the tall, lanky, taciturn, string-black-haired sheepherder with the unbelievable set of handle-bar mustachios and air of unassailable dignity; the ruddy-faced, blue-eyed handy man, who refused bacon for breakfast because it "tasted too much of silver." And after the blizzards of winter there were the colors of spring, with the sage blossoming vivid yellow-green against the silver sands under the clear blue sky.

One exceptionally severe winter, during a blizzardy spell, with the mercury at 40 below, illness struck, rendering Harry Crampton helpless with fever. Completely housebound while the icy blasts whipped about the plains, Mrs. Crampton nursed her husband back to health through long, dark grueling days, her heart heavy with worry over the freezing stock. "I remember looking out the window day after day and thinking I could stand anything but the sight of the poor horses starving, and each day another lying dead in the snow," she said. "That winter was the worst ordeal of our ranch life, but we came out of it."

Medical and dental care are always a problem in these isolated areas; where prompt attention is an issue, permanent disabilities may result from what otherwise would have been a slight matter. In Crampton's case, an infected tooth spread poison throughout his system; an ensuing operation on his leg left him permanently lame. As he could no longer ride horseback he used his car like a steed, rounding up cattle by driving over the trackless desert.

Under the Sub-Marginal Land Act, the federal government for years has been acquiring land unfit for human use. The Fort Rock Valley, which had looked so promising to homesteaders a few decades earlier, now became classified as sub-marginal, and more of the settlers took advantage of the chance to sell out. Those who remained, among them the Cramptons, found they could no longer graze their herds at will on abandoned acreage. There was a landlord now—his name was Uncle Sam, and he sent agents around regularly to collect rental. When World War II began, problems increased to the point where the Cramptons reluctantly gave in to the course of natural and historic change. They sold their Fort Rock land to the government and began a new life, settling this time in Bend, on the Deschutes River. Now the second largest town in Oregon east of the Cascades, Bend sixty years ago was nothing but a range-land outpost, a stopping place on the Deschutes River for stockmen herding their cattle and sheep to and from mountain pastures.

With change so constantly in the saddle, the Cascade Range is dotted with ghost towns, deserted mining and logging settlements. These battered relics of human enterprise lie deep in the wild recesses of the mountains, some of them hardly detectable in the encroaching thick, jungle-like vegetation. Northeast of Seattle in the Mount Baker forest area is Monte Cristo, rich in historical interest and dramatic in physical setting. Monte Cristo is located in the basin of the Sauk River headwaters, ringed by the perpendicular, eroded walls of three 7,000-foot mountains: Wilman's Peak, Silver

Tip, and Monte Cristo, as though it were cupped in a great jagged stone hand.

A small plank bridge over the boulder-strewn bed of a foaming creek leads you into the alpine pocket where silvered buildings still perch on rocky ground, the skeletal remains of Monte Cristo, flourishing mining town of the nineties. Ragged peaks, streaked red with minerals, against cerulean skies; crystal-clear air fragrant with mountain balsam, cedar, black hemlock, and heady with altitude; the sound of rushing waters and occasional bird notes—this is Monte's setting, the same on a summer afternoon today as before that Fourth of July of 1889 when two prospectors, Frank A. Peabody and Joseph Pearsall, first discovered the region's potential riches.

They had hiked over Poodledog Pass from Lake Chelan east of the mountains, when on Silver Lake Ridge they paused and gasped at the richly colored panorama opening before them. "Why, Peabody!" Pearsall exclaimed in high excitement, "It's as rich as Monte Cristo!" "Then that's just what we'll name it," Peabody answered, "Monte Cristo of the Cascades."

During the next few years natural sounds at Monte Cristo were mingled with the ringing of pick and shovel against hard rock, the trundling of wheelbarrows and the clanking of machinery, as prospectors began a small frenzy of claim-staking, working, and in a few cases, jumping. They packed in over a long trail in those days, for the nearest railroad stop was Hartford some forty miles west. Freight teams operated between Hartford and the mill town of Granite Falls, located on a flat, rather swampy area between the Stillaguamish and Pilchuck rivers. From Granite Falls to

Monte Cristo the miners packed over about forty-five miles
of trail, and it was rough going at times.

Construction of a railroad was begun immediately, to operate between Hartford and Monte Cristo, and one great
day in 1893 the first trainload of thrilled sight-seers puffed
and roared its way along a roadbed spectacularly beautiful,
but insanely difficult both to construct and maintain. In the
narrow, beautiful gorge of the Stillaguamish, whose black,
fern- and moss-decked walls press the river to a deep, green,
whirl-pocked ribbon, seven tunnels had been blasted through
solid rock. Slides hampered the workers constantly, and old-
timers say there is one unmarked spot where the bodies of
several Chinese laborers, trapped by falling rock, remain en-
tombed.

What with slides and washouts, the railroad was constantly
in need of repair during the years it was operated; finally
an unusually violent flash flood wiped out the trestle, which
crossed the river at Verlot. This whim of nature spelled finis
for the Monte Cristo railroad. As the richest and most accessible of the ore deposits had been removed by this time,
operations came to a standstill. The population, which had
reached a peak of one thousand, began a rapid exodus. The
five hotels lost most of their occupants; the jarring rhythms
of crusher and concentrator, the constant creaking of ore
buckets moving along overhead cables, were silenced; and
again the soft plashing of waterfalls, the sharp, thin calls of
mountain birds held sway.

In this rapid rise and fall of a human settlement in the
lap of primitive nature, a rather complete pattern of activities mushroomed into being. Starting with the establishment of a post office, the community produced in rapid order

a general store (the Monte Cristo Mercantile Company) housed in a log cabin, a public school, a volunteer fire department, a newspaper (the *Monte Cristo Mountaineer*), several saloons, a church, and—almost—a jail. During the course of its construction, the jail house was torn down one dark night by "unknowns," thrown into the river, and replaced by a crudely painted sign, replete with skull and crossbones, which warned: "We want no jail here. If you want to ride a rail go ahead." The numerals of the signature, "4–11–44," were those of a famous old vigilante committee of the "wild west."

Among present claim holders at Monte Cristo is a slight, silver-haired prospector in her 70's named Kate Knoulton, who has never given up hope of a mining comeback for the region. Kate Knoulton formerly was a nurse, having served with the Red Cross during World War I. It so happened that during the final illness of Frank Peabody, Miss Knoulton became his nurse. In gratitude for her faithfulness Peabody left her in his will several of his Monte Cristo mining claims. Kate had never envisioned a career of prospecting, but when, a few years later, she was threatened with a breakdown in health due to overwork, and was told to throw herself into some form of outdoor activity, she put two and two together and made tracks for the mountains with pick and shovel on her back.

Her new interests and enthusiasm, combined with plenty of mountain air, had the desired result. Kate has worked her own claims ever since, living, when snow conditions permit, in her small cabin beside the winding trail. Her thin, straight body, clad in trousers and scarlet jacket and always carrying a pack, is familiar to those who live along the road between the Puget Sound town of Edmonds and Monte Cristo. Kate, never having owned a car, customarily hitch-hikes the sixty miles between her Edmonds home and Monte Cristo, her wiry, erect figure striding along the highway with all the resilience of a willow sapling.

The motorist who hails Kate Knoulton with the offer of a lift will find that her sociable chatter keeps pace with the ceaseless throb of the motor. Her sharp blue eyes, behind spectacles, look as though they would never tire; the merry spirit of her hearty laughter is eternally young.

Because the Cascades are extremely rugged, the valleys narrow and precipitous, timber growth heavy, soil shallow, and rock slides common, the settlements within the range must carry on a constant battle with nature to exist; consequently when the mineral wealth of an area is exhausted, towns die rapidly unless there is some other source of maintenance, such as tourist patronage. At the mouths of the main mountain valleys there are more stable towns, with from several hundred to a few thousand inhabitants, who depend for their livelihood on logging, lumbering, truck farming, dairying, fruit growing, or small business establishments catering to the surrounding countryside.

Typical of these is the town of Granite Falls, at the mouth of the valley in which Monte Cristo is the last outpost. These towns, too, ebb in size and activity, depending on the condition of the land, but the thread of their existence carries on. Granite Falls, for instance, dependent chiefly on logging and lumbering, dwindles when these activities slacken for any reason. A prolonged shutdown of the logging camps may be caused by labor trouble or by severe weather—deep snow in winter or fire-hazard dry spells in summer.

At the turn of the century Granite Falls was still in its 'teens as a settlement, with a population of only 75. By 1905 the population had increased to 800, and the town was incorporated. Today, with a population of 1,200, Granite Falls has these assets: one shingle mill, one lumber mill, one limestone quarry, a handsome, modern high school, an elementary school, and a main street about four blocks long bordered by a drugstore, three grocery stores, a bank, two taverns, a feed store, a hardware store, a soft drink establishment called the Palace of Sweets, and the Jewell Novelty Art Shoppe. The busiest spots in town are the three gas stations which service the constant stream of enormous log trucks en route from the hills to the mills; and on Saturday nights the taverns, which face each other across the main intersection.

These foothill towns still have a frontier atmosphere; they are bleak, elemental, and somehow real in a life sense, as big cities are not. Their weathered frame buildings, leaning a little, wear their timbered false fronts with tipsy dignity.

The backbone of social life in a community like Granite Falls (and there are hundreds such dotted throughout the Cascades) is strung along these main vertebrae: the Lions Club, the Lady Lions, the American Legion, the Ladies' Auxiliary of the Legion, intercommunity basketball and baseball games, church socials, the Saturday night dance, the grange, family gatherings celebrating anniversaries, and "Stanley parties." Stanley parties are a chain institution at which groups of ladies meet, play games, absorb refreshments, and purchase the company's household products such as cleaning paste, spot remover, mops, window cleaners, and scrub brushes. Through an elaborate system of prizes, the Stanley Company has incorporated their customers into their sales service.

Reports of these functions are carried fully in the weekly paper, an eight-page publication with four pages devoted to local news and four filled with "boiler plate." Publishing a newspaper on this scale is a marginal sort of thing, with the owner-editor doing everything including the sweeping up. The local items have a refreshing directness and down-to-earth quality, and there is a tolerant insouciance toward typographical errors. After all, if half a column goes in up-side down, you can turn the paper around, can't you?

You may find in the "Robe News" column that "Forty Watts is still hot on the trail of that wolf that's been hang-ing around Big Four. It must be a monster by now, as each time he tells about the animal it gets bigger and bigger"; or that "Bull-Block Mike was visiting in the valley on Tues-day and reports his rheumatism is much improved"; or, in the Riverside column, "There seems to be quite a lot of boys out enjoying scouting the woods for cascara bark these days. Some get home with a full bag and some seem to be getting hi-jacked coming out of the woods, losing bag and all."

Death and life collide frequently in the foothill towns. The logger, of all men, is vibrantly alive—tanned, mus-cular, his skin and clothing pungent with the pitchy juices of the great trees. Few men are more apt to meet instan-taneous death. The accident rate in logging and mill work is high, although not so high as it used to be. The big com-panies now enforce safety rules, prohibit "highballing," and

Sunrise side of Mount Rainier from Naches Pass

Aerial view of Mount Hood, with Mount Saint Helens (left)
and Mount Adams (right) in background

Mount Baker

keep their equipment in good shape, but the small-scale independent logger still puts his trust in haywire.

In Granite Falls, should you drop into Fieldings' grocery
store at almost any hour of the day, you are apt to hear discussions of some recent catastrophe. The Fieldings have the
reputation of carrying their customers along through tight
periods; the store has an easygoing air reflecting the
friendly, generous nature of the proprietors. A waiting knot
of customers stands about patiently amid a degree of confusion, for the counter is small and crowded with orders in
process of assembling. Behind the counter in the heart of it
all is Bud Fielding checking lists and generally struggling
to bring order out of chaos, while his pretty blonde wife
pounds away at the adding machine.

Discussions are seasonal; in the fall of hunting, at elec-
tion time of politics, in the spring of gardening, but at any
time likely to be of an accident. The logger, perhaps, who
was sandwiched between two logs during loading operations
on the side of a mountain; the choker setter who was hit on
the head by a falling block; the rigger who fell from the
spar tree; the mill worker crushed beneath the load of lumber when the cable snapped directly over his head, his life
snuffed out as when a boot squashes an ant.

Loggers fall from spar trees, they are decapitated by
writhing steel cables which sometime snap when over-
stretched, they are crushed by rolling logs, hit by "widow-
makers" (loose limbs suspended so precariously that any
breeze may drop them), knocked out by dangling tongs,
chains, or blocks. These are just a few of the hazards; it's
an occupation in which exact co-ordination of every movement of every man on the job is essential. To see expert log-

gers at work, handling the great trees as though they were
so many matchsticks, is as exciting and fascinating from the
standpoint of skill and poetry of movement as to watch any
ballet; perhaps some day before the big trees are gone the
process may be photographed adequately.

In each of the towns, too, there are the old men; the men
who, in their youth, cut the great centuries-old trees of the
virgin forests in the valleys where now small farms cluster
or second-growth conifers jostle one another for light and
soil. You will see them playing pinochle around a tavern
table under the conical green shade of a hanging globe, or
swapping stories as they watch the scene in the morning sun
from a vantage point at the crossroads. Some of them you
will have to seek in rest homes or county hospitals, and
until you have talked with these once robust old-timers in
the drab, impersonal rooms of these institutions you have
not known the meaning of the word resignation.

The pioneers cling to their homesteads until physical dis-
ability forces them to seek other shelter. Even then, worried
relatives must intervene to bring about the move. These are
the people who stayed because they loved the land and enjoyed its beauty, although when they talk about it they
don't put it that way. In the early days there were some men
who had an eye only for timber wealth, who took out homesteads to avoid purchasing the trees. They performed the
minimum of improvements required to establish ownership
—built a cabin, planted an orchard and a row of raspberries.
Once the trees were cut, they moved out. "Cut out and get
out," the phrase goes.

All through the back country now you may come upon
small glades of fruit trees in the most surprising and in-

accessible spots. Surrounded by fast-growing hemlock, cedar, and fir, the little apple and plum trees have grown tall, too, reaching for sunlight. Their twisted limbs are festooned with moss and pocked with woodpecker holes, but each spring they make a bit of magic in the deep woods with the pink and white of their blossoms. In the fall they drop their small, rusty, puckery fruit to the ground, a welcome feast for deer, bear, squirrels, and mice.

The men who cut out and got out made the money, and probably still have it. Those who stayed in the hills have something else, something it's hard to put your finger on. Speaking of the death of an old-timer, a storekeeper in a mountain town said to me, "They're going pretty fast these days, the old fellows, and it's sad to lose them. There's something about them you don't find any more. They got a kind of flavor—I don't know exactly what it is, but you miss them mighty bad when they're gone."

Grandma Otto is a very small (something under one hundred pounds), very white-haired, very black-eyed great-grandmother, a widow now for many years, who lives quite happily by herself in the prim white frame building facing Mount Pilchuck in which she and her husband, Robert Otto, raised their three children. One cool rainy August afternoon Grandma Otto told me her memories of the pioneer days. She is the earliest settler still living in the valley.

We sat in the neat old-fashioned kitchen (for there was a fire in the friendly cookstove), with the light through the windows green from filtering through the many leaves of the fifty-year-old cherry tree which spread its unpruned branches clear to the back porch. Julia Otto's voice has a sweet, rather resonant quality, and her dark eyes shone with

memories. I think the notes I made in their original, con-
densed form will convey more information than I could
include were I to round out the sentences. Here is the story
as I jotted it down to the sound of the wood fire, the pelting
rain, and the soft voice.

"Came up the valley in 1890. Originally from Michigan.
By wagon from Hartford to Granite Falls. From Granite
Falls on first day of October over new trail. Had boy,
Charles, six, and little girl, Florence, three and one-half.
First day the trail had been used, not very well cleared yet.
Both children had whooping cough when they came. Played
outdoors all the time. Ponies packed everything over new
trail. Were preparing mines at Monte Cristo; steady stream
of pack ponies. Ponies tied together. Cost two cents a pound
for packing. Ponies had to swim creeks. Beaugarde made
money ferrying people over river in boat.

"First cabin close to river, temporary, soon washed out.
River washed sometimes one side, sometimes the other.
Moved into log cabin in forest during winter. Wasn't
chinked up, door not on. Cabin 14 x 16. Fireplace of cedar;
if it took fire, doused with water. Two bunks in corner, one
on top of other. Furniture was folding canvas camp chair,
little girl's rocking chair and high chair, and most important item, cookstove. Horse fell down hill with stove. Horse
not hurt, but afraid stove broke. Some pieces broken but
mostly all right. After stove arrived, fireplace used for wood
box.

"Few necessities shipped by trunk from Michigan to
Getchell. By road to Granite. Repacked at Granite for horse.
Husband and brother with one horse packed the things

(few dishes, oil lamps, clothes) to cabin. Cow, wool mattress, and bedding sent out ahead. Cow very important.

"Neighbor had dried blackcaps (mountain raspberries). 'Best thing I ever tasted.' Husband worked with neighbor clearing land. Bonfire never went out, day or night. Never had forest fire. Dug and blasted stumps out. No way to move logs out, just burned them on the place. Douglas fir and cedar.

"Made trip out one Christmas time. Walked from Granite to Hartford, seven miles. Took morning early train to Seattle, evening train back to Hartford. Trip took three days.

"Ray born in '95. Delivered own baby. Delivered many babies in valley.

"Homestead was 160 acres. Proved up in seven years. All materials for first house taken directly from woods. Flooring split by hand. Draw shave—wide knife with two handles—could get floor smooth and white. Split all lumber with froe. Boards about six feet long. Could split either fir or cedar. Had raising-bees, rolling up logs. Door fashioned of one piece of cedar.

"Ran out of kerosene one time. Decided to make candles. Had brought tallow. (Had also brought rag bag for patching clothes and sewing quilts.) Tied wicks on stick, melted grease. Dipped and dipped Set them on stump to cool. Cat dragged them under house. Night coming on, no light. Had to work fast. Cut out tin with scissors, hammered it around broom. Soldered it with stove handle and piece of wire. Melted tallow, had mustard-bottle cork to bung it up. Had good candles before nightfall. Had to be made fast. Made blue and white ones for Christmas tree, used bluing for color.

"Songs around bonfire on summer nights. Expeditions for cranberries. Marshy area where wild grasses grew, no trees. Cranberries plentiful there. Picked all day, took lunch. Small lake with fish. Thick moss. All changed now. Overgrown with bushes, lake dried up.

"Picnics up-river. Used to hurry to get work done. Boys would go fishing. Lots of big trout in river. Would make big bonfire, take potatoes along. Big feed. Camping parties where Green Gables resort is now. Made beds of hay. Cows came back to sleep, nibbled on beds. Card parties, singing, and dancing. Wirt Robe's blackface songs, jokes, banjo. 'Why'd You Go and Make Them Goo-Goo Eyes?' Never locked up, nobody ever robbed.

"Shortly after Ottos arrived much land in valley was made National Forest Reserve. Later reopened for settlement. Pack-saddle man put fictitious names on claims, located others on false claims. Lots of trouble. Claim jumping.

"First road into Granite was made of puncheons, split cedar poles. Men earned one dollar a rod for laying puncheon road. Tent saloon on old road, called Blazing Stump. Teamsters and mailman used to stop at Blazing Stump. Stay out late. Mrs. Otto had to prepare their meals. 'Oh, that old Blazing Stump! I used to get so mad.' After road went through, never knew how many she'd have at meals. 'We always had something to eat. I don't know how we did it, but we always did.' Difficult when cow went dry. Dinners at noon. Two mail carriers changed horses at Ottos'. One to Silverton, one to Getchell.

"First mail delivered by men with pack trains. Had to put it in oven before reading, so wet from horses wading and swimming river. One horse drowned in whirlpool. All mail lost.

"Eager for garden plants. Ordered plant slips, rosebushes; pack man left them at cabin where he stopped to eat. Husband made special trip to get them. Yellow rosebush on fence brought from Michigan. Hard to find clearing big enough for planting.

" 'There was a man died on the trail that first fall.' Lovely mild fall and winter, '91. Julia Otto outdoors helping husband fell trees, pull cross-cut saw, cut wood. MacKenzie, surveyor, on way to Silverton. Had mining claims. Just married. Stopped at Ottos' late in afternoon. Wouldn't stay over. Not much snow. Body found about a quarter mile from Silverton. Had dragged through creeks, died on hands and knees. Body had to be carried out, insurance company insisted. Was big man. Robert Otto and others took lantern, started out. Julia Otto lonely, left with two children. Read to children as long as they'd stay awake. Took men all night to get to Granite with body. 'Never did feel so out of the world as I did that night.'

"First Christmas didn't have a thing. Things sent from Seattle arrived after New Year's. Cradle for Florence's doll. Gun that would shoot arrows for Charlie. Made cookies. Children delighted. 'You'd think they had the best there ever was.'

"Julia Otto's sister, Ella Theurer, first schoolteacher in valley. Husband had mill at Robe. Private school, handful of pupils. County school superintendent said if there were five children they could have public school. Florence went year early, to make quota. Men built log schoolhouse. Each parent built seat and desk for own child. Men joined in making teacher's desk.

"Dr. Gibson fine doctor, but didn't stay in valley much. Not much sickness. One man died, Robert Otto made coffin. Delivered box, refused to put corpse in it. When Dr. Gibson returned, said it was smallpox. Could have been serious, heavy rain kept epidemic down. One little girl died of jaundice.

"Ella Theurer helped with nursing. Pulled small boy through pneumonia. Man with bad case of inflammatory rheumatism. Out of his head, shouting in delirium. When normal stuttered badly. When delirious never stuttered at all.

"Had plenty of food. Fresh fish, game, canned meat, pheasant, wild rabbit. Had own smokehouse for fish, bacon, ham. Root-house full of vegetables, preserves.

"Neighboring homesteader was Negro named Rogers. Wife was full-blooded Cherokee. Had ten children. Could do any sort of odd job, but never stopped talking. 'He was just the worst old blow.' No prejudice on part of community.

"Many men killed in slides when railroad being built. Riverside graves washed out. Homesteader Davisson lost leg in building railroad. Granite Falls known as the Big Burn. Had saloon on each corner, literary society, debating club. 'Now there's so much going on all the time if we wanted to we could never be at home.' "

Grandma Otto loves to fly. She has flown to California to visit her daughter. But she can't be satisfied long away from her own home. The occasions she loves best are when her children, her grandchildren, and her great-grandchildren gather together beneath the old roof. "We had such a big crowd," she will say happily, her eyes dancing.

A near neighbor of Mrs. Otto is great-great-grandmother Baker. Since the death of her husband years ago she is sole proprietor of "Dad Baker's Pioneer Auto Park," a group of rustic cabins scattered through a riverside forest. Mrs. Baker has a birdlike quickness of manner, a hearty laugh, and a brisk step. She arrived in the valley with her three little girls when the puncheon road was in use. She remembers that at times the mud was so thick the only way to get over it was on sleds drawn by oxen.

One of the little girls, now a great-grandmother herself, lives in a brand new cabin a quarter mile up the valley from her mother's acreage. Susie Buchanan is postmistress of Robe, has her own gift shop, and writes the news of her locality for the *Granite Falls Press*. Susie, like her mother, has a quick sense of humor which can be gritty at times, a philosophy that bears her uncomplainingly through vicissitudes, and a full realization that she never wants to leave the mountains.

A short distance away lives Bob Buchanan, Susie's husband. Bob and Susie Buchanan have been married a long time, but a few years ago they decided their strongly individualistic personalities were better accommodated under different roofs. They are good friends, just independent. Bob loves cats, hates dogs; Susie likes dogs, dislikes cats. Bob can't stand the radio; Susie likes it for company. Bob likes a drink of beer; Susie is a teetotaler. They like each other fine, and this way there's no quarrel.

On up the river, miles from any neighbor, lives Bob's older brother, Bill Buchanan, a bachelor nearing the age of ninety. His cabin is in a clearing across the river from the road; to reach it he has a flat-bottomed boat on a cable strung between two trees on either side of the river, which is very swift and rocky. Both Bob and Bill are excellent gardeners, and each year share with neighbors their crops of beans, peas, chard, spinach, carrots, and beets. For years Bill has used a pair of bulls to plow his ground in the spring. For a time he owned a pet monkey whose persistent vice was sneaking up on the chickens and yanking out their tail feathers.

Silverton is the last and highest year-round settlement in the mountain valley in which it perches. Fifty years ago Silverton boomed as a mining town. Its buildings, all of them survivors of the boom era, are beautifully weathered and nestle contentedly at the base of 1,500-foot perpendicular cliffs like a colony of mussels on a dock piling. The valley here is just wide enough for the gravel road, the Stillaguamish River, and, on the west side of the river, a narrow strip of bottom land.

Silverton is the last spot in the narrowing valley where gardening is possible. The growing season is short, with severe frosts occurring late in May and early in September, but the few year-rounders manage to grow peas, beans, root vegetables, strawberries, and blackberries in small well-tended plots. The brown soil is apparently rich, for all the vegetation has an unmistakably lush appearance.

On one side of the narrow suspension bridge which spans the river at Silverton is Erik Schedin's tavern, a leaning frame structure about 12 x 14 feet. Erik sells beer, soft drinks, candy bars, tobacco, and a few canned goods, principally to hikers, sportsmen, and the loggers and truck drivers who work in the forest areas of the surrounding mountains. He and his brother, Albert, both bachelors, came to America from Sweden as young men. Erik has lived at

Silverton for the last twenty-five years, with Albert joining him off and on. As a lad of fifteen in Sweden, Erik began going to sea, continuing his school studies after working hours and between trips. He had then, and still has, a strong, vital interest in history, philosophy, world affairs, and politics; he is a consistent liberal, with a sound basis of reasoning which stems from reading, talk with friends and strangers, hard physical labor, and long hours of solitary meditation.

As Erik relates experiences out of his past you realize that his life has been motivated by that hardy, intrepid quality characteristic of these mountain people. His wanderings have taken him to Alaska seven times, he tells of a 3,000-mile journey by foot across Siberia to Kodiak, Alaska, the last five days of which he endured without food. For the most part he has followed construction work as powder monkey. Dynamiting is a hard, dangerous occupation and Erik has a back injury sustained in a road-building accident some years ago. "You gotta be tough," is Erik's motto when things go wrong.

Eyes of that very blue color outdoor people so often seem to have; straw-colored hair; ruddy, weathered skin; a once powerful frame shrunken a little now from the 70-odd years; a hearty, kindly manner; an excitable way of talking, flavored with a strong Swedish accent: this is Erik Schedin. From his grandmother in the old country he learned fortitude, a homely philosophy, and a good deal of useful information about medicinal plant lore. He explains how he cured himself of diabetes by drinking quantities of tea steeped from dried red-huckleberry leaves, which contain insulin.

Erik remembers vividly and with horror an experience he

and his brother had one severe winter years ago getting the body of a dead neighbor out of the mountains down to the coroner. The neighbor, isolated by flood conditions, had died several days before he was discovered. There was no road into Silverton at that time, which meant hauling the body on a sled about twenty-five miles. At Red Bridge, about one-quarter of the distance, the log which at that time served as a span was submerged about a foot under the angry waters of the Stillaguamish. With Albert pulling the sled and Erik pushing and steadying it from the rear, they attempted the precarious crossing. A few hard-breathing moments, the ripping torrents pulling at their legs, and then the swift current pushed the sled from the slippery log. Erik lost his footing and fell in too, right across the grim cargo.

The memory of that moment still brings a wild look to his eyes. "There I was in the water hugging the corp," he said, pronouncing it without the "s." "I couldn't get a footing, the water was too swift, so all I could do was hold onto the corp and Albert held onto the railing for dear life and pulled us out to shore."

Solid misery accompanied the rest of the journey, for they were soaked and their clothes were chill shrouds flapping about their blue and aching limbs. Where the trail joined the road the coroner was waiting. In view of their condition, Erik and Albert decided to ride into town with him. Erik, being the wetter, rode in front with the driver; Albert crawled into the trunk and lay down beside the sled and its dripping burden.

Once in Granite Falls they drove into Frank Asche's garage. "When Frank opened up the back of the car he thought nothing but the corp was in there," Erik said. "Albert sat up and started to climb out. Well, Frank jumped back with his face as white as a sheet and yelled, 'Hey, it's coming to life!' I never saw any man look so scared. We felt terrible, but we had to laugh at the look on Frank's face." The brothers stayed the night with friends, who fed them a steaming meal, first warming them with quite a lot of hot drinks.

Just as the land has many moods, so the people of the Cascades are of many types, but one characteristic is common among the hill folk which differentiates them from town and city dwellers: they do not have a regard for money, as such. They live for the process of living; they enjoy contact with the earth, with trees, with animals, and they absorb knowledge of these matters as naturally as they breathe. Obviously they must earn a living, and this they do in the manner which comes handiest, but they work in order to live and to care for their children, not to accumulate wealth, even if they could.

"I figure I am rich in proportion to the number of things I can get along without," a logger, the father of five sons, told us.

"I don't see the use of what people call progress," said Harold Engles, a district ranger whose thirty years with the Forest Service have given him every type of mountain experience. "It looks to me like just more and more people doing more and more things they don't want to do."

Engles, a mixture of Irish and German descent, is a man of varied moods and subtle humor. "Ah, civilization!" he exclaimed one day at Darrington's Timber Bowl Festival, a midsummer celebration which attracts hundreds of visitors.

"It will be a sorry day when they have to pay the boys to get drunk at these affairs. I was just uptown," he added quickly, "and I don't think they need to worry about that yet awhile."

In their background, the Cascade mountain people are for the most part of mixed "American" vintage. The majority of the early settlers came from the broad Middle Western region: Illinois, Wisconsin, Indiana, Ohio, Oklahoma, Nebraska. Occasionally colonies of settlers from other countries sprang up, spearheaded by one or two families who attracted others by enthusiastic letters.

"Swede Heaven" at the foot of Mount Higgins is an example. The Scandinavians settled throughout the Pacific Northwest in large numbers, attracted principally to logging and dairy farming. Most of them, however, stayed in the lower coastal plains and waterfront towns.

Many German families moved into Snohomish County in the eighties and nineties; the roster of pioneers in such areas as Getchell, Machias, Granite Falls, Lake Stevens, and Lake Roesiger bristles with names like Mueller, Speichiger, Menzel, Beckmeyer, Steinke. A number of French Canadians settled on the south side of Mount Rainier in the logging, mining, and farming country near what is now the town of Mineral.

From their hill homes in the southern Appalachian mountains have come large numbers of North Carolina and Tennessee families, all of whom gravitated either to portions of Skagit and Snohomish counties in northern Washington or to Lewis and Cowlitz counties in the southern part of the state. The migration started about 1910 and has continued steadily to grow; about three thousand people have now settled in the two regions. They are referred to as "tarheels" by themselves and their neighbors and are extremely clannish, keeping to their old ways and customs, retaining their twisted drawl and colloquialisms.

The Cascade mountain valleys have much in common with the Appalachians, and the pioneers make their livelihood in their new homes much as they did in their old, although the western area is fresh, new country, and affords a good deal higher living standard than the tired soil of the eastern range.

Their cabins and barns are built of native lumber, usually covered with hand-split cedar shakes grayed by the weather. They keep a few chickens, raise and smoke their own bacon and ham, fish, hunt, pick berries in season, peel cascara bark, work in the logging camps and, during fire season, at Forest Service lookout stations. They are fond of their liquor jug and of the songs they have brought west with them—the folk songs handed down through the generations. In religion they retain their own Baptist services, in some cases bringing west their own clergymen. The tarheels love to sing, at their services they sing with such vigor that they make the whole community resound with the rhythmic fervor of "that old-time religion."

These southern mountaineers add a generous dash of color to the lore of the regions they colonize. They contribute a spark of temperament to the more stable atmosphere created by the folk of Middle Western descent. Stories abound of fights between the Indians and the tarheels, both of whom are apt to exhibit fiery tempers when in their cups. Things are calmer now, but not so many years ago scarcely a Sat-

urday night dance passed without a knifing and fights by
the dozen.

Wilderness areas during the early prospecting and homesteading days were to some extent beyond the limits of the
law. Supposedly they came within law enforcement districts,
but the arm of the law, while long, didn't reach to many
parts of the back country. That pioneer community was fortunate which had an individual with the capacity to preserve
order and resolve crises. Such a man was Henry Keenan,
a French Canadian who settled in Darrington with his petite,
dark-eyed wife in the nineties. Keenan was never legally a
law enforcement officer, but he was called upon by frantic
citizens on many occasions to quell the unruly and to resolve
fierce disputes. He was not an unusually large man, but he
possessed great physical strength combined with an inner
force of character stemming from a resolute sense of justice
and complete lack of fear.

Henry Keenan operated a hotel in Darrington, one of the
iron-bound rules of which was that complete quiet must
prevail after 10 o'clock in the evening, for the sake of those
who had to arise at 5 o'clock in the morning for a day of
hard labor. Usually a few aptly chosen words from Keenan
could silence a roomful of roisterers, but there were times
when sterner measures were necessary. Keenan could take
hold of a couple of tough customers by their collars and
eject them as neatly as though they were stuffed with
sawdust.

They still tell with awe of Keenan's defeat of the trouble-
some Indian who, after a long period of distressing behavior, appeared one morning in one of the town's eating
places quite drunk and with a long glittering knife. Ob-

viously enjoying the effect of his sinister entrance, he held everyone in the room at bay by sauntering about, flipping the blade into the air, catching it between his fingers, flourishing it dangerously close to ears and noses, and generally making himself impressive but not popular. The sheriff was called, but after a hasty look at the situation he was convinced of his inadequacy to handle the matter without bloodshed. He called Keenan, who said, "If you'll deputize me for the next half-hour, I'll take care of that character. He's been asking for it too long." The desperado's eyes glittered as evilly as the long blade he was twirling when Keenan entered the door. One well-aimed blow of Keenan's fist, however, ended the threat.

A certain amount of moonshining has always gone on in some of the remote fastnesses of the Cascades. They say that if the quality of the product is satisfactory, operations are fairly safe from interruption by raiders. But should the quality drop, the irate customers will take matters into their own hands even if the law doesn't interfere.

I ran across a cheerful young man of southern Appalachian stock on our acres one fine summer day, and during the course of a friendly chat he looked around approvingly, winked, and said, "You've sure got a nice, lonesome place way out here in the woods. You'd ought to git yourself a little old copper boiler and cook up some mash"—ending with a delighted leer. I have considered looking up recipes.

The early history of the Cascades so abounds in heroics that they become commonplace. Best known, of course, are the occasional acute flare-ups of Indian trouble, such as the famous White River massacre. Undoubtedly the Indians did cause the immigrants much uneasiness and occasionally an-

guish, but the aid they contributed as guides and providers
of food in the wilderness more than offset their shortcom-
ings. Indeed, the earliest expeditions of trappers, explorers,
and railroad surveyors would have suffered severe loss of
life without the services of the native tribes.

An outstanding example of man's teeth-gritting endurance pitted against formidable nature is the building of the
first road over the Cascade Range. The Oregon Cascades,
that section of the range south of the Columbia River, were
explored a decade earlier than the Washington range, as was
consistent with the earlier development of Oregon's rich
Willamette Valley, goal of the earliest immigrants over the
Oregon Trail.

The Cascade Range loomed to the travel-weary immigrants like some immobile granite behemoth; by the time
they had traveled the two thousand miles from their homes
to this coastal area they thought they had seen and had been
through everything, they found, to their dismay, they hadn't
seen anything yet.

"The crossing of the Rocky Mountains, the Bear River
range, and the big hill of the Brules, with the Blue Mountains, was insignificant in comparison to the Cascades," wrote
George Curry, one of Oregon's earliest journalists, in 1846.
"Here is no natural pass. You breast the lofty hills and
climb them; there is no way around them, no avoiding them,
and each succeeding one you fancy to be the dividing ridge
of the range."

William Barlow, who with his father, the redoubtable
Samuel Barlow, and a small company of fellow Illinois Ore-
gon-trailers, built the first wagon road over the Cascade
Range, said in his reminiscences, "All went well with the

emigrants until we started down on the Oregon side of the Cascades. Then the real simon-pure hard times commenced."

Until the Barlow road went through the immigrants had to take their wagons apart at The Dalles on the Columbia, stack them and their belongings onto Hudson's Bay Company rafts, and gamble on shooting the rapids of the Columbia, taking advantage of the natural gorge which the river has cut through the mountains. They then reassembled their wagons for the remaining trip to the Willamette Valley. They had either to drive their livestock over a narrow Indian trail south of Mount Hood, or to swim them across the mile-wide Columbia, drive them down-river on the north side to Fort Vancouver, then ferry them across to the Willamette side.

All this sounded far too tortuous to Samuel Barlow, who as captain of his wagon party had scouted the way across the plains, bringing the entire expedition through without loss of life to man or beast. As the party approached the Cascades, Captain Barlow kept resting a speculative eye on a certain low spot south of Mount Hood. A wagon road would simplify everything.

"God never made a mountain," he reasoned to his companions, "that he did not make a place for a man to go over it, or under it if he could not find the place. I am going to find that place."

At Fort Hall on the Snake River during a two-day stopover for repairs and rest, Captain Barlow announced his final decision to drive his teams straight over the mountains into the Willamette Valley. If there was an Indian trail over the Cascades south of Mount Hood, he and his men would widen that trail into a road.

"Well, we have been here many years," Superintendent Grant at the Hudson's Bay station told him, "and we have never taken a pack train over those mountains yet, but if you say you will take your wagons over the mountains you will do it. The damned Yankees will go anywhere they say they will."

And they did. They started south from The Dalles in October, stopping at Five Mile Creek for a final rest before the ordeal. Here grass, wood, and water were plentiful; the blue autumn skies and crisp, clear air caused spirits to soar. Wide vistas of rolling highlands opened before the traveler in that north-central Oregon country, with its occasional streams causing the dry grasslands to break into patterns of willow, cottonwood, and aspen, golden in the fall.

Refreshed, the party rolled on thirty more miles in a day, arriving at Tigh Creek in beautiful Tigh Valley where they faced their first major difficulty, the crossing of a precipitous canyon. In the party were about twelve men able to do hard work, and about thirty women and children. A heifer was killed for meat; bacon and flour supplies were good, but tools were few and in bad condition, with only one small grindstone to sharpen the axes and saws, worn with many months of hard usage.

November was nearly gone when the exhausted party arrived at the summit of the pass. Snow had not yet fallen, but the near promise of it was in the air. Scouts reported that the toughest terrain of all was still to come, for the great tangled forests of the western side made the eastern flanks seem simple by comparison. They decided to make camp, build a house, cache the wagons and supplies, then make the rest of the journey on foot, driving the stock over the trail. Two men would remain with the cache until spring, when work on the road would be completed.

The western descent plagued the party with cold (for snow was falling now), hunger (supplies were nearly gone), illness, death of stock from the poison leaves of laurel which they nibbled for lack of grass, great fallen logs, and swampy huckleberry bogs in which the horses and cattle floundered and sank to their bellies.

Spirits reached their lowest depths during the encampment on Laurel Hill, with some of the women tearfully asserting they would all surely freeze or starve or both. "Nonsense!" scoffed William Barlow's sister, Mrs. Gaines. "We are right in the midst of plenty. Plenty of wood to make fires, plenty of horses to make meat, plenty of snow to make water."

She turned to one of the crying women. "When it comes to starving," she added, "here is your old dog as fat as butter. He will last us at least a week."

"Would you eat my old dog?" Mrs. Caplinger sobbed.

"Yes," Mrs. Gaines snapped. "If he were the last dog in the world."

But the bravest talk could not quell the growing spirit of alarm. Early the next morning William Barlow and his friend J. M. Bacon set out on a fast trip for relief supplies. With only four small biscuits, a little coffee, a pair of blankets and a dull ax to ward off the rigors of winter wilderness, they went down Laurel Hill "like shot off a shovel." At dusk three days later they rejoined the anxious group, who had been making short moves forward each day. Reinforced with adequate food, the Barlow party continued on the last lap of its expedition, arriving at Oregon City on

Christmas Day, 1845, just eight months and twenty-four days from the time they rolled out of Fulton, Illinois.

As soon as snow melted that spring, Samuel Barlow and his crew commenced work on the western half of the road, from Clackamas Valley to the summit. Funds for road building were subscribed by the settlers, all of whom were eager for the benefits they knew would ensue, but only a small fraction of the pledged money was ever collected. During the following two years Captain Barlow collected toll from the immigrants, keeping the road open each year until the last wagon of the season had rumbled over the pass. His records state that during the first year the road accommodated 145 wagons, 1,059 head of horses, mules, and horned cattle, and one drove of sheep. The Barlow Road is said to have been a greater spur to the settlement of western Oregon than any other one enterprise up to the building of the first railroad.

The first road over the Washington Cascades was not built for another eight years. (Washington, of course, was at that time still part of Oregon Territory.) Oregon's peaceful, lush Willamette Valley, designed by nature in a gentle, affable mood, had absorbed the immigrants bent on settling quickly into an ordered existence. The more restless, who had still a taste for adventure, pushed farther into the wilderness, into the far northwest corner of the territory, where indeed they could go no farther, where the long fingers of Puget Sound lapped quietly at the pebbly shores of islands and peninsulas to form myriad coves and bays.

To reach the Sound the immigrants had to take their wagons apart at The Dalles, travel by boat to the mouth of the Cowlitz River, then up the Cowlitz by Indian dugouts, by pack trail over rough, hilly country until they came to the prairies. There they reassembled their wagons and struck out across low grassy prairies for "Whulge." (This Indian name for Puget Sound seems to me to describe something of the calm, placid quality of the great bay.) It was a rather devious and difficult route for the cross-country travelers; it took money, which few of them had; and it involved more adventure, with which most of them were satiated.

Those who did penetrate to the Sound were wild with enthusiasm for the richness of the new land. With untiring zeal they hacked away at the wall of giant trees which closed in about the water's edge, turning the great trunks into log houses, forts, stores, and mills. Boatloads of prime Douglas fir were shipped to lumber-hungry markets in California.

Earliest reference to a road over the Washington Cascades is in the Fort Nisqually Hudson's Bay Company's *Journal of Occurrences*, the entry for August 6, 1850, stating, "A party of men here today on their way to cut a road across the mountain to Wally Wally, the expenses incurred to be paid by a subscription among the settlers. Mr. Robertson, the deserter from Fort Victoria, was among the working party."

Two years later Congress, under President Fillmore, passed an appropriation of $20,000 for building a "military road" over the Cascades, and the following year Washington's first governor, Isaac Stevens, relegated the job to the leadership of a Captain McClellan, who, the governor pointed out, had served his country gallantly in Mexico. Apparently Captain McClellan's experiences in Mexico had not fitted him for pioneering in the Cascades, for his sole contribution to the road was to consult with the Indians and to accept their verdict that the project was impossible, that the Cascades offered no practicable opportunity for a road because of the great depth of snow and other engineering difficulties.

Already, however, a handful of settlers had collected $1,200 in cash and numerous contributions of supplies, and on July 10, 1853, they had begun to build the road. One group of workers, under Whitefield Kirtley and Nelson Sargent, crossed the mountains along the old Indian trail over Naches Pass to begin at the Yakima River and work toward the west; the other, led by Edward Jay Allen, a brilliant young engineer, began on the coast side by improving the six miles of "trail road" constructed along the Puyallup River by deserter Robertson and his comrades in 1850, then whacked a clearing through the dense timber along the White and Greenwater rivers to the very foot of the mountain range.

All summer they pursued their gargantuan labors, felling and bucking the great trees by day, eating enormously of beans and flapjacks around crackling fires, sleeping in the blackness of the forest night while the blue smoke from the fire's embers mingled with the pitchy branches to make a fragrance better than any other in the world. Behind them they left a chaos of resinous wreckage—enormous trunks and bristling branches overlapping in a welter of confusion which the Indians eyed gravely, shaking their heads over the hopelessness of the "Boston hooihut."

Late in August the road building reached a crisis. The eastern party had completed a steep corduroy affair following the river to its source at the pass. The western crew, however, had exhausted their funds, their supplies, and a good percentage of their energy, and they had come to an impasse, a formidably steep ridge leading to the summit. They had worked furiously in an effort to complete the road for a wagon party they had heard was on its way. As they were contemplating that final ridge they received word that the immigrants had changed their course, and were heading for the Willamette.

Color in the woods bespoke the season; the vine maples were flaming; the cottonwoods and alders sailed an occasional golden message downward with the breeze; nights held a hint of frost. Early autumn storms in the mountains can be death-dealing in severity.

The road builders decided to wait one more year to complete their project, hoping that in the meantime congressional funds would at last be made available.

No sooner had Allen and his crew returned to the shores of Puget Sound than they learned that they had been misinformed, that a large pioneer caravan was approaching, laboring up the east side of Naches Pass over the new road. Accepting the challenge, some members of the crew, Allen among them, hurried back to the mountains, where they found thirty-six wagons on a painfully slow and difficult ascent of the east side. Ninety-six times the caravan had crossed and recrossed the torrents of the river; now at the summit they looked down upon an apparently impossible descent of the west side.

The job, then, was to build the road as they traveled; to inch forward day by day, a few feet at a time, trusting that fall storms would hold off. There was but one possible route to follow on the descent; this led over a long ridge between the canyons holding the two forks of the Greenwater River as they flow from the summit of the pass. This steep, rocky ridge had long been the Indian's route; now over its dramatic alpine contours the white man's road, the Boston hooihut, must be constructed.

James Longmire, whose family settled in the superb forests on the southern slopes of Mount Rainier, where Longmire Lodge now stands within the National Forest, described for the Oregon Pioneer Association the descent of the caravan so tersely that it almost sounds easy, until your imagination begins to fill in between the lines:

"One end of a rope was fastened to the axles of the wagons, the other thrown around a tree and held by our men. Thus, one by one, the wagons were lowered gradually a distance of three hundred yards, when the ropes were loosened, and the wagons drawn a quarter of a mile farther with locked wheels. All the wagons were lowered safely save one, which was crushed by the breaking of the rope . . . We made the road as we went along. We crossed the Greenwater sixteen times and the White six times."

Eying that perpendicular wall on the west side, Captain McClellan said to Allen: "My boy, you have done well so far. You and your crew have done wonders with the amount of money you have expended. But this ends it. You're up against a stone wall, so to speak."

Allen heatedly replied, "I will make up that almost perpendicular twelve hundred feet not only a road that an emigrant can get down, but one that six yoke of cattle can haul one thousand pounds up."

Some months later Allen invited McClellan to return for a look at the finished job. "We had constructed a road," Allen related in a letter to a friend, "up which I hauled, with four oxen, fifteen hundred pounds. It was buttressed up an average of fifteen feet, and in some places forty feet, with the huge trees that covered the mountainside, and was stayed down the mountain, from tree to tree, with thousands of braces. It was impossible, but we were ignorant, and not fully conscious of this impossibility; and so we did it."

McClellan, standing on the highest point of the buttress, did not hesitate to express his admiration. "Young man," he said, "do you know what you have done here? Under the conditions, Napoleon's passage of the Simplon was an engineering feat no greater than this."

Those who insist, as I have heard many do, that it takes war to bring out men's real abilities, do not realize the accomplishments brought about through the peaceful desires of a handful of hardy settlers for ease of travel and trade with their neighbors on the other side of a mountain range. This, it would seem, is the traditional American way, a spirit to cherish and preserve.

While the Cascade mountains are predominantly wild and rugged in character, the range is not without its gentler aspects. The western flanks are, to my knowledge, entirely free from poisonous snakes and insects. (There are occasional rattlers on the east side.) You can hike along forest trails, plunge into dense thickets of underbrush, or fling yourself to the fragrant, needle-carpeted ground among mosses and trailing vines without worrying about breaking out in rashes or welts. While poison oak has made its presence felt in the lower coastal regions, I have never heard of anyone encountering it in the Cascades.

An amazing variety of Lilliputian plant life exists in the western Cascades, the floors of the rain forests are carpeted with a delicate pattern of mosses, ferns, brilliantly colored fungi, and a great many little green creepers, which manage to stagger their blossoming season from early spring until fall, so that there are always starry petals gazing up at you from the ground.

For every torrential river there is a serene little brook; for every giant waterfall, a dainty, plashing spray tolerant of the tenuous campanula and maidenhair ferns its droplets play upon. The most terrifying cliffs harbor nests wherein baby black swifts sprout their first down; the mist-strewn heights enfold in their rocky bosoms miniature alpine gardens seemingly planted with painstaking precision and infallible taste. Nature in the Cascades is like some powerful, ancient goddess who with one hand shakes a mountain to shower down tons of giant boulders, while the fingers of the other hand close gently and protectively around a nest of pinkly naked baby deer mice.

THE CASCADE RANGE

by Grant McConnell

DISCOVERY

On the afternoon of the thirtieth of April, 1792, two ships flying the ensign of the British navy were sailing southeastward into an arm of the Pacific Ocean on the coast of North America. The sea, though by no means calm, was moderate after the tumult of the squall-ridden entrance where the ships had anchored the previous night. A light northwest breeze filled the sails and hurried the vessels onward. All day the weather had been clearing, but there still remained a bank of cloud lying low over the water ahead. The shore to starboard a few miles away was rough and covered with dark forest. The land in the opposite direction was more distant and little could be made of it. But the day was pleasant and there was good reason to suppose that a harbor would soon be found for the much needed refitting of the ships.

Aboard the larger of the two vessels there was a restrained excitement. The coastline which they had been following for days had shown none of the large rivers and bays which had been reported to exist. But here at last was a large inlet, perhaps even the inland sea that had been rumored. There was, for example, the story told by a Greek pilot in the service of Venice some two hundred years before, one Juan de Fuca, about just such an inlet and near this latitude. Perhaps—and here was greater cause for excitement—the inlet would turn out to be the much sought Strait of Anian, the water passage across America whose location it was a primary mission of the little squadron to find.

Late in the day high land appeared above the clouds in the east. It did not seem to be continuous at first. The land ahead might be no more than a cluster of islands or it might be merely high in places, low in others. Then the much anticipated safe harbor appeared, a bay protected by a long curving sand bar. At almost the same time the third lieutenant reported a new discovery. In the words of the journal of the expedition, "A very high, conspicuous, craggy mountain, bearing by compass north 50 degrees east, presented itself towering above the clouds; as low down as it was visible it was covered with snow; and south of it was a long ridge of very rugged snowy mountains, much less elevated, which seemed to stretch to a considerable distance."

By his discovery the third lieutenant achieved a kind of immortality, for his name was given by his commander to the "high craggy mountain," and it has remained Mount Baker, the northernmost of the high Cascades.

The commander of the squadron, Captain George Vancouver, did not succeed in finding the Strait of Anian but he did learn enough on his voyage to be able to report that no inland sea existed connecting the Pacific and the Atlantic. The discovery was one of the most important of Vancouver's achievements and it is altogether probable that his view of Mount Baker and the long "ridge" to the south was one of

Glacier Peak

Cratei Lake showing Wizaid Island in centei The waters of
this lake are among the cleaiest and bluest on the continent

Mountaineers camping at Indian Henry's Hunting Grounds
The west side of Mount Rainiei can be seen in the background

the most convincing reasons for believing the strait was not to be found.

Vancouver repaired his ships in the harbor he had found and sent out parties in the ships' boats to explore the inlet. The major outlines of Puget Sound were mapped and two more high snowy mountains were discovered. The first of these appeared to be at the southern end of the range extending southward from Mount Baker. It was remarkably high, round in form, and like its neighbor, covered with snow. Captain Vancouver, being in a position to distribute compliments on a grand scale, named the mountain after a naval friend, Rainier. A little later Vancouver sighted a third high, round, and snowy mountain much to the south. This he named Saint Helens, after a British diplomat.

Vancouver's first lieutenant, Broughton, later rounded out the expedition's record of mountain discovery while on an exploration of a large river reported that same year by the skipper of a Yankee fur-trading vessel. Vancouver was surprised, after eight months at sea without seeing any other ship than his own, to meet the "Columbia." His surprise turned to chagrin when he learned from her captain that the "Columbia" had already found and entered the mouth of a large river which the British ships had passed without seeing. Vancouver accordingly dispatched Broughton on an independent journey to explore the river. Broughton found the river quite as reported by the Yankee and sailed up it more than one hundred miles. Near the far point of his voyage, Broughton climbed a hill and from it discovered another high peak to the east. He named the peak, in Vancouver's manner, after Hood, another high-ranking British naval officer.

THE NAME

Captain Vancouver was the first to record the existence of high mountains east of Puget Sound and along the Columbia River. Aside from a casual observation that Mount Baker and Mount Rainier were connected by a ridge, however, he did not suggest that the peaks he had found were parts of one of the major mountain chains of America. Appreciation of this fact did not come until much later, and even then the naming of the range itself was less act than evolution.

The first white men to penetrate the Cascade Range were those in the remarkable expedition of Lewis and Clark. Through the years 1804, 1805, and 1806 this party, led by two unusually able young men, crossed the continent to the Pacific and returned with a wealth of information about the new lands of the nation. Their route through the Rocky Mountains was poorly chosen, but the way they followed through the Cascades was incomparably the best, and was the one followed by all but a few of the early pioneers to the land of Oregon.

It was late in the year 1805 that the party came to the Oregon or Columbia River—President Jefferson had been a little uncertain in his orders to the two leaders what the river should be called. Since most of the summer had been spent in threading a way through, around, and over moun-tains, Lewis and Clark were not astonished to see ahead of them still more mountains. They noted several snow-capped peaks and duly entered the bearings. The important thing for the expedition, though, was that it had come at last to the great river which was an avenue to the sea.

On October 25 they passed the Great Falls of the Co-

lumbia (near the present town of The Dalles). Then they
were in the mountains. For the next few days they rode
through a deep cleft which if smaller would be called a
canyon. They paused at several Indian villages and with
great diplomacy maintained friendly relations. On November 2 they came to a spot where one last portage was necessary. With their usual precaution the leaders scouted out
the difficulties before attempting it. They made the portage
successfully and in another day's time were through the
mountains.

During the next three decades a succession of rivals in
the fur trade, the Astorians and the men of the British Hudson's Bay and Northwest Fur companies, passed up and
down through the Columbia River Gorge. Gradually they
were joined by growing numbers of less expert travelers,
the home- and land-seekers. Not all of these had as easy a
time in the last stretch as Lewis and Clark. The place where
Lewis and Clark had made their final portage became known
as one of the chief difficulties of the entire transcontinental
journey.

It was a passage to be approached with foreboding. Cliffs
of black rock rose high above the river, and beyond the cliffs
were steep forested slopes that disappeared into the clouds.
Here and there small streams emptied into the river, and
on the cliffs were their cataracts as they made the final
plunge from the mountains. There were occasional Indian
villages along the shore, and on a few islands were Indian
burial grounds with vaults built on poles above the ground.
Behind lay the endless distances of the Great Plains, the
severe high crossing of the Rockies, and the long descent of

the river. Ahead, the river swept majestically on toward the Pacific.

Two mountains on opposite sides of the river crowded close to the channel. Rock had fallen from their walls, and the bed of the stream was strewn with the debris. Boats could descend these rapids but only with great danger. The alternative was a portage, but this led through the territory of Indians who had an evil reputation for extortion and banditry.

Here were the Cascades of the Columbia. For the caravans of the nineteenth century's westward migration they were the final barrier before reaching the fertile western valleys. The actual rapids were not tremendous; they have since been submerged by the water impounded behind Bonneville Dam. In the scale of the gorge through which the river passes, they were almost insignificant. Yet these rapids with their attendant danger from the Indians were the only serious difficulty involved in crossing the last great range. The mountains themselves were identified as *the mountains by the Cascades* and ultimately the entire range came to be known simply as *The Cascades*.

There was something almost providential in the existence and early discovery of the Columbia River Gorge. The mountains which stand on either side of the deep gap extend for hundreds of miles to the north and to the south. Nowhere else in the range is there a comparable passage. The word brought back by Lewis and Clark was that the only part of the territory west of the Rocky Mountains fit for settlement was the Multnomah—or Willamette—Valley. This became the objective of thousands of pioneers. That valley lay just beyond the Columbia River's opening

through the Cascades. Travel by water was the most practical method available in the early 1800's, and the Columbia
with its big tributary, the Snake, led directly toward the
Willamette and to the one point at which the Cascade mountains could easily be crossed. Except for two points on the
river, at the Great Falls and at the Cascades, the Columbia
was a thoroughfare and one of the finest waterways of the
continent. The portages around the Great Falls and the
Cascades would have been easy if it had not been for
the primitive monopolists in possession there. At the point
where the Columbia passes by the crest of the mountains its
altitude above sea level is little more than one hundred feet.

Although the name of the Cascades came from a spot
which was almost an incident in the long sweep of the range,
it is curiously appropriate. These, more than most, are well-
watered mountains. This is something seen: in the thousand
streams that rush down into the valleys, in the multitude of
lakes that lie wherever there are hollows to hold them, in
the waterfalls that course over the cliffs, in the bright greens
of luxuriant vegetation, and in the snow and glaciers of the
high peaks. It is also something heard. Through much of
the range there are few places where the sound of water
does not reach. It is a sound that is sometimes deafening, as
when one stands by a large waterfall or a glacier-fed torrent. Sometimes the sound is only a murmur reaching from
a deep valley to the mountains above. But always it is a
sound of movement, hurried, turbulent, melodious.

DIMENSIONS

The Cascades are an integral part of the vast complex of
mountain ranges that parallel the Pacific shore of the conti-

nent. To the north there are the arctic giants of Alaska and
the Alaska Canada boundary and the mysterious Coast
Range of British Columbia. To the south there are the Sierra
Nevada and the lesser ranges of southern California. There
are few gaps between these chains and it is difficult to say
where one ends and the next begins. Some of the ranges lie
completely within the limits of single political units. Some
are geologically simple and their common structure defines
them. The Sierra, for example, are almost entirely within
California and are in outline a single ridge with characteristic
forms etched upon that ridge.

The boundaries of the Cascades, however, are not obvious. Most of the Cascades lie within the states of Oregon
and Washington. Yet Lassen Peak and Mount Shasta, peaks
that are clearly a continuation of the line of volcanoes of
the northern states, are in California. At the other end of the
chain, peaks similar to Shuksan, the close neighbor of Mount
Baker, continue on into Canada. There are volcanic indications of a type common in the Cascades in the mountains of
Garibaldi Provincial Park and in the cones near Mono Lake
on the east side of the Sierra. The mountains of the Cascades, moreover, are not exclusively volcanic. The natural
boundaries that best mark the limits of the Cascades are
the Fraser River in Canada and the Feather River in California. From the Canadian boundary to the Fraser, the Cascades dwindle rapidly. Near the Feather River, the gradually rising uplift of the Sierra begins.

The Cascades are a long chain of mountains, nearly seven
hundred miles. In this distance the Cascades have probably
more variety of mountain forms than any other range of the
continent. The north-south line of the divide is fairly

straight for most of the length of the range, but in the northern part it becomes twisting and devious. In places the range is very simple, in others exceedingly complex. In their width the Cascades vary from an average 50 miles in the southern and central parts to 120 in the north.

East and west, the Cascade Range is one of the most definite climatic boundaries of the world. Standing at a distance of a little more than 100 miles from the Pacific, it is the first large barrier to the humid air currents that flow inland. The lesser coastal ranges absorb some of the force of the storms that sweep out of the sea, but the greater part of the moisture which the heavy clouds carry is intercepted by the Cascades. This determines much of the character of the range and divides the land on either side into separate regions. In a hundred ways it sets the quality of life in the vast area dominated by the range.

On the west side of the Cascades there is a heavy annual rainfall. Temperatures are mild, and the span of their variation is small. The vegetation on the west side is dense and luxuriant. The bulk of the timber resources of the area are on the west side. The agriculture is varied, and farms tend to be small. The largest concentrations of population and most of the industry are there. The commercial life of the entire Pacific Northwest is centered in the cities of the west side.

On the east side the rainfall is slight. Winters are cold and summers hot. Much of this region is swept by high winds. Except in irrigated areas, the vegetation is sparse. The timber of the region is limited to the hills, and the forests are open stands of pine. Agriculture is specialized— fruit, wheat, and cattle—though in a few districts there is

greater variety. Towns are few and small; it is a land of
distance and space. The general temper is more conservative
than in the west.

Not all these differences are caused by the Cascades alone.
The range, however, is the dividing line between the two
regions. There is nothing indistinct or intangible about it.
Start from any of the cities of the coastal side and travel
east. The sky perhaps is overcast with a low-hanging mass
of cloud. The outlines of distant hills are dull, and the sil-
houettes of nearby trees do not stand out against the air but
merge with it. Along the way there are forests whose in-
teriors are dark and where the undergrowth is thick and
green. Everywhere the color is green: dark green of Douglas fir, light green of grasses and deciduous trees. There
are many streams carrying white water down through moss-
grown canyons. The ascent over the divide is gradual, or if
the way is through the Columbia Gorge, there is no climb
at all. Then in the space of ten miles or so a change occurs.
The sky grows lighter, the undergrowth is less abundant,
and the bright reds and yellows of the trunks of pines stand
out among the firs. Through a sudden break in the clouds
there is a field of blue sky, and standing against it is the
snow slope of some high mountain. The air sharpens. Firs
disappear. There are new shades of brown. At last, a little
past the crest, the sky becomes clear except for long fingers
of light-fringed cloud reaching out over the rolling plateaus
of the inland region. Below and beyond the mountains are
the light-brown wheat fields, the gray-green groves of orchard, and long stretches of sagebrush and rock.

Perhaps the most likely impression of the range to be
gained by a newcomer to the Northwest is that the Cascades

are not a range of mountains at all, but rather a series of grand but isolated volcanoes rising above a line of rolling hills. This was probably the impression carried away by Vancouver and by many of the early travelers. It is the impression that anyone will get by approaching the range in its central or southern portions. It is the appearance seen on coming to the range anywhere from the west. The high isolated peaks completely dwarf the hills from which they rise. Then, as so frequently is the case, low banks of cloud traveling eastward from the Pacific come to rest against the parts of the range between the great volcanoes, and only the latter are seen shimmering loftily through the soft moist haze. They seem apart and dissociated from the surrounding country, and they are frequently mistaken for unusual billows of cloud or for some unbelievable apparitions of an atmospheric nature.

The volcanoes are massive. With several exceptions they do not stand in groups. From few places is it possible to see more than one at a time. The great ones are separated from one another by dozens of airline miles. In the neighborhood of any one of the volcanic peaks, that one dominates everything within sight, and although other mountains may be seen in different directions or in the distance, the personality of the nearby peak obliterates the sense that other mountains can exist. Thus each of the big volcanoes has its tributary region for which there is only one mountain in the world, and that one is *The Mountain*. It is painful for a Portlander to hear a person from Seattle mention *the mountain* and to comprehend slowly that the mountain indicated is Rainier. As for the Seattlite, the Portlander's colloquial reference to Mount Hood as *the mountain* is a piece of insufferable

provincialism. And yet, the Seattlite and the Portlander may
trade homes and each will come under the unique spell of
the nearer mountain. The volcanic peaks are jealous gods.

At times this jealousy finds a strange but understandable
response. For many years the people of the city of Tacoma
engaged in a crusade to have the recognized name of the
Cascades' highest mountain changed to "Tacoma" in place
of the outlandish syllables "Rainier." Against the fiery op-
position and ridicule of other communities within the sway
of the big mountain, the Tacomans carried their fight to the
Board on Geographic Names, to Congress, and to the public.
The dispute became bitter and the meanest motives were
imputed on both sides. Amid much derision, the Tacomans
lost, but it would not be safe to say that the name Mount
Rainier is finally and universally accepted. The battle fought
by Tacoma was at root a struggle to possess the mountain
—not just for the better advertisement of the city, but for
the satisfaction of something deeply rooted in the people
who look up from their homes to the sight of a twilight lin-
gering on the heights of the mountain.

There have been other attempts in the history of the Cascades to gain possession by the magic of a name. Hall J.
Kelly, probably the original western booster, visited the
Northwest in the first half of the nineteenth century and
became concerned over the menace of the British. One of his
many projects for the country involved renaming the Cascades the Presidential Range. The attempt failed.

The volcanic peaks, then, are the aspect of the Cascades
that is best known. They are the highest in the range; they
are the largest and the most conspicuous. They are located
so as to be visible from the largest cities and from many of

the most traveled highways. There is nothing in the nation remotely resembling any one of them, let alone their long stately procession. And yet the Cascade Range is much more than this line of great volcanoes. The long ridge that Vancouver observed would be one of the big ranges of America even without the volcanoes. In the valleys and on the hills of the lower parts of the range lies one of the greatest belts of evergreen forest that is to be found in the country. Its stand of Douglas fir is one of the first resources of the land. The hills below the volcanoes contain water-power reserves that are scarcely touched.

There is, however, another aspect of the range that is little known and very different. The Cascades are in reality two separate but interwoven mountain systems. One system, that of the volcanoes, extends the length of the entire chain from Canada to northern California. The other system is non-volcanic. It begins near Mount Rainier and extends northward into Canada. This second system is a labyrinth of high broken ridges, heavily glaciated peaks, and deep narrow valleys. Its mountains are among the most beautiful and the most imposing in America. It has scores of glaciers, fierce torrents and waterfalls, high meadows, and virgin forests. While it is shorter than the volcanic system, it is considerably wider, so that it is by no means a small part of the range. This division of the range into two distinct mountain systems is one of the outstanding facts about the Cascades and is one of the reasons for its great variety. What may be said of the volcanic peaks is frequently untrue of the northern system. Thus it is most convenient in outlining the range to discuss the two parts of the chain as though they were quite separate ranges.

Around the rim of the Pacific there are many volcanoes. Some, like Katmai and Krakatao, have erupted in historic times and are remembered for their cataclysmic violence. They are awesome curiosities and objects of fear. There are others, like Fuji, which now stand as mute quiescent monuments to the latent fires within the earth. Some of these possess a serene and lonely grandeur which seems to deny their origin or the possibility of new outbursts from their depths. It is difficult to conceive of them as having spewn smoke and cinders and molten rock. Covered with snow and in their great isolated heights, they seem not of the country in which they stand, scarcely of the earth.

The volcanoes of the Cascades are such mountains. Their form and their beauty seem complete and final for all time, and as though they had always been as they are now. Moreover, they have not, in the short time white men have been living in their shadow, erupted so as to cause the loss of life or great destruction. There are vague Indian legends of smoke and explosions from some of the peaks, but there is little definite fact to be learned from these. The evidence of the mountains' fiery past lies on the sides of the peaks and in their distinctive shapes.

Of the big volcanoes of the Cascade Range, Mount Saint Helens, in southern Washington, is perhaps the one which best typifies the remote and ethereal quality that is in some way common to them all. In outline this mountain is a very nearly perfect cone with rounded summit and slopes almost unmarred by any break in their smooth, even curves. When it is seen from a distance in the fall or spring, rising above the rolling expanses of green forest at its foot and whitened with snow from base to summit, it has an air of peace and of great age.

Yet Mount Saint Helens is one of the youngest of mountains and one of those for which there is a record of eruption. In 1842, when there were still few settlers in the region, the mountain sent up clouds of black smoke and ashes. Pumice was reported falling from the sky as far away as The Dalles, sixty-three miles by air from the mountain. Within the last few years live fumaroles have been discovered on its sides. It is probable that in the course of geologic time the mountain will awake again and that new deposits of lava will appear among its glaciers.

From time to time since the last explosive activity from Saint Helens there have been reports of smoke rising from others of the volcanoes. Mount Baker and Mount Rainier are said to have been smoking through the middle part of the nineteenth century. The crater on Mount Baker was smoking as recently as 1903. The climax of the Cascades' volcanism in modern times, however, occurred at the very southern end of the range. In 1914 Lassen Peak burst into activity, and between May and September it had forty-seven eruptions. At the largest of these dust rose to eleven thousand feet, and fragments four feet in diameter were ejected with the dust and smoke.

Though there is no concern that any of the Cascade volcanoes will reduce the communities about them to modern Pompeiis or Herculaneums, the fires inside the peaks are not extinct. Anyone who has climbed either Mount Hood or Mount Rainier can testify that these are not "dead" volcanoes. A thousand feet below the summit of Hood and directly on the summit of Rainier are steam fumaroles. None of them can be reached without a long hard trudge, and they are at an altitude where there is perpetual wind and, more often than not, cloud and storm. Nearby are fields of snow and ice-hung rock sloping down to glaciers. A layer of cloud, perhaps, has formed far below at the level of timber line, six thousand feet. All the land save that of the mountain and the other distant sentinels of the range has been obliterated. Overhead is a sky of such brilliance and clarity that it is blinding to unshielded eyes. Against the blue of this sky a wisp of white vapor rises from the rock of the mountain and is dissipated. Or perhaps the cloud lies not at timber line but upon the whole of the mountain. The snow and ice blend with the dense white of the cloud and there is neither distance nor foreground. The only reality is sound—of the wind and then, on suddenly arriving at a small patch of bare pumice, of a deep rumbling from underground. The pumice and rock are warm to the touch, and it is good to rest there after exposure to the cold wind.

Although the volcanic peaks had the same type of origin, they differ markedly in form. Mount Saint Helens is the prototype for its simplicity of outline; no one of the others is so symmetrical or so unmistakably the same mountain when seen from its different sides. Since the first lifting of each mountain's mass there have been intermittent side eruptions which have altered the conical form. Mount Adams and Mount Rainier, both mountains of enormous bulk, have irregular projections from this cause. Mount Shasta has a satellite on its flank, almost a separate volcano in its own right.

More important than these secondary lava flows in de-

fining the highly individual personalities of the peaks is the
work of their many glaciers. The entire range is so located
that it takes the first heavy impact of the frequent storms
carried inland by the warm moist air currents of the Pacific.
As a result the snowfall in the Cascades is very heavy. It is
not unusual for a winter's snow to pile fifteen and twenty
feet deep in the medium altitudes of the range. This has
caused the formation of glaciers wherever the snow accumu-
lates from year to year. On the older peaks these glaciers
have cut large cirques bounded by slender spines of rock.
The summit of Mount Hood has become a long thin ridge
largely as a consequence of glacial action. From Portland,
where the ridge is seen end-on, the mountain appears to have
a fine sharp point. From the south the ridge is apparent, and
the mountain might easily be taken for a different peak.

The largest concentration of glaciers in the United States
is on the sides of the northern volcanic peaks of the Cascades. Rainier has an area of forty-five square miles in its
twenty-four glaciers. Some of these are like rivers of ice falling from the summit down over cliffs and flowing to an elevation of four thousand feet, well below the level of some of the
resorts. The Emmons Glacier on Rainier is five and one-half
miles long, small in comparison with those in Alaska and
Canada, but still the longest in the forty-eight states. Mount
Baker is even more completely covered with ice than Rainier,
and the lovely volcano bearing the name of Glacier Peak
is poorly named, so common are glaciers on all the mountains in its vicinity. The volcanic peaks to the south are
covered with ice only to a slightly lesser degree, and some
of their glaciers are among the most interesting.

The glaciers and the snow fields of the Cascades are re-

sponsible for a great deal of the character and the charm of
the whole range. Without the glaciers, the volcanoes would
be mere mounds of rock and pumice. Without the heavy
snows of the range, none of its mountains would have the
rugged form and grandeur that is their general feature. The
well-watered meadows, the abundant streams and waterfalls
would be lacking. But more important, without the shining
white of snow and ice the range would be without the characteristics that distinguish it among American mountains.
The Cascades are not the only mountains of perpetual snow,
but of all the great ranges they are the most heavily snow
covered and it is this more than anything else that accounts
for their peculiar beauty.

In the long, nearly straight line of the volcanic system
there are eleven mountains over ten thousand feet high.
Two, Shasta and Rainier, top fourteen thousand feet. The
figures in themselves, however, do not account for the impressiveness of these mountains. Ten thousand feet is a
quite moderate elevation in the Rockies or in the Sierra.
Colorado alone has fifty-two peaks above fourteen thousand. The explanation of the lofty appearance of the volcanoes of the Cascades lies in the fact that most of them
display their entire elevation not from a high plateau, but
from sea level or near to it.

Rainier is the climax of the volcanic system. It is both
the highest and the largest in the range. With its many sides,
it is the equivalent of a range of mountains in itself. From
some places it appears as a rounded dome, from others as a
sharp-pointed summit or as a long ridge above wall-like
cliffs. The trail which goes around the mountain is ninety-

five miles long—and that at the highest practicable elevation near timber line.

The glory of the southern part of the range is Crater Lake. It lies in the crater that is all that remains of a mountain posthumously named Mount Mazama. It is six miles in diameter and is surrounded by brightly colored volcanic walls two thousand feet high in places. It is just four feet less than two thousand feet deep and has no visible outlet. Its most dramatic feature, however, is the color of its water, a brilliant blue. One of the most awesome experiences that may be had in the range is to go boating on Crater Lake and to drift about one of the crags that reach up out of its depths. Though the water is just as blue when seen from the rim, its remarkable clarity is more apparent from the lake's surface. From far below the rock is seen to soar upward, and the boat seems suspended alongside it in a medium no denser than air.

The lake was discovered in 1853 by a party of prospectors. Two groups of gold hunters had met in the region, one of which held the supposed secret of the "Lost Cabin Mine." The objective of this group was told in a moment of drunken confidence to a member of the second group, and there followed a long pursuit and eventual joining of forces. When the search for gold was resumed, the leader of the interloping party made the big discovery of their somewhat comic expedition. The leader, John W. Hillman, was riding rather inattentively over a gently sloping hillside through open forest when his mule stopped abruptly. Directly in front of him and far below, Hillman saw the brilliant color of Crater Lake. His reported reaction was that he was glad the mule wasn't blind. Hillman found more than the average seeker of lost mines, though it is scarcely necessary to add that he never got to dig in the Lost Cabin Mine.

Between Crater Lake and Rainier are many areas which, although less famous, are as worth visiting as these two. In a triangle around the Columbia River Gorge is the well-known group of Hood, Adams, and Saint Helens. To the south of these are Mount Jefferson and the cluster about the Three Sisters. This area is one of the most distinctive parts of the volcanic system. It has the sharp contrasts of desolate lava fields and gentle meadows, of rocky spires and undulating plains, of dark evergreen forest and sparkling lakes. Much of it is a sunny open mountain country with nearly level land between the peaks. Most of its forest is ponderosa pine. Through groves of these trees it is possible to see for long distances, and there is no sense of being shut in by foliage. There are many park lands—high meadows dotted by shallow pools and small groups of alpine trees. Perhaps the finest of all the park lands of the range is at the northern foot of Mount Jefferson. It lies on the floor of a small hidden valley which runs squarely across the divide. Mount Jefferson, architecturally an almost perfect mountain, on this side rises suddenly from the level, flower-covered floor of the valley, and there is complete harmony in the combination of sharp icy rock and soft grassy fields.

This valley, Jefferson Park, can be reached only by trail. Its beauty, like that of many similar places in the Cascades, is fragile and could easily disappear before a road. The trail system of the Cascades makes most of these places accessible with relatively little effort. For people with unlimited time, the Pacific Crest Trail follows close to the top of the range and through spots such as Jefferson Park. Much of the range,

however, does not permit trail building along its summit. No
single trail, moreover, could touch all of the range. Yet by
taking parts of the Pacific Crest Trail one at a time and by
using the trails that lead in through the foothills, very
nearly all of the Cascades can be seen progressively on short
holidays and week ends.

THE NORTHERN SYSTEM

In the northern part of the state of Washington the character of the Cascades changes abruptly. There is a hint of
nonvolcanic structures in Goat Rocks north of Mount Adams,
and near Mount Rainier there are striking though small
peaks that are clearly not of volcanic origin. The main transition, however, occurs between Rainier and Stevens Pass, the
most northern of the usable routes across the range. Within
this distance, a little more than sixty miles, the range becomes wider, more complex, and more rugged. More to the
north these characteristics become even more pronounced.
The mountains are larger, and the valleys deeper and
wilder, until the region at the head of Lake Chelan is
reached. From here to the Canadian boundary there is no
break in the mountains of this different system.

This region has been described as the most alpine of our
American mountain areas. Certainly the mountains are as
numerous, as precipitous, and as abundant in glaciers—
though most of the glaciers are small—as those of the Alps.
On one very important score, however, this region is the
antithesis of the Alps: it is a wilderness. There are few parts
of the United States in so completely wild a state. Roads
are few and poor; there are not many trails, and those which
exist receive little attention. From the valleys, which are

the main lines of such travel as does pass through the country, it is not often possible to see much except dense forest.
There is much wildlife—deer, bear, cougar, mountain goat,
marmot, grouse, and ptarmigan. To see the region it is necessary to go by foot or by horse to the high passes, and even
this does not permit more than a sampling in a single trip.
The country is accessible for only a short part of the year.
During the winter months, which extend from October to
May, the trails are closed by snow and there is repeated
danger of avalanches. A few skiers penetrate into the high
regions in March and April and are rewarded by seeing the
mountains at their best. During the summer many tourists
approach the area and some fishermen and climbers enter it,
but only a handful discover for themselves the singular appeal of this loveliest part of the Cascades.

The northern system is relatively unknown. Part of the
reason lies in its inaccessibility. This is not a complete explanation, though. With the expenditure of a little energy
and at no great cost it is possible to see some of it. One of
the causes is that there is no hint outside the area of what it
contains. On the map the region does not seem particularly
impressive. The altitudes that appear on the map are between 8,000 and 9,500 feet. There are many undistinguished
areas with such elevations. But perhaps nowhere else is the
convention of measuring the scale of mountains by reference
to sea level more deceptive. Repeatedly in this area, 8,000-
foot mountains seem large by comparison with peaks of
14,000 feet in other ranges. Dome Mountain rises 6,400
feet from the West Fork of the Agnes in a horizontal distance of two and one-half miles. Mount Eldorado rises 7,000
feet above the Cascade River in a little more than two miles.

There are many such examples. The depth of the valleys perhaps gives a more accurate impression of height than the mountains' elevation above sea level. The valleys, which are largely U-shaped, continue at nearly sea level far into the mountains on the west side. Then they rise in a series of sharp steep steps or end suddenly at the foot of towering cliffs. The same is true on the east, though there the valleys are slightly higher. This mountain system, unlike the Sierra, is equally developed and rugged on both its east and west sides. Glaciers tend to be more numerous on the eastern slopes, but this is the only significant difference in the structure of the mountains.

Although this northern system is intersected by many deep valleys, its average height is considerably above that of the volcanic section. For this reason the number of streams that characterize the entire range is greater than in the southern regions. At the final cirque of any valley there are many lines of water streaming down the cliffs. In early summer there may be two dozen of these waterfalls at the head of one valley. They will dwindle as the season advances, but even in early autumn most of them will remain. During the summer the streams of the region are often barriers to travel. A creek which in the morning is easily forded can become an impassable torrent by late afternoon.

There is little in the way of recorded history of the region. The trappers of the Hudson's Bay Company penetrated the area, and occasionally an old rusted beaver trap is discovered, or the ruins of a log cabin out of which large cedar trees are growing. A minor prospecting boom flared early in the century. Trails were built into many valleys which are now inaccessible because of the dense undergrowth

of alder. The boom collapsed under the cruel difficulties of
working in the country, but a few of the faithful kept on.
Not many years ago two men making a snow survey for one
of the power companies were staying in the middle of winter at a tiny cabin near Lyman Lake. They had had a long
trip by snowshoe, and so far as they knew they were the
only men in many miles. They heard a strange and startling
sound outside. Opening the door, they found Blue Mountain Ole, who had come to visit his "mine." Blue Mountain
Ole had good samples to show, but his diggings were somewhere above the Lyman Glacier. Now that he is dead people
occasionally go out to look for his mine.

As the price of metals rises and falls, mining activity in
the region grows and dwindles. A few companies have succeeded in working the largely low-grade ores of the range,
but the typical history is one of a small stock company
founded on high hopes and deep illusions. It spends its resources in cutting a road or trail to its claims and in blasting
a small hole in the ground. A few rich samples are taken
from small fissure veins and there is much excitement. Then
the harsh winters and the hard rock of the country take their
toll, and as the costs of bringing out the ore are realized
the undertaking fails. The visible accomplishment is only an
ugly mound of refuse in what had once been a pleasant spot.
Antiquated mining laws still permit adventurers to lay claim
to regions in which they can find minerals and to gain possession of the land for their own ends, whether for stock
promotion, commercial resorts, or even private lodges. It is
no longer possible for miners to set fire to the forests of
whole valleys to make prospecting easy, as they once did,

but the existence of outcrops of brightly colored rocks remains a curse on the country.

From the summit of any high peak of the northern system there are views of an apparently limitless expanse of mountains. Unlike the mountains of the volcanic system, these peaks lie in ridges or ranges. Some of the largest of the peaks can be identified, but many are either unnamed or have only collective names. Glaciers by the score hang on the sides of the cliffs. These glaciers are small compared to the vast streams which existed during the ice age. The prehistoric Chelan Glacier was nearly ninety miles long. This glacier, which receded long ago, left one of the deepest canyons of the continent in its place. Most of the canyon is filled with a lake whose surface is at an altitude of eleven hundred feet but whose bottom is over three hundred feet below sea level. Mountains as high as eight thousand feet rise above the lake.

In every direction there are mazes of radiating valleys. Some seem to lie athwart the axis of the chain, but none furnish easy routes through the range. These valleys are often somber places to enter. In some of them the forest arches completely over the trail, so that on the brightest days little sunlight reaches the ground. A thick mat of needles and decaying wood is underfoot, and there is little sound except that of running water. Tracks of animals are frequently seen on the trails, but seldom the animals themselves. A few birds pass like shadows among the tops of the trees, but they are silent. On days of bad weather, dark clouds flow down the valleys and each needle drips with moisture, though there may be no rain.

There are other valleys which open at an elevation of

about four thousand feet to meadows of grass and small shrub-like plants. Small groves of spruce, fir, and hemlock divide these fields. The mountains which surround the valleys rise directly from the meadows, first in short steep rockslides and then in sheer cliffs. Such valleys are delightful in summer but are often terrifying during winter, when avalanches pour off the cliffs on either side.

At the head of nearly every valley there is a zone of "high country" similar in some ways to the parkland areas of the volcanoes. Here at elevations of five to seven thousand feet are the high passes. Near the passes there are again meadows, but they are more delicate and more given over to flowers and heather. The trees are smaller and more stunted. Small clumps of white-bark pine, mountain hemlock, and alpine fir are scattered among the meadows. Gaunt twisted larches grow in lines along the tops of the lower ridges. Each of the passes is a window to long reaches of the country—to the walls and glaciers of the nearby peaks, to waterfalls from the upper snow fields, and to series of peaks and ridges which continue indefinitely toward the horizon.

Two volcanoes, Mount Baker and Glacier Peak, rise in the midst of the northern system. From any high summit, their massive rounded forms are landmarks on the jagged skyline of the area. In the mingling of the two systems there is the same harmony of contrast that is the continual surprise of the range. Fittingly, the northern system reaches its culmination close to these two volcanoes. From Cloudy Pass the symmetrical outline of Glacier Peak in the west is balanced by long lines of sharp rocky peaks extending north, east, and south. With the foreground of meadows, streams,

and deep evergreen valleys, here are found all the elements
of the Cascades.

THE PUBLIC DOMAIN

Throughout the length of the Cascades there are few
areas that are not the property of the people of the United
States. Because of the wisdom of a relatively few men, near
the turn of the century, the best of our mountains and the
natural resources which they hold have been preserved for
the nation. Today, with the exception of several state parks,
various small islands of private property and other land
exploited for private interest, the Cascade Range is under
the care and supervision of the federal government.

Three areas in the range have been made National Parks.
These, Mount Rainier National Park, Crater Lake National
Park, and Lassen Volcanic National Park, have been established by Congress and are administered by the National
Park Service of the Department of the Interior. In all the
National Parks the interests of conservation are paramount,
and the only permitted use of the parks is for the public's
enjoyment. The Park Service supervises the concessions
which serve visitors, and itself provides many facilities such
as roads, trails, museums, and guide service. In general, the
regulations of the Parks are more stringent than those of
the National Forests. No firearms are permitted, for all
game in the Parks is protected against hunters. Visitors are
more carefully supervised, and less commercialization is allowed. The policies of the Park Service have been criticized
at times, but it is true that the cause of conservation has been
well served by the National Park system.

Most of the Cascades, however, are in the National For-

ests. Beginning with Mount Baker and Chelan National
Forests on the Canadian line and extending to Lassen National Forest in California, there are twelve such forests
(*see* Appendix). The heavy responsibility for protecting this
large area against fire and pests and of administering its use
lies with the Forest Service, a branch of the Department of
Agriculture. This agency, one of the oldest of the career
services and one of the most competent, has an exceedingly
varied task.

The most familiar job of the Forest Service is fire protection. The forests of the Pacific Northwest are in a zone
of very low humidity during the late summer months, and
among the curses of the region are the all too frequent pillars of smoke that rise out of the mountains to spread like
clouds over the entire area. The cost of these fires is something that can seldom be assessed fully. When the forests
are destroyed there is a loss not only of usable timber but
of water resources as well, for the forests are the reservoirs
from which a large part of the Northwest draws its water
for irrigation and for life.

The Forest Service is committed to a policy of multiple
use of the forests. Since the war a strong emphasis of the
Service has been to make timber available for building homes
that are needed throughout the country. The objective is
to place the forests on a "sustained yield" basis, so that the
maturing trees will be harvested as a crop, leaving the
younger trees to grow and maintain the forest. This policy
should prevent the devastation that has fallen on some of
the once pleasant valleys of the range. There have admit-
tedly been places where the policy of sustained yield has
not been strictly followed, and there is continual clamor

from mill operators for more "liberal" cutting privileges.

Sheep and cattle graze in large areas of the forests. This is one of the most difficult interests to satisfy. There have been attempts to gain large tracts for exclusive use for grazing. The attempts have been discredited, but there is no assurance that they will not be repeated. Overgrazing, particularly by sheep, can destroy not only the beauty of the high meadows where the animals range but the water supplies which rise among the grasslands.

Recreational use is one of the primary purposes of the forests. A wide range of facilities, from open-trail shelters to a million-dollar hotel on Mount Hood, are offered by the Forest Service. There is an increasing demand for "development" of the wilderness areas of the Cascade forest, so that picnickers may arrive in cars and skiers may ride uphill on cableways. This demand is being met to a considerable degree. However, a few areas have been set aside as Wild and Wilderness Areas, in order that a little of the original flavor of the Cascades may be preserved. These areas, though, are only a small part of the range.

Much of the finest of the Cascades is in the National Forests. None of the National Parks contains anything superior to the mountains of the Stehekin River watershed. That such areas are not federal parks is owing not to any inferiority in beauty, but to public support of the Forest Service policy: that the forests shall be used to serve various purposes. This is a good policy, but only when wisely administered. It cannot be wisely administered unless there is a realization by the people of America that the forests and all they contain can be destroyed, and that there are always special interests willing to despoil the forests for selfish ends.

The National Forests are not so well protected by law against such depredations as the National Parks. The Forest Service, as an arm of a democratic government, is responsive to the desires of the public. If the public grows indifferent, its desires can be confused with the variety of special demands. The mountains of the Cascades are a part of our natural heritage, and it is a public responsibility to see that they are protected and used wisely.

CASCADE HOLIDAY

by Weldon F. Heald

The Cascades in summer offer to the mountain enthusiast the richest and most varied fare of any range in the United States. Along the seven-hundred-mile crest from northern California to the Canadian border are our greatest remaining forests, our fairest alpine meadows, our largest glaciers, and our grandest peaks. And the follower of Cascade trails, whether he be hiker, fisherman, mountain climber, hunter, camper, or leisurely automobile tourist, can find in a lifetime more diverse kinds of topography, vegetation, climate, and scenery than in any other mountains in the country.

For the Cascades are not a single, homogeneous range like the Sierra Nevada to the south. Stretching through ten degrees of latitude—which corresponds on the East Coast to the distance from Philadelphia to southern Labrador—the Cascades show three distinct climatic and topographic provinces, each quite different from the others.

In the northern California section the range starts hesitantly in thinly wooded, semi-arid lava plains with the giant cones of Mount Shasta and Lassen Peak dominating a haphazard group of round, dead volcanoes. Through Oregon the Cascades hump up into a broad, mile-high, eroded plateau, surmounted at intervals by a chain of symmetrical, dormant fire-mountains, streaked by snow and streaming with glaciers. Northward the forests thicken and lakes multiply, and in south-central Washington the alpine section begins. Although much of this region is still little-known wilderness, nevertheless it is the climax of the Cascades. Within an area of 10,500 square miles—equal in size to nine Rhode Islands—is a maze of jagged, glacier-hung peaks and ridges. Far below, deep narrow valleys twist and turn, carrying milky torrents which rage between towering fir forests of almost tropical luxuriance.

But different as they are, all three sections offer some of the best fishing, hiking, camping, and climbing on the continent. Here is a mountain banquet spread out in three lavish courses—enough to satisfy the most exacting outdoor epicure season after season. But with such an overflowing menu of superlatives, how can the average mountain-hungry vacationist be sure to get the most out of his short Cascade summer holiday?

Of course, the best way to know and savor mountains is to leave civilization behind, hit the trail on foot or horseback, and camp out under the stars for a few days, a week, or a month. And there are thousands of miles of trail in the three sections of the Cascade Range. They thread silent forests, climb to high-perched lakes, cross velvet parks, and circle the fire-mountains just below the glaciers. Following these trails with knapsack or pack train is the chosen way of the true mountaineer.

But the Cascade banquet is lavish enough so that the automobile tourist can partake of his share. He, too, can find high passes to cross—in a sedan; climb to timber line in his convertible, or park his trailer in a campground beside a rushing trout stream. And even the hurrying train traveler through the Cascades can catch quick glimpses of thundering waterfalls, snowy peaks, and forest-bordered lakes from the astra dome of his streamliner.

So if you are a mountain lover—afoot, on horseback, or behind a steering wheel—there is your particular kind of outdoor summer holiday awaiting you in the Cascades. The banquet table is set. Let us scan the opulent bill of fare and from it you can select the choice morsels which appeal to you the most.

FIRST COURSE—NORTHERN CALIFORNIA

Northward from Sacramento, U.S. Highway 99 and the Southern Pacific's Cascade Line lead up California's wide-sweeping Great Central Valley to Oregon. As you approach the little town of Corning, nestled among miles of olive groves, a ghostly white cloud appears on the horizon ahead. Farther on, the cloud grows and materializes into a huge, symmetrical volcanic cone sheathed in shining snows. It is Mount Shasta, the great southern sentinel of the Cascades. This soaring peak is the first of a stately procession of eleven ice-clad giant mountains which extend northward along the axis of the range through Oregon and Washington to the Canadian border.

Shasta dominates the head of the Great Central Valley, but it has not always held the center of the stage. Seventy miles southeast, where the volcanic Cascades merge with the granite Sierra Nevada, stands Lassen Peak. It appears as an undistinguished, rounded hump rising above the rolling mountains east of the valley. But suddenly on May 30,

1914, without warning, Lassen Peak burst into violent eruption. The crater belched mushrooming clouds of smoke accompanied by explosive ejections of dust, rock, and super-
heated gases. Later, lava poured down the west slope while
the whole mountain shook and rumbled.

For seven years Lassen Peak was the only active volcano
in the United States. Altogether, about three hundred eruptions occurred before the outburst spent itself in 1921. Today Lassen is peaceful again, but the region roundabout
exhibits such remarkable examples of recent volcanic action
that it was set aside in 1916 to be preserved in its natural
state.

Lassen Volcanic National Park, southernmost and smallest of the three national parks in the Cascade Range, has
an area of 163 square miles. Besides the mountain itself, it
includes groups of hissing steam vents, boiling mud springs,
miniature geysers, and other dramatic indications that the
fires of Lassen are not dead. In the park, too, are scores of
mountain lakes, wild-flower meadows, evergreen forests,
waterfalls, and trout streams. From Red Bluff you can take
an all-paved loop to include Lassen, returning to Highway
99 either at Redding or Mount Shasta City.

The Lassen road leads east to the little forest resort of
Mineral, forty-seven miles east from Red Bluff. There it
turns north and climbs through magnificent fir forests for
eight miles to the park entrance. In another mile you reach
the Sulphur Works, some 7,000 feet up on the south slope of
Lassen Peak. You are now close to the heart of the sleeping volcano. Steam vents, boiling mud pots, and hot sulphur
springs line a canyon bottom stained by chemical action into
pastel shades of pink, green, and blue. Five miles farther

on, a foot trail leads in a little over a mile to another volcanic inferno called Bumpas Hell. In a steaming ten-acre hollow are mud springs, small geysers, boiling pools, and scorching gas vents.

Besides these two easily reached exhibits of volcanism, there are several others accessible by longer trail trips. Devils Kitchen, Boiling Springs Lake, and Willow Creek Geyser are all within hiking distance of Drakesbad, a small resort within the Park at the end of a fifteen-mile spur road from the lumber town of Chester. Another road, poor but passable, leads from Chester thirteen miles north to beautiful Juniper Lake, largest in the park, and Horseshoe Lake, two miles beyond, where the Park Service maintains improved campgrounds. Trails lead from these lakes into the roadless eastern section of Lassen Volcanic National Park.

Beyond the Sulphur Works the main loop highway continues to wind up the mountain's southern slope. It passes Emerald and Helen lakes and crosses the southeastern shoulder of Lassen Peak at an elevation of 8,475 feet, the greatest height reached by an automobile road in the entire Cascade Range. At the high point a foot trail climbs to the summit of the volcano, 10,453 feet. It is a boulevard among trails, wide and gentle enough for lovers to stroll up arm in arm, and it makes Lassen the most painless Cascade fire-mountain to ascend.

Snow lies deep and long on Lassen's upper slopes. The area has become a popular winter sports center, each season closing with a ski meet on the Fourth of July.

The road dips down from the high point through lush Kings Creek Meadows, passes pleasant, forest-fringed Summit Lake with its two improved campgrounds, to the Devastated Area. Here during the violent 1915 eruptions, horizontal blasts of hot gases swept down Lassen's northeast slope. The snow cover was instantly melted and the water and gases swept everything before them for a distance of ten miles. Vegetation is again beginning to take root on the barren hillsides, but the evidence of the complete ruin of forests, brush, and meadows is still a striking example of the power of our only active volcano.

At Manzanita Lake, which reflects the cone of Lassen in its quiet waters, is the National Park headquarters and museum. The northern Park entrance is a mile beyond. From here you can complete the Lassen loop to Redding, fifty-two miles, or you may continue on State Route 89 by way of McArthur-Burney Falls State Park and McCloud to Highway 99 at Mount Shasta City. This latter is an interesting trip through rugged volcanic country, and Burney Falls, 128 feet high, is one of the most beautiful in California.

Ten miles north of Redding is one of the greatest structures ever built by man. Just below the confluence of the Sacramento, Pit, and McCloud rivers stands gigantic Shasta Dam, the principal unit in California's $400,000,000 Central Valley Project. Planned for irrigation, power, and flood control, the massive concrete dam took seven years to build and is 560 feet high and 3,500 feet across at the top. Behind it stretches the blue waters of artificial Shasta Lake, which winds up the three river canyons among the hills for over twenty miles.

Highway 99 and the Southern Pacific Railroad are carried across an arm of Shasta Lake on a high, double-decked bridge. Nearby are boat landings and bathing beaches on the new lake, which is rapidly becoming a popular recreation center. After crossing another smaller inlet, the highway ascends the narrow, wooded canyon of the brawling Sacramento River and comes out on the open plateau at the foot of towering Mount Shasta.

Rising in majestic isolation, over ten thousand feet above the forested uplands at its base, Mount Shasta is the second highest peak of the Cascade Range but is second to none in impressiveness. "Lonely as God and white as a winter moon," its vast, shapely bulk dominates the region for scores of miles in every direction. Like all the great peaks of the Cascades, Shasta is a dead or dormant volcano, built up through ages of time by successive eruptions of ashes and lava. Its main summit is 14,161 feet in elevation and Shastina, a secondary crater, a mile and a half to the west, attains 12,433 feet.

But it is unfortunate that most visitors see only the south side of Mount Shasta. Early-day lumbering and repeated forest fires have given the mountain a less attractive setting than any other major Cascade peak. Then too, from the little-known north and east sides Shasta itself is much finer. The upper slopes are sheathed in glistening ice fields, and five glaciers stream down the mountain's sides. A poor back-country road traverses the wild region northeast of Mount Shasta and is worth taking for a revelation of the real majesty of this great snow-capped volcano.

The ascent to the summit is laborious rather than difficult, and it requires no technical acrobatics of advanced alpinism. From Mount Shasta City the recently built John Everitt Memorial Highway now permits you to drive your car up the south slope to an elevation of 7,600 feet. A mile and a half by trail brings you to the Sierra Club's Shasta Alpine

Lodge, four hundred feet higher. During the summer there is usually a custodian in charge and camping space is available. The summit climb takes eight to ten hours round trip from the lodge, depending upon snow conditions. But if you start around 2·00 A.M. and make Thumb Rock for sunrise you will see one of the grandest sights of your life.

At the lumber town of Weed, nine miles north of Mount Shasta City, U.S. Highway 97 branches northeast from Highway 99. From here to the Canadian line the two major roads parallel each other along the east and west bases of the Cascade Range. At intervals, crossroads climb over the crest, joining the two highways. Thus the Cascade road system on a map resembles a ladder, with routes 97 and 99 the sides and fifteen or so transverse roads forming the rungs.

Highway 99 follows the green, forested west side through the thickly inhabited part of the agricultural and lumbering Pacific Northwest. Farther along it are the cities of Portland, Tacoma, and Seattle as well as scores of smaller pleasant and prosperous communities. Highway 97, on the other hand, lies along the high, thinly populated, semi-arid plateau at the east base of the Oregon Cascades. It traverses a yellow-brown land of vast distances, open pine forests, jagged lava flows, and rolling wheat fields. In Washington, 97 crosses several eastern spurs of the mountains, dips down into broad valleys famous for their irrigated fruit, then hugs the west bank of the Columbia River almost to Canada. It would be difficult to find two parallel routes with but a single mountain range between them which show a greater divergence in climate, scenery, and human activities than these two Cascade highways.

North from Weed, Highway 99 crosses the Klamath

River, climbs over the Siskiyou Mountains, and drops down into the sheltered, tree-shaded town of Ashland. You are now in Oregon. There is a greener, more northern look to the countryside. And to the east the high, even plateau of the Cascades begins, with the snow-splashed cone of Mount McLoughlin, 9,493 feet, rising to a point above it. At Medford a crossroad heads for the high Cascades. Its destination is Crater Lake, and the chances are a hundred to one you will take it.

SECOND COURSE—OREGON

Once, not so many thousand years ago, the Cascade Range possessed a twelfth great volcano rivaling Shasta and Rainier in size. One day this 12,000-foot peak vanished. Seventeen cubic miles of mountain disappeared completely in the fires, smoke, and dust of a gigantic eruption Geologists, who know about such things, call the prehistoric volcano Mount Mazama, and explain how it came about that we lost a mountain and gained one of the continent's superb natural wonders—Crater Lake.

When the upper part of the majestic, ice-clad peak exploded or fell in upon itself during a prodigious eruption, it left a stupendous circular crater five to six miles across and 4,000 feet deep, walled by precipitous, jagged cliffs. For hundreds of years this steaming, fiery caldron gradually cooled, then water seeped in and filled it halfway to the brim. Thus was Crater Lake born where once a great volcano stood.

Although there is no visible inlet or outlet, the lake today maintains a constant level and its waters are clear, cold, and unbelievably blue. When you stand on the rim, looking

down on Crater Lake enclosed in an almost perfect circle
of color-stained cliffs one to two thousand feet high, you
are not only struck by its unique beauty, but also with a sense
of mystery and awe. The titanic forces which made this lake
are stilled, but they have left their impress on every detail
of the landscape.

Crater Lake National Park was created in 1902 with an
area of 251 square miles. At the Park village, on the southwest rim at an elevation of over 7,000 feet, are a lodge,
housekeeping cabins, cafeteria, and public campgrounds. A
zigzag trail descends 900 feet to the lake and another leads
to Garfield Peak, 8,060 feet, one of the finest viewpoints in
the Park. Each day a ranger-naturalist conducts an automobile caravan around the 39-mile road which circles the
rim. He stops at all the spectacular viewpoints and explains
the fascinating story of the suicide of Mount Mazama and
the birth of Crater Lake.

But perhaps the lake is at its best seen from a launch
skimming across its blue waters. If you have an explorer's
instinct you can spend days pushing into the many small
coves at the foot of the cliffs, visiting Wizard Island with its
crater, and circling the lava pinnacles of the Phantom Ship.
Your fisherman's urge may be satisfied at the same time,
fly casting or trolling for rainbow trout. For Crater Lake is
in good fishing country. The Rogue River which has its
source near the Park is one of the most famous trout-fishing
streams in the world and the home of the gamy steelhead.

From the Park village on the rim, the crossroad from
Medford drops down through the pine, fir, and hemlock
forests which clothe the sides of old Mount Mazama and
joins Highway 97 on the east side of the range thirty-eight

miles north of Klamath Falls. A few miles below the junction, the main highway follows the east shore of Upper Klamath Lake, forty miles long and eight miles wide. Almost every kind of North American waterfowl can be seen on Klamath Lake during spring and fall migrations, and its waters are the home of hundreds of giant white pelicans.

Klamath Falls, somewhat below the lake's southern outlet, is a busy modern city, center of a rich lumbering, agricultural, cattle- and sheep-raising area. Mountain roads lead west into the heart of the Cascades. Among deep forests at elevations of five thousand to seven thousand feet are many little lakes and streams stocked with rainbow, cutthroat, eastern brook, and silverside salmon, while bass and catfish can be taken at Hyatt Lake and Lake of the Woods. The latter, evergreen-bordered and dominated by the great cone of Mount McLoughlin, is one of the most beautiful in the southern Cascades. On its shores are resorts, campgrounds, summer cottages, and bathing beaches.

But the greatest concentration of lakes in the entire range lies north of Crater Lake. For a distance of sixty miles on both sides of the crest are scattered a dozen large bodies of water, ranging in length from one to six miles, while scores of smaller ones are tucked away in the green folds of the mountains.

The lake region is traversed both by a high-speed, trans-Cascade highway and the Southern Pacific's Cascade Line which crosses over the mountains from eastern Oregon to the Willamette Valley. But the mountain lover who is willing to leave paved boulevards can take State Route 209 directly north from Crater Lake.

This leisurely forest road crosses the barren expanse of

the Pumice Desert, legacy of Mount Mazama's eruption, to charming Diamond Lake, cradled between needle-sharp Mount Thielsen and the rounded dome of Mount Bailey. Fishing and swimming are excellent, and there are rustic resorts and improved campgrounds. North of Diamond Lake the road penetrates the wild, heavily wooded headwaters of the Umpqua River, climbs the divide at Windigo Pass, then drops down to Crescent Lake and the trans-Cascade highway, fifty-four miles from Crater Lake Village.

Besides Crescent Lake, backed by snowy Diamond Peak, and Odell Lake on the railroad and highway, there are Davis, Summit, Big and Little Cultus, and Waldo lakes reached by fair mountain roads. A network of foot and horse trails cover the mountains and lead to many smaller lakes.

The famous Oregon Skyline Trail, too, runs through the center of the region. From the Columbia River to the California line this superlative pathway in the wilderness follows the high backbone of the Cascades. For four hundred miles it winds up under snowy peaks, crosses exquisite flower meadows, passes more than seven hundred lakes, and leads through vast silent forests. The Oregon Skyline Trail is a link in the 2,150-mile Pacific Crest Trail which traverses the length of the Cascade Range, Sierra Nevada, and southern California mountains from Canada to Mexico. The Cascade Crest Trail in Washington, the Oregon Skyline Trail, and Lava Crest Trail in northern California now furnish a continuous knapsack and pack-train route through a thousand miles of the finest scenery in the high Cascades.

The next cross-mountain road to the north is the well-known McKenzie River Highway, connecting Eugene on the west with Bend in eastern Oregon. The road is named for the rushing, foam-flecked McKenzie River, one of Oregon's famed fishing streams, which it follows for fifty miles on the west slope. Near the mile-high crest of the range the highway winds through lake-dotted alpine meadows and fields of desolate, black lava at the base of a trio of imposing snow-capped peaks. These are the Three Sisters.

Rising to more than ten thousand feet, the great dormant volcanoes carry numerous glaciers on their broad shoulders; the Collier Glacier, between North and Middle Sister, is the largest in Oregon. Surrounding the Three Sisters is a region of mountain parks, fir- and hemlock-fringed lakes, cascading streams, and a veritable show-window exhibition of recent and intense volcanism.

The highway crosses McKenzie Pass, 5,325 feet, and meets Highway 97 at Bend, a thriving lumber town lying at the east base of the Three Sisters. Its hungry, whining sawmills are fed from hundreds of square miles of ponderosa pine roundabout. But Bend is also a recreation center from which roads lead into the mountains to Suttle Lake, Metolius River, famed for its fishing, and the Three Sisters country.

The ninety-mile Century Drive circles the southeastern part of the last-named region. It is a good graded road which climbs to over six thousand feet to a mountain gateway between Bachelor Butte and rugged Broken Top, then descends into a broad upland valley at the foot of the towering South Sister. At pine-bordered Sparks and Elk lakes are resorts and pack stations where you can outfit for a week's or a month's camping trip. There is plenty of variety and elbow room for a wilderness vacation in this section of the Cascades, for nearly four hundred square miles have been set aside by the United States Forest Service as the Three Sisters Primitive * Area.

One of the most intelligent and farseeing policies of the Forest Service is to preserve a small part of the magnificent National Forest Area as wilderness. Beginning in the 1920's, some of the nation's wildest and most rugged areas of mountain and forest were set aside as examples of primitive America as God made it. As far as possible these last bits of wilderness will be preserved as samples of a world undisturbed by man. They are havens of camp and trail life where roads, buildings, and commercial resorts are taboo. The modern city dweller, on foot or with pack train, may catch his fish, sit by his fire, and live an outdoor life in surroundings comparable to those of the pioneer trappers and mountain men of a century ago.

Today there are nine Forest Service Primitive Areas in the Cascade Range—three in Washington, four in Oregon, and two in northern California. These representative pieces of our once great western wilderness, wisely preserved by the Forest Service, are not advertised as are the National Parks. Their trails are still uncrowded; their remote lakes, meadows, forests, and peaks are visited only by those few who seek out the peace and inspiration which can be found to the fullest degree only in nature's wildest places.

There are many such places in the Three Sisters region. But perhaps the most perfect bit of unspoiled country in the Oregon Cascades is Jefferson Park in the Mount Jefferson Primitive Area, thirty miles to the north.

* Since this manuscript was sent to the printer, the United States Forest Service has declared the term "Primitive Area" obsolete; henceforth Wild and Wilderness Areas will be the accepted terms. "Wild" indicates an area under 100,000 acres, and "Wilderness," one over 100,000 acres.

If I were asked what was the most characteristic feature which distinguishes the Cascades from all other mountains on earth, I think I would vote for the subalpine parks just below timber line which line the crest of the range like a string of emeralds. Cascade parks are nature's landscaping brought to faultless perfection, and to camp and wander in such exquisite flowery sky-meadows is, to me, one of the greatest pleasures in following Cascade trails.

Jefferson Park is among the finest of these mountain meadows. Cupped in a westward facing basin high up under snowy Mount Jefferson, it spreads a full two square miles of lush greensward enameled with beds of blue lupine, delicate pink shooting stars, and the carmine points of Indian paintbrush. Among the flower gardens small crystal-clear streams gurgle between mossy banks, and still pools reflect groups of dark, spiry alpine firs and feathery mountain hemlocks. Over the rocky rim of the basin to the south, Mount Jefferson stands incredibly tall against the sky. From its lava, summit pinnacle, brilliantly shining snow fields sweep down the long slopes, their surfaces broken by cold, steely blue outlines of glacial crevasses.

Surely, when good mountaineers die they must be transported to some Elysian alpine abode resembling Jefferson Park.

The Mount Jefferson region is reached by the north branch of the Santiam Highway which crosses the range from Bend to Salem. Going west, the road forks from the McKenzie Highway at Sisters, twenty-two miles from Bend. After passing around the north shore of charming Suttle Lake, the road climbs to Hogg Pass and forks again two miles below Lost Lake on the west slope. The main highway continues down the long valley of the Santiam River to Albany; the right-hand branch crosses a broad, flat divide to the headwaters of the turbulent North Santiam River which it follows to Salem.

Around the road junction is an interesting region of forests and lakes dominated by the rocky spires of Mount Washington to the south and Three Fingered Jack on the north. Big, Fish, and Clear lakes, with improved campgrounds, are reached by short spur roads. This section of the Cascade crest is streaked with hardened streams of black lava from the geologically recent volcanic field which centered around Belknap Crater, ten miles south.

The North Santiam Highway penetrates a heavily timbered area, until recently known only to lonely trappers, hunters, forest rangers, and hikers. For twenty miles the road roughly parallels the west boundary of the Mount Jefferson Primitive Area. This 135 square miles of roadless wilderness includes 10,495-foot Mount Jefferson, Oregon's second highest peak, as well as twenty-two miles of the Cascade crest. A pack station is located at Marion Forks on the North Santiam River from which point good trails lead into the Primitive Area to Marion and Pamelia lakes, Hunts Cove, and Jefferson Park.

At the junction of the North Santiam and Breitenbush rivers is Detroit, a mountain village which has long been an outfitting center for parties packing into the Jefferson area for fishing, hunting, and climbing. Here you may take a scenic road to Breitenbush Hot Springs resort, then on over the summit to Olallie Lakes Recreation Area. Olallie Lake, with cabins, campers' supplies, and boats, is the largest of more than one hundred small lakes and tarns lying in an upland basin at the foot of Olallie Butte. The road continues north along the Cascade crest, following the route of the Oregon Skyline Trail through forests and meadows to the Mount Hood Loop Highway, sixty-five miles from Detroit.

At Salem, capital of Oregon, the North Santiam Highway joins Highway 99 which you once again follow down fertile Willamette Valley to Portland. But long before you reach the suburbs of the state's largest city, the slim, white, ethereal cone of Mount Hood appears in the northeast. The peak seems to be lightly floating in the sky above the long green swell of the Cascades.

For a century Mount Hood has been one of America's best known and most famous mountains. From the earliest immigrants seeking a route westward over the mountains, to the modern automobile tourist, Mount Hood has stirred the imagination of all who have beheld it. Rising with graceful symmetry to a pointed, snow-capped crown, the peak stands in magnificent isolation—calm, aloof, peaceful. Although early settlers estimated that Mount Hood was at least 18,000 feet in elevation, accurate surveys have ignominiously reduced the summit to a mere 11,225 feet. But the peak has suffered nothing from this mathematical amputation; it tops everything else in Oregon and still looks every inch of 18,000 feet high.

Portlanders affectionately call Mount Hood "Our Mountain." They take an intense civic pride in the great white volcanic cone which can be seen from every part of the city. Although forty miles distant, the mountain is as much a part of Portland as the downtown office buildings, Union Station, or Public Library. Mount Hood is pre-eminently a "people's mountain." Its streams and lakes furnish water, power, and

light to a half million Oregonians and its slopes are visited
annually by more than a million people for summer and
winter recreation.

You can take your car close up under the snows and
glaciers of Mount Hood from Portland by a 165-mile circle drive which for variety and grandeur is not surpassed
anywhere else in the United States. The two sections making
the circle back to Portland are the Columbia River Highway
and the Mount Hood Loop.

The former follows the south bank of the Columbia, together with the Union Pacific Railroad, through the immense gorge which the river has cut completely across the
basic lava rocks of the Cascade Range. Completed in 1915,
before the heyday of the ravaging bulldozer, this highway
is a classic of American road building. Every cut, fill, and
bank is carefully and artistically built up with concrete and
rustic stone retaining walls; each bridge is designed to har-
monize with the landscape; and part of the way is even
finished with neat cement curbing and gutters. Certainly the
Columbia River Highway is a remarkable monument to the
progressive, public-spirited citizens of Oregon who con-
ceived a road through the great Columbia River Gorge more
than forty years ago.

For fifty miles the highway climbs, dips, and loops beside the majestic blue river. Huge Douglas firs and lacy
maples arch overhead, and the underbrush is green and cool.
The brown basalt southern walls of the gorge, topped by
domes and pinnacles, rise a sheer one thousand to two thousand feet above the roadway. The cliffs are cut by narrow
ravines and lined with foaming waterfalls. Every bend re-
veals a new vista across the river to the forested hills of

Washington, a plumy cascade, or a deep fern-lined canyon. It is a road of a thousand fascinating details—one to drive slowly, to savor, and to enjoy fully.

Latourelle, Waukeena, Horsetail, and Multnomah falls are the finest of the many cascades. The waters of Multnomah make a perpendicular drop of over six hundred feet into a tree-fringed pool. From the falls a six-mile trail leads to Larch Mountain, 4,038 feet, from which there is a widespread panorama of the gorge, miles of rolling fir-clad mountains, and the three snowy mountain peaks: Hood, Adams, and Saint Helens. Other forest trails radiate from Eagle Creek Park recreation area to Ghost Falls, Chinidere Mountain, and Wahtum Lake.

At Bonneville, forty-three miles from Portland, is the $74,000,000 federal dam and hydroelectric project which harnesses the waters of the Columbia. The dam is 1,100 feet across to the Washington shore and impounds a reservoir behind it nearly fifty miles long. Seagoing ships pass through the huge lock beside the dam, enabling them to reach a point 176 miles inland. One of the interesting sights at Bonneville is the fish ladders where salmon actually climb stairs from the river to the lake behind the dam.

With a capacity of more than half a million horsepower, this gigantic power and navigation dam is a remarkable piece of engineering and is of inestimable value to the Pacific Northwest. But those who knew the Columbia Gorge before its erection regret that the ruthless demands of economic progress have destroyed some of the river's most beautiful spots and interesting historic sites.

At the pleasant little city of Hood River we leave the Columbia and head south on the Mount Hood Loop. The road ascends wide Hood River Valley through miles of apple and pear orchards. Straight ahead is the great shining mountain, its slopes mantled with ice and snow.

One of the finest views of Mount Hood—and certainly the most photographed—is from Lost Lake, reached by a fourteen-mile side road up the West Fork of the Hood River. With the lake as a foreground mirroring the almost perfectly symmetrical snow peak, the picture forms a balanced composition of water, forest, and mountain. At the lake are campgrounds, good swimming, and fair fishing.

Approaching the head of Hood River Valley, orchards and farms give way to evergreen forests. The loop road climbs rapidly through heavy timber to the base of the mountain and enters Mount Hood Recreation Area. Twenty-four miles from Hood River a paved branch road winds up Mount Hood's north slope to Cloud Cap Inn. The surroundings of this famous old resort lodge, built in 1889, are utterly magnificent. It is situated near timber line, six thousand feet up, at the foot of Elliot Glacier which sweeps down from Mount Hood's summit in a frozen cataract nearly three miles long. East, north, and west is a panorama over hundreds of square miles of mountain and valley, backed by three snow peaks lining the horizon. Saint Helens and Adams, each sixty miles distant, stand at either side of the giant bulk of Rainier, 115 miles away.

Cloud Cap Inn is the starting point for the north side, or Coopers Spur climb of Mount Hood. It is also on the Round-the-Mountain Trail which completely circles the peak near timber line. This 37-mile foot and horse trail passes below ten glaciers, leads through subalpine parks, over skyline ridges, and by fir-bordered lakes. From early July to the first week in August the Round-the-Mountain Trail puts on its biggest show of the year. Then the way becomes a colorful journey through banks and fields of wild flowers.

Back on the Mount Hood Loop Road you continue around the east base of the peak, following the rushing East Fork of the Hood River. Along its banks is an area of resorts and campgrounds crowded with vacationists during the summer months. The road winds up through forests and meadows, with ever-changing views of the mountain, to historic Barlow Pass. There the first wagon train of emigrants crossed the Cascades in 1845. Just beyond the pass is a junction with State Route 50 which comes up the east side of the range from U.S. Highway 97 north of Bend.

You now begin the long sixty-mile descent around the south base of Mount Hood. This area has seen amazingly rapid development in recent years as a winter sports center. But in summer the south side of the mountain cannot compare in interest and beauty with its north and east slopes. However, perched high on the broad south slope is one of the finest resort hotels in America. Timberline Lodge, opened in 1937, was a WPA project sponsored by Portland businessmen during the depression. The architecture of the long, rambling, gable-roofed building with its graceful hexagonal cupola, has been called "Cascadian" and has the feel and atmosphere of the high mountains about it. The design and construction of the lodge gave to hundreds of skilled craftsmen and artists, then on relief, the opportunity to express themselves in stone, wood, textiles, furniture, glass, and paint. Together, these anonymous workers created a co-operative masterpiece of native American art.

Timberline Lodge in summer is the starting point for the

popular south side climb of Mount Hood and the Round-the-Mountain Trail; in winter it is headquarters for some of the finest skiing in the country. In fact, the entire upper valley of the Zigzag River is a winter sports paradise with resorts, ski tows, ski trails and ski "bowls." Government Camp is the center of this south side region and is a busy place the year round. At the camp there is a settlement of hotels, tourist cabins, cafes, and service stations.

Below Government Camp the loop road descends the Zigzag River to the Sandy, which it follows almost to Portland. Mile after mile you pass forest resorts, lodges, and summer cabins. In late June masses of white, rose, and cerise blossoms of the rhododendron bring light and color to the somber fir woods by the roadside. It is a pleasant, gentle, restful country after a trip so crammed with superlative horizontal and vertical scenery.

When you drive into the suburbs of Portland after circling Mount Hood you will understand the pride and affection Oregonians have for their great white peak. You have made an acquaintance with one of the most distinctive mountain personalities in America.

THIRD COURSE—WASHINGTON

As we said at the beginning, the Cascades share their abundant riches with the mountaineer behind a steering wheel. The Mount Hood Loop is an example. But a far better way to explore, enjoy, and to know intimately its peaks, forests, meadows, lakes, and streams is to join one of the many Pacific Northwest mountain clubs. These organizations of outdoor enthusiasts range from informal groups of twenty congenial people who like to fish, hike, climb, or ski, to the Mazamas of Portland and Mountaineers of Seattle with more than a thousand members apiece.

These clubs offer the easiest and cheapest way to get out into the mountains. Most of them conduct scheduled, guided walks each Sunday to a nearby mountain or scenic spot. Week-end camping trips are taken into the back country during the warmer months. The larger clubs feature summer outings, a longer mountain vacation lasting two to four weeks. Each year a different region is visited and many enthusiasts return season after season to accompany these amiable, democratic caravans to the Cascade wilderness.

Some of the clubs also maintain lodges, cabins, and huts in the mountains, open the year round to members at nominal fees. In the cities are club headquarters, most of them with meeting and lounging rooms and well-stocked mountain libraries. A list of Cascade Range outdoor organizations will be found in the appendix. No matter which club you may join, the rewards will be far in excess of the small annual membership fee.

Each summer the Mazamas of Portland conduct climbs to the summits of Hood, Adams, and Saint Helens—the three "Guardians of the Columbia"—all visible from the city. Until recently Mount Adams was a retiring mountain, requiring a pack trip to reach the circle of alpine meadows below the glaciers. Today you may drive up to timber line on Washington's second highest mountain in half a day from Portland. Via the North Bank Highway through the Columbia River Gorge to White Salmon, then north on the Trout Lake road to Bird Creek Meadows, Mount Adams is a little over one hundred miles from Portland. The road ends high on the south slope of the huge peak in a region of parks watered by streams from the snowbanks. It is a delightful place for a leisurely camping holiday.

Mount Adams, 12,307 feet elevation, is the third highest in the Cascade Range. It is a mammoth, sprawling hulk of a mountain which humps up to four gently rounded summits. The south side climb from Bird Creek Meadows is, in mountaineers' parlance, a "walk-up," but the eleven large glaciers streaming down Adams' cone have provided experienced climbers with some of the most sporting snow and ice work in the Cascades.

The mountain is the center of a heavily wooded region penetrated by several Forest Service roads which wander for miles through the wilderness. Fishing is good in Goose, Council, Takhlaks, Bench, Mount Adams, and Walupt lakes, and automobile campgrounds are numerous in the area.

Thirty miles west of Adams, Mount Saint Helens rises in white, flawless perfection above the green swell of mountains at its base. Although the smallest of the eleven Cascade fire-mountains, and but 9,671 feet high, Saint Helens has the most evenly symmetrical cone of them all. Most of the year the mountain resembles a giant scoop of vanilla ice cream. As recently as the 1840's Saint Helens is believed to have been active. During the last eruption pumice cinders were blown out from the crater, burying the cone to a depth of ten to twenty feet. Forests were destroyed and streams were dammed into lakes. Vegetation is slowly reclaiming the devastated area, but there still remain many interesting evidences of recent volcanic action.

Mount Saint Helens is reached from Highway 99 by two spur roads extending to the base of the mountain on both the northern and southern sides. The south route is the way to go for the easiest climb to the summit; the northern road leads forty-six miles in to Spirit Lake, one of the most beautiful in the Cascades. In fact, there are few finer combinations of lake and mountain anywhere, for directly above the primeval forests on the south shore Saint Helens' glacier-clad cone towers a full 6,500 feet.

Spirit Lake lies in a primitive, unspoiled region at the north base of the mountain. Trails radiate in all directions to a score of sparkling little lakelets tucked away in the hills, where good fishing is to be had. On the south and east shores of the lake are two resorts and three improved campgrounds. Boats are available, and rainbow, eastern brook, and Montana black-spotted trout can be taken from the clear cold water.

As you travel north from Portland on Highway 99, past the neat model lumber city of Longview, to Centralia, the massive bulk of Mount Rainier looms ever larger to the northeast. When the details of rock, ice cliffs, and shining snow fields become clearer you will probably whistle and exclaim, "This is a mountain!" Thus do we mortals express admiration for the indescribable.

For Rainier is one of the world's greatest mountains and by far the largest, if not the tallest, in the United States. Even a recital of dry statistics is impressive in the case of such a gigantic feature of the earth's surface. Carl P. Richards of the Mazamas has computed that the volume of Mount Rainier above the 5,000-foot level is forty-nine cubic miles. If you could take the three "Guardians of the Columbia" and roll them into one, you would still be short nine cubic miles of material to build Mount Rainier. In sheer bulk the Big Mountain is seventeen times bigger than Saint

Helens, five times greater than Hood, and nearly twice the size of Adams.

Mount Rainier, the Indians' "mountain that was God," rises in rounded majesty from valleys two thousand feet above the sea to a total height of 14,408 feet. On its broad slopes are twenty-four glaciers clutching the cone like the radiating tentacles of a huge white octopus. Forty-five square miles of ice cover the mountain, and glacier tongues push down into the forest belt ten thousand feet below the summit. There are several ice streams five miles in length, while the six-mile Emmons Glacier is the largest and longest in the country.

The Big Mountain is the central feature of Mount Rainier National Park. With an area of 377 square miles it is the largest of the three national parks of the Cascade Range. The Park has four major entrances and two minor ones. In fact, for lovers of unspoiled mountain wilderness, Rainier's road system is becoming much too extensive. An all-paved highway branches east from Highway 99 eleven miles south of Chehalis and ascends the Cowlitz River Valley, entering the Park at Ohanapecosh Hot Springs. This road then skirts the east side of the mountain, leaves the Park at the White River Entrance in the extreme northeast corner, and continues on to Tacoma and Seattle. Where the road crosses Cayuse Pass it is joined by the Naches Highway which climbs the east slope of the range from Highway 97 at Yakima. In the southwest corner of the Park the oldest and best-known road comes in from Tacoma by the Nisqually River Entrance and winds up the mountain's south side to near timber line at Paradise Valley. Unpaved roads also reach the Park via the Mowich and Carbon rivers on the northwest side.

There are already eighty-five miles of road within the Park boundaries. Yet "cats" and "dozers" continue to bite into Rainier's flanks; a new mountain road now leads to the magnificent park country at the head of Puyallup River, and is destined to reach the Mowich Entrance; a link highway is being built to join Paradise Valley with Ohanapecosh; and there is persistent talk of a loop road to circle the mountain.

Paradise Valley and Yakima Park are the two main tourist centers in Mount Rainier National Park. Both have alpine lodges, housekeeping cabins, cafeterias, and nearby campgrounds. Similar accommodations are also available at Longmire and Ohanapecosh Hot Springs in the low forested valleys at the mountain's base.

Paradise Valley is a rolling, floral park land interspersed with groups of pointed alpine firs just below the vast glaciers and snow fields on the south side of Rainier. The rounded, white summit rises about nine thousand feet above the valley. Few places in the Cascades offer so many fascinating short walks and rides. Trails lead to Nisqually and Paradise glaciers, Reflection Lake, Sluiskin Falls, Glacier Vista, and Mazama Ridge. Ranger-naturalists conduct daily foot and horseback trips in the valley; longer all-day excursions are made twice a week.

Here is also the starting point for the summit climb. This strenuous trip, for which a guide is essential, requires two days. The night is spent at the staunch rock shelter at Camp Muir, located at ten thousand feet. The view from Columbia Crest, the highest point on the summit rim, is one of the

most extensive on the continent. A maze of Cascade peaks,
valleys, and ridges stretches north and south from the Canadian Coast Range to Mount Hood. The snowy Olympic
Mountains are outlined on the western horizon above the
blue waters of Puget Sound, while in the opposite direction
the tawny, semi-arid hills and plains of Washington's "Inland Empire" shimmer through the heat haze.

One of the top pack trips in the Cascades is around Mount
Rainier by the Wonderland Trail. For over one hundred
miles this superlative pathway traverses a region of breath-
taking grandeur. Along the route are dense "rain forests"
of fir, hemlock, and cedar, miles of high-perched flower
meadows, little lakes, streams, waterfalls, airy timber-line
ridges, deep valleys through which rage milky torrents from
the glaciers. And always the great, white mountain against
the sky with its cliffs and snow fields, frozen icefalls, and
soaring ridges. The Wonderland Trail can be made in a
week, but it is better to spend ten days or more taking some
of the many side trips. Every few years one of the mountain
clubs spends its annual summer outing hiking the Wonderland Trail; dunnage, food, and equipment are carried by
pack train.

Yakima Park is situated in a hanging valley 6,400 feet
up on a northeast spur of Mount Rainier. On that side the
dome of the mountain is an unbroken field of ice from which
the Emmons Glacier sweeps down ten thousand feet in six
miles into the forested White River Valley.

At Yakima Park, as in Paradise Valley, ranger-naturalists
conduct short walks each day to nearby points of interest.
One of the most impressive close-ups of Mount Rainier's
icy crown is from Burroughs Mountain, 7,830 feet, four

miles by trail from Yakima Park. There the Winthrop Glacier pours down the north slope past you in a silent, frozen flood a mile wide, more than five miles long, and hundreds of feet deep. You are so near to the glacier's wrinkled, riven surface that you can look into yawning crevasses and see groups of fantastic towers and pinnacles of ice. The "riffles" in this vast ice river can be likened to rapids in a stream of water: they are caused by the ponderous, slow-moving glacier's riding over rough places in its bed.

From Burroughs Mountain you may be fortunate enough to see an avalanche fall from the ice cliffs lining the top of Willis Wall high up on Rainier's north face. Periodically, thousands of tons of snow and ice break away and cascade down the 2,500-foot precipice onto the Carbon Glacier. The roar of these avalanches can be heard for many miles.

But wherever you go or whatever you do—whether you spend a month or a day in the National Park—Mount Rainier will be one of the high points of your Cascade holiday. For our biggest mountain can proudly hold its own in size, beauty, and grandeur with the great peaks of the world.

At Rainier you have entered the third, or alpine, section of the Cascade Range. Thirty-five miles southeast of the mountain the broad, mile-high, eroded plateau we have been following from southern Oregon suddenly comes to an end. Instead of isolated volcanic cones strung at intervals along the crest, the range northward now becomes a labyrinth of jagged peaks and twisting ridges, 6,000 to 9,500 feet in elevation, cut by deep, narrow winding valleys.

Even the summer climate of this northern section is decidedly sterner stuff. Although summer is the dry season, as in the south, you often discover while trying to dry your socks by the campfire that this is strictly a relative statement. Lassen Peak averages less than one-quarter inch of rain in July and August, but four and one-half inches are apt to fall at Mount Rainier during these two "dry" months. The northern peaks may be cloud-capped for days at a time, and your trip marred by zero visibility and persistent chilly drizzles which dampen the ardor of the most zealous mountaineer. On the other hand, if you are lucky the glaciers may shine brilliantly under cloudless blue skies for two weeks at a stretch. The northern Cascades are fickle and unpredictable, but they are well worth wooing. And the ardent pursuer is always rewarded sooner or later.

With increased elevation and ruggedness, the range is a formidable barrier between eastern and western Washington. North of Mount Rainier only three roads cross the crest in the 150 miles to the Canadian border. Each of them follows a transcontinental railway line. A rambling, unpaved mountain road climbs over Stampede Pass with the Northern Pacific; hard-surface U.S. Highway 10 parallels the Chicago, Milwaukee & Saint Paul and crosses the divide at Snoqualmie Pass; Route 10A goes over Stevens Pass above the eight-mile Cascade Tunnel of the Great Northern Railroad.

But these roads follow lines of least resistance over the lowest passes. True, they do traverse deep valleys among heavily forested mountains, but they are only moderately scenic, giving little hint that nearby is the most magnificent alpine wilderness in the United States. However, it is incredibly rough country. In order to see the finest of the northern Cascades, you must leave roads and civilization behind and take the trails on foot or with pack train.

There are six of these alpine areas in the northern Cascades. The southernmost is the region around Goat Rocks. Included within a 115-square-mile Forest Service Primitive Area is a ridge of sharp, flinty pinnacles more than eight thousand feet in elevation, enclosing a deep, semicircular basin of meadows and forests. On the north side of the ridge dazzling snow fields and glaciers descend to a belt of timber-line parks, sparkling with crystal streams and carpeted with wild flowers—penstemon, saxifrage, lupine, larkspur, mimulus, avalanche lilies, and paintbrush.

Here is the most southerly home of the rare and elusive mountain goat. These sure-footed, horned rock climbers, with coats of long silky hair, range northward throughout the high peaks of the Cascades. They are usually seen only as white dots moving across some impossible looking cliff far up near the skyline. Since being protected by law from hunters, mountain goats are increasing. But that other more ponderous native mountaineer, the grizzly bear, having been given no such consideration, is making a last stand far north near the Canadian border.

The Goat Rocks Primitive Area is reached from Packwood on the Cowlitz River road to Mount Rainier, or from Yakima via Tieton Reservoir on the east side. Six miles up the western approach trail is Packwood Lake. With its quiet waters, picturesque little island, and steep mountainous shores, it makes a beautiful camp site for a day or a week.

The next alpine region to the north extends along the Cascade crest for eleven miles between Snoqualmie and Stevens passes. The peaks are not high, ranging between seven and eight thousand feet, but their sharp, jagged summits stand impressively above deep radiating valleys on both sides of the range. There are a dozen small glaciers, more than fifty lakes, forests of almost tropical luxuriance, and miles of lush sky-meadows. The Cascade Crest Trail traverses the area, and numerous trails lead in from all directions. One of the best pack trips to this high country is from the Stevens Pass Highway south up the Foss River Trail to the lakes on the north side of glacier-capped Mount Daniel, highest peak of the group. Three sizable lakes, four to six miles long, all popular fishing resorts, lie southeast of the area and are accessible by car. U.S. Highway 10, the Snoqualmie Pass Highway, skirts the shore of Keechelus Lake, while Kachess and Cle Elum lakes are reached by short side roads.

Farther to the east, fifteen miles from the Cascade divide, the rocky pinnacle of Mount Stuart, 9,470 feet, dominates a detached cluster of rugged granite peaks. Geology and climate combine to make the scenery of the Stuart Range unique in the Cascades. Unlike the typical brown rock of the divide, these mountains are a cream-colored granite, and because they are situated on the dry, eastern side, vegetation is sparse and open. The combination is striking, but gives the region a very un-Cascadian appearance. Profound, gorge-like valleys are enclosed by gleaming granite walls rising to barren, splintered ridges, towers, and spires; under the peaks bare rock basins hold lakes and isolated oases of pocket-sized meadows; glaciers are small, and by midsummer the snow fields have dwindled to ragged patches in the shadow of the highest pinnacles. These east-side mountains have a sharp, bright, clean-swept appearance quite different from those of the humid west slope.

Approach to the Stuart Range is from Leavenworth near

the junction of U.S. 97 with trans-Cascade Highway 10A. A narrow seventeen-mile dirt road leads up the stupendous, V-shaped canyon of Icicle Creek, from which trails branch south into the heart of the Stuart wilderness. One of the most popular trail trips ascends Snow Creek to its head at well-stocked Nada and Snow lakes in a rocky basin surrounded by 8,000-foot peaks. Another trail leaves the road at Bridge Creek Camp, branching to Eightmile and Stuart lakes. Above the latter towers the precipitous north face of Mount Stuart—a 3,000-foot broken granite wall spread with hanging glaciers. From the road end in Icicle Creek canyon, trails also lead north into the wild Chiwaukum Mountains and northwest to Chain-of-Lakes near the Cascade crest.

The mountains of Washington are rich in minerals. Wherever you go are signs of past mining activity. You run across rotting buildings and ore dumps in the most surprising places—on cliffs high above timber line, beside the icefalls of glaciers, deep in remote valleys, and on the shores of lonely lakes. Around many of these abandoned mines are rusty boilers and broken machinery amidst scattered wheels, ratchets, and cogs. Some of these have been standing idle for fifty years. You marvel that this equipment, often weighing many tons, was laboriously brought in by man-and-mule power over rough wilderness trails. And you wonder, too, who were the disappointed eastern investors who spent thousands of dollars on useless machinery. For in spite of the prevalence of mineral veins and rosy promises, few have made fortunes in Cascade mines.

The most interesting mining district, and at one time the most active, is the Monte Cristo section on the west slope

thirty miles east of Everett. In the middle and late 1890's
men dreamed of an Eldorado among the snowy peaks. One
of them was John D. Rockefeller whose gold, silver, and
copper mines flourished for several years. As a result the
town of Monte Cristo suddenly rose from the forests fully
equipped with saloons, gambling halls, and brothels. Fever-
ish activity accompanied by general hell-raising featured the
formerly quiet alpine valley under the glaciers. Today all
is quiet again—a few moldering buildings along a weed-
grown street are all that mark the brave town of Monte
Cristo.

The district is among the most beautiful in the northern
Cascades, and is one of the two alpine sections which can be
traversed by automobile. A graded road has been built on
the abandoned right of way of the old Hartford & Eastern
mining railroad up the South Fork of the Stillaguamish
River almost to Monte Cristo. It connects with another road
down the Sauk River to Darrington. This loop enables you
to see some of Washington's finest mountain scenery from
your car.

Big Four Inn on the Stillaguamish, named for the giant
number outlined in snow on the steep face of the mammoth
mountain above it, is the chief resort of the region. Monte
Cristo itself is reached only by a six-mile trail from the road
at Barlow Pass. A scenic pack trip can be made among the
peaks above the ghost town: to Glacier Basin, Columbia
Glacier, Silver, Twin, and Blanca lakes. But the gem lake
of the Monte Cristo district is easily reached on foot in a
nine-mile round trip from the Sauk River road at Elliott
Creek.

It would be difficult to argue down anyone who main-

Timber felling, vintage 1900 Note the ten-foot crosscut saw

Timber felling, 1949

Logging camp near Mount Rainier

tained that Goat Lake has the most perfect mountain setting of any body of water in the entire Cascade Range. And it would be impossible to prove him definitely wrong. Cradled in a basin rimmed with ice-sheathed peaks, Goat Lake is strongly reminiscent of Lake Louise on a smaller scale. It is only a little over a half mile long, but its glacial waters are a shimmering expanse of emerald green, bordered by luxuriant forests of fir and cedar. Behind are cliffs lined with white threads of waterfalls from the glaciers above and, on the skyline, the enclosing ridge sweeps around in a lofty semicircle to culminate in the aspiring, snowy summit of Cadet Peak, four thousand vertical feet above the lake in a distance of a mile and a half.

High up under a blue ice cliff on a shoulder of Cadet Peak is all that is left of the Penn Mine. In its heyday during the late 1890's miners worked in the shafts summer and winter, their only contact with the outside world an aerial tramway down the sheer cliffs to the lake. Old-timers in the Monte Cristo district tell of twenty to thirty feet of snow up at the Penn Mine, and of being marooned for two months at a time with their food supply close to exhaustion.

Twenty-five miles northeast of Monte Cristo, deep in the heart of a complicated complex of mountains and valleys, is Glacier Peak. This graceful, 10,436-foot white cone is the most elusive and retiring of all the Cascade fire-mountains. Even to obtain a passable view of Glacier Peak you must seek a lofty vantage point miles from the nearest road; to reach its base requires a pack or knapsack trip of several days, either from the east or west.

For Glacier Peak is, in fact, the southern sentinel of the stupendous, primitive wilderness of the northern Cascades.

In an area measuring seventy miles north to the Canadian line, and almost as wide across, there is not a railway, paved road, or town. It is a wild, untamed piece of original America so rough that even horses cannot penetrate some of the more remote valleys or cross the higher passes.

The northern Cascade wilderness is packed solidly with hundreds of square miles of soaring peaks massed together in lines, groups, and knots. They rise steeply thousands of feet from narrow valleys clothed in a jungle-like growth of huge evergreens and tangled underbrush. Literally hundreds of glaciers mantle the summits, hang high in cirques under rocky ridges, and stream down the mountainsides into the valleys. There are probably twice—possibly three times—as many glaciers in this one area as in all the other ranges of the United States put together.

The peaks of the northern Cascades offer the alpinist superb, but often dangerous, rock climbing, and the finest snow and ice craft in the country. The fisherman can catch his limit of unsophisticated but gamy trout from different waters each day in the week. And hidden away among these twisted, convoluted mountains are enough lakes, meadows, waterfalls, alpine basins, and sweeping panoramas to keep the lover of the outdoors busy for a lifetime.

There are numerous trails leading into the wilderness from both sides of the range, but perhaps the most impressive gateway is Lake Chelan on the east. From the town of Chelan, on Highway 97, you start from dry, brown foothills and penetrate the heart of the Cascades by boat. Lake Chelan is one of the wonders of the continent; it rivals the fiords of Norway or the Alaskan inlets. Fifty-five miles long and never more than a mile and a half wide, the lake fills the bottom of an enormous glacier-carved valley to a depth of fifteen hundred feet. Mile after mile you skim over the blue water, the mountains rising ever higher until, around the last bend, the upper part of the lake stretches before you like a gigantic corridor shut in by precipitous rock walls seven to eight thousand feet high.

On the upper lake are Lucerne and Stehekin resorts, starting points for pack trips into the alpine wilderness beyond. The most popular are the Railroad Creek and Agnes Valley trails to Lyman Lake and Lyman Glacier. The fine group of rock peaks and glacier basins at the head of Stehekin River and North Fork of Bridge Creek are also well worth exploring. Plans are under way to build a scenic road over the divide at Cascade Pass, connecting Lake Chelan with Marblemount and the Skagit River Valley on the west slope. When completed, you will be able to drive your car through some of the wildest and most rugged country in the Cascade Range.

On the west side man rivals nature in producing lakes almost as spectacular as Chelan. The city of Seattle has dammed the Skagit River in three places for power and light. Gorge Dam, Diablo Dam, 389 feet, and Ross Dam, eventually to tower 650 feet above the river bed, have created three artificial lakes which wind up the Skagit Valley for many miles. Before World War II, two-day excursions, including a boat ride on Diablo Lake, were conducted during the summer season. These trips, extended to the new lake behind Ross Dam, will be resumed in the near future. When Ross Dam is completed you will have an opportunity to explore twenty miles of the upper Skagit by boat.

Southeast of Diablo Lake a trail leads up Thunder Creek

to Park Creek Pass on the divide. The glaciers of Thunder Creek are particularly fine: the McAllister Creek, Inspiration, and Boston are among the largest and most beautiful in the Cascades. But it takes considerable strenuous bushwhacking to see the best of this magnificent region. Another trail follows up the Skagit into the enormous 1,250-square-mile North Cascade Wilderness Area lying along the Canadian border. The west part of this Forest Service primitive preserve, between the Skagit and Mount Baker, contains the thickest forests and snowiest peaks in the Cascades.

Dominating the extreme northern end of the range, six hundred miles from Lassen Peak where we started, is the swelling dome of *Komo Kulshan*, the white, shining mountain. Thus the Puget Sound Indians named the eleventh Cascade fire-mountain which we know as Mount Baker. Although but 10,750 feet in elevation, Baker's forty-square-mile mantle of gleaming ice and snow rivals Rainier's in extent. In fact, the almost unbroken purity of Mount Baker's snow fields far surpasses that of the greater mountain.

In the near future you will be able to circle Mount Baker by a loop similar to that around Mount Hood. Road builders have only to close a gap of a few miles between Baker Lake and Austin Pass on the east side of the mountain to make such a loop possible. The most scenic part of the future circle is already completed. A sixty-mile paved highway branching east from Highway 99 at Bellingham on Puget Sound follows the North Fork of the Nooksack River to Austin Pass.

Near the end of the road, at an elevation of 4,200 feet, is Mount Baker Lodge, a chalet-type hotel with cabins and restaurant service. From the wide porch you look across Heather Meadows, a hanging green garden perched high above the deep valley of the Nooksack. The meadows are dotted with mirror-like pools and groups of veteran mountain hemlocks which here reach their finest development. Sharp, red-hued mountains along the Canadian border rim the northern horizon, while directly east, bold-prowed Mount Shuksan thrusts its knife-edged summit a vertical mile above its skirt of glaciers. Shuksan is one of the most distinguished examples of mountain architecture in America. You are apt to be incredulous when you learn that this peak with its tremendous precipices and hanging ice fields is but 9,030 feet high. The road ends at Austin Pass, 4,630 feet, with a view of Shuksan on the east and the snowy north face of Mount Baker to the west.

Short trails radiate from Heather Meadows to a score of delightful spots between the two great mountains. Or you can take longer trips over Hannegan Pass to the little-known peaks and valleys northeast of Mount Shuksan—to Whatcom Pass and the Challenger ice fields, to Chilliwack Lake, just over the line in Canada, and to the wild border region on the upper Skagit River. Heather Meadows is also a good climbing center: Shuksan is for experts only, but competently guided ascents of Mount Baker are often taken by ordinary mortals.

Beyond Mount Baker the Cascade Range suddenly ends at the broad trench of Canada's Fraser River. We have scanned the rich bill of fare of the Cascade banquet from beginning to end. Possibly you have chosen some titbits here and there which particularly appeal to you, and have planned a trip next summer to northern California, Oregon, or Washington to sample them.

But it won't be all as smooth and easy as our armchair Cascade holiday. We had to leave out the details. There will be heat, dust, wind, and chilling rains; mosquitoes will hungrily attack you in July, gnats and black flies will swarm around you in August. You may be scratched by the pestiferous devil's-club and blistered by rocky trails. But you will forget these things, remembering only the glories of the mighty Cascades. And you will be content, for:

"Happy is he who, like Ulysses, hath made a goodly journey."

LOGGING AND MINING
by James Stevens

The Indians logged the red cedar for canoes and houses and the alder for their fires. In 1792 the exploring British captain, George Vancouver, tried the Douglas fir (as it was later named) for ship's masts and yards and found it good. Real logging began at Fort Vancouver in the early 1820's. A sawmill was set up there, and by 1825 cargoes of clapboards were being shipped to the Sandwich Islands. In that year Governor Simpson of the Hudson's Bay Company inspected Fort Vancouver and ordered that the "coasting timber trade" be given priority over the fur business.

The sailing ships came up the Columbia and down Puget Sound from the gray seas toward a green ocean of trees. For many years it was hard to see the logging because of the trees. Then axmen hewed out a trace for the covered wagons that wheeled around Mount Hood. Water-powered sawmills were set up on the banks of the Willamette. In 1845 the Simmons party turned north from the Columbia because among its members was one colored family, and a provisional legislature had barred Negroes from the territory south of the Columbia. "Colonel" Michael Simmons built a sawmill on Puget Sound in 1847.

Real-quill logging began on the bottoms of the Cascades' foothills with the California gold rush. More than a million board feet of Douglas fir lumber was shipped from Oregon City to San Francisco in 1849.

A bigger splurge of the kind was in 1906. Soon after the great San Francisco fire, trainloads of lumber were backed up all the way between the stricken bay region and Oregon. All ships, too, were turned into lumber carriers as the Columbia River and Puget Sound mills ran night and day and the yells of "Timber-r-r-r! Down the hill!" rolled all along the western slopes of the Cascades, and from not a few places among the east-side pines, too.

By 1906 the logging business of the Cascade country was well into the transition from the pioneering phase to that of industrial forestry. It was a way from old forests to new. Timber was still treated as a mine. Timber was cheaper than dirt. Every summer Seattle, Portland, Tacoma and other towns that the Cascades looked down on were clouded with the smoke of land clearing. Giant stumps dotted real-estate developments and the new farms. The second growth came on in waves when fire was kept off the cut-overs. It was looked on as a major nuisance. Nobody dreamed that loggers might ever *try* to grow trees among the stumps. The Douglas fir forest was still a green ocean between the Pacific and the Cascades, and the pines made the east slopes of the great range an evergreen land.

By 1906 the products of the Douglas fir log were being shipped to sixty-seven countries. Three railroads ran through the Cascades to the Midwest and to eastern connections, and a fourth was building. The line to California had new branches into Oregon forests. The Yukon gold rush, the world's fair at Portland, a series of land booms that rose with plans for scores of other branch railroads through the Pacific Northwest, the beginning of the Panama Canal project, and kindred wonders of the day, had all served to cast new values on the forests. The federal government had set up the U.S. Forest Service as administrator of many millions of acres of forest reserves which were to be managed as future sources of supply for local industries. The loggers and lumbermen were organizing for co-operation on traffic and forest-fire problems. The donkey engine and the logging railroad had succeeded the bullteam and the skidroad.

In 1910 Paul Bunyan was but a half-forgotten name in the woods. The times were yielding better tall tales than any old pinetop could invent. The flying machine was a story of the day. So was the submarine and the wireless. There were logging donkey engineers in the woods who had done turns on the digging of the big Panama ditch. Henry Ford was famous among men of the woods from the Skagit to the Rogue, from the Klamath to the Okanogan. Steam machines were not enough. Tractors were in the timber, pulling big wheels on the east side, snorting along on distillate and gasoline. More jobs! Railroads building to Tillamook and Coos Bay on the coast, the Natron Cutoff * starting through the Cascades, Hill and Harriman racing lines up Deschutes River canyon to the central Oregon pineries. Irrigation dams

---

* The Natron Cutoff, begun in 1910, gave the Southern Pacific Railroad its present Oregon-California main line through the Siskiyous and the southern flank of the Cascade Range.

and ditches under way everywhere, too. Thousands upon
thousands swarming all over the dry lands east of the mountains to take up homesteads, thousands more buying "stump
ranches" from the lumber companies at four bits an acre.

The young man came west, not to grow up with the country but to seek his fortune. When fortune failed, there was
always work in the timber. It was hard work, and the young
men who could handle it commonly took jobs at a logging
camp only to keep them while looking for something better.
Sometimes a man would find himself making his fortune
out of trees, almost before he knew it. Sometimes, as in
1907, hard times came, the young men saw hope darken
and they turned to revolt. Then there was an organization
ready for them—the Industrial Workers of the World, the
fighting "Wobblies." By 1917 there was war in the woods
as well as in Europe. The struggle grew, until it surged
three ways after 1936, with the C.I.O and A.F. of L. timber unions fighting not only the boss loggers but among
themselves.

The history of logging in the Cascade country is one that
heaves and roars with epic drama. All that I have attempted
to do in this note is to sketch an outline for a few stories of
the region's woods and woodsmen which may illustrate this
life of trees and men, touching on times past and on today.
My own life has been in it since 1902. I write a little from
things heard, mostly from things experienced.

DAY OF THE BULLTEAM

The wet winter wind wheeled over the Oregon Coast
Range, crossed the Willamette Valley and blew hard up the

Mamook * for the snow peaks of the Cascades. It was a dark day in the canyon. The dense forest of Douglas fir and western hemlock and western red cedar dripped from the fine rain. The sixteen oxen—the "bullteam"—stood with heads down, the log chain slack under the eight yokes. John Larrity, the bullpuncher, and his second man were heaving the turn of logs together by the power of screwjacks. The skids, small logs sunk in the earth at intervals of four feet, were smeared with oil, and the riding side of the log was peeled and slick.

The shod hoofs of the big spotted bulls slipped in the soaked earth between the skid logs. It was always tough going around this bend of the skidroad. The turn was stuck, and John Larrity, being in a fair humor, was giving his team the best of it by screwjacking the logs together and slacking the coupling chains, just as a locomotive engineer jams the cars of his train for an easy start.

It was a ten-minute job for the bullpuncher and his helper. Then Larrity shoved a brown plug under his sweeping, coaly mustache, ground off a chew that bulged his right cheek, returned the plug to a pocket of his mackinaw, and picked up his oxgoad.

The goad was a thick hickory stick over six feet long and tipped with iron. A club, yet in Larrity's giant gloved hand it seemed a switch. He held it straight up while he scowled and figured over the bullteam and the turn of logs. He broke his rumination by firing tobacco juice in a shot that

* Fictional place names in this chapter are "Mamook River," "Illahee," and "Swan Creek." This device has been used where the purpose is to project features common to the whole region, in terms of general description.

hit the butt log squarely in the heart. Then he swung spring-
ily for the bulls.

"Yee-ay!" His growly bellow brought a shiver from the
low-headed brutes. "Yee-ay, Tamper, you, Hogan, haul
wheelers, on that slack! Snub and Sawbuck, h'ist! Leaders,
steady up! H'ist, swingers! H'ist, ye all!"

He bellowed on, lurching from yoke to yoke, the sharp
tip of the goad raking ribs and jabbing shoulders. The
wheelers leaned into the yoke and lumbered forward, the
swingers tightened the chain, the leaders took hold. Then
a lunge by all sixteen bulls in a single effort yanked the butt
log ahead. The eyes of the animals rolled as the pull of the
coupling chain caught the weight of the second log, but they
kept going. The long team began to labor with the tighten-
ing of the chain on the third log. The bullpuncher's profane
roars and the bite of his goad made the brutes grunt, groan,
and paw mud.

"There she skids! Gee, Hols! You ape of an ox—gee,
Hogan! Swing, swing!"

Now they were logging, hauling the turn around the
tough bend. Up and down the skidroad Larrity made his
prodding and bellowing way. But there were slips, then a
slowdown. Vaulting on the goad, the bullpuncher leaped
the five feet to the top of the butt log. In another second
he had jumped on to the hips of Hogan, the near wheeler.
Yelling like a crazed cougar, Larrity dug into quivering
hide with the sharp calks of his boots. He jumped to the
off wheeler's back, then to the yoke ahead, using his goad
as a balancing pole, sounding that wild cougar squawl. Blood
trickled where his boots struck. The beasts of labor hit their
yokes in plunges of desperation. The haul picked up speed.

Larrity lit on the ground as the turn of logs passed the worst spot of the skidroad.

"All right, bulls," he said. "Slog along. We can do the rest of 'er to the river rollways standing on our heads."

That was logging in the *good old days*, on the wet-weather side of the Cascades.

FALLING THE ROUND STUFF

Catty Dan chopped from the left, Nels from the right. The first thing for them in squaring off at a Douglas fir was to notch for springboards, their working footrests. At times (in the old days) they might notch and stairstep their way up ten feet before setting in clear above the store of pitch and the flare of the tree's trunk to its roots. Then each planted his calk-booted feet far apart, sprung his knees, bowed his back, and swung from his hips with the ax.

Shunk-shink! Shunk-shink! Shunk-shink!

Catty Dan took the lead, Nels followed his stroke. On then, swing and swing, the thudding clang of the axes a powerful beat, boot-size bark chips flying; then a richer ring in the ax beats, with soft, white sapwood chips fist-big a-sailing; and then the cut into the true tree, the gold and red heartwood of the old-growth Douglas fir of the uplands.

The chopping went on until the undercut was notched rightly to guide the fall of the tree, the lower plane of the cut horizontal, the upper line slanting down, all slick and clean.

Then the springboards were stepped up on the other side of the tree and mounted with ten-foot crosscut saw. Timing was the thing for good sawing. Muscles needed to be loose and working easy, fast though, pulling the saw, then letting it slip smoothly into the pull from the other end, pulling again, touch and go in split seconds.

The swing of teeth and rakers from one angle to another in the kerf, the stop to slush coal oil along the saw blade against binding pitch, the sense of when to stop and maul in wedges to make room for the saw and guide the lean of the tree, the response to the tree's first faint death shudder —Catty Dan and Nels had to feel and act on these things without parleys, with no hesitation.

When Dan yelled, "Timber-r-r-r! Down the hill!" it was also Nels giving voice. The two would come down with freed saw and go as one man for shelter from limbs broken and flying.

So the tree harvest went on, tree by tree, from the time of the pioneer to the time when two men came into the woods carrying a rig with a narrow oval frame belted with linked saw teeth which could be spun like fury through big timber by the power of a motor. Then time was past for one of the hardest kinds of toil on the good, green earth.

LOGGING CAMP BUNKHOUSE: OLD STYLE

It was the main building of a camp in which two outfits had gone broke. The layout had stood idle and rotting for years in the times between loggings. The shakes, rafters, walls, double-barreled bunks, and calk-pitted floor planks of the bunkhouse held the smells of many winters of steam from drying clothes and of many summers of sweating bodies. Smells of tobacco smoke and juice were permanent fixtures. Old scents of death were here, too. Men had been taken mortally sick in this place. Men smashed in the woods had been brought here dead, or here to die, or to wait for

a while on the way to death. Men without homes, lost to
their people.

Human life at its lustiest had left its spirit here, too.
Night after night the shapes arose, in the hour or two between supper and sleep. The talk of the old-timers brought
them forth and up, mightier than life, through stories of
bullpunchers, axmen, and fighters who had lived here in
other years.

One regular night: Wire swung the coal-oil lamps and
their reflectors from the cedar ridgepole. Wire lines held
the mackinaws, shirts, socks, and drawers nigh the roof to
catch the ballooning heat from the pot-bellied heating stove.
Some loggers lolled in their bunks, reading or writing letters by the light of candles from the commissary. Others
sat hunched on benches along the bunkhouse rows, heads
bowed, studying the life that was theirs to live in this place.
More were in quiet card games. It was a low-toned scene
of weary and none too hopeful men at peace. There was
seldom an argument here, never a fight.

The loggers were mainly in their sock feet. All wore over-
alls or ducking pants stagged just below the knee. Red strips
of drawers legs were revealed between the frazzled ends
of pants legs and sock tops. Suspenders as wide as the belly-
band of a horse's harness stretched over wool-shirted shoulders. Pipe smoke drifted thickly over shaggy heads and
fogged the lamps and candlelight. There were no cigarette
smokers in camp. Tobacco juice puddled the ashes of the
heater bed. The light was so dim right there that the heater's
fat sides shone red and sparked yellow.

At nine o'clock the lights were doused. The gut-hammer
would ding-dong the men out of their blankets at five. Soon

the bunkhouse sounded with a chorus of hearty snores. The glow of the heater faded. The smells thickened and settled in the chilling air. The shapes sank down to rest, also. The ghosts of old loggers might roam through pleasures and palaces, but only in a ripe and seasoned bunkhouse could they truly rest in peace.

LOGGERS' SALOON: 1910

The stern-wheeler brought a tow of log rafts down the Columbia and up the Willamette to Portland. Four men and a boy had paid for rides down from the camp on the green skirt of Mount Hood. The boy was sixteen now, he had held his own as woodbuck to a donkey engine in the camp, and he hoped to go along with the four as another man in Portland city. Ashore, he trailed them along Front Street in the rain of a March night. Their way led to Ericsen's Saloon.

At that time Ericsen's had a world-wide fame. Easing in behind the four big loggers, the boy peered around them and into wonderland. His imagination exaggerated every detail of the scene. The brown and shining bar curved away from the door and down a room that seemed as big as a circus tent. Row after row of card tables, each one crowded with gambling men, reached into corners that, to the boy's peering eyes, were mysteriously far in the smoke drift. Slot machines stood in many colors; they clacked and whirred as men played them, and coins jingled forth now and then. From far deeps rose sounds of piano and fiddle music. The boy found himself moving ahead, swimming through a mellow glow.

The bar had the length of a city block in all its curves and turns. Back of it white lights shone on mirrors, pyramids of glasses, and rows of queer-shaped bottles labeled with vivid colors, and these stood on a back bar draped with the snowiest cloths. The diamond-like dazzle of white was half-blinding. Bright white light was also reflected from the varnished columns and beams about the mirrors, from the brass of bar rails and from the nickel of spigot handles. The seventeen bartenders were all in white jackets. Polished brass spittoons, which to the boy's eyes were fit to serve as huge vases for flowers, stood all along the massive brass footrail. Above the glittering brasswork swung snowy towels.

The sights were unbelievable, a dream, to the boy who had seen little that was grander than a homestead shack in the junipers and sagebrush east of the mountains, and small shanty camps in the pineries. He stood back in a shadow and looked and marveled and was glad to have come this far in life. He heard music while the glasses clinked, the gold and silver jingled on the bar, and the talk of men from the woods surged through the vast, shining cavern of Ericsen's Saloon. He did not even venture to ask for a small beer. This life in the saloon was intoxication enough. All he wanted was to be a Cascade Range logger from now on and to come in once in a while to see the sights in Ericsen's Saloon.

THE SHORT LOG COUNTRY

From the northern nub of the Siskiyous the Southern Pacific Railroad had a branch that ran into the Klamath pine area, on the east slope and southern end of the Cascade Range. Only rock peaks stood between Swan Creek here and the Douglas fir forests that spread away downward

from timber line on the west side of the range; but the forest
species, the climate, and the life of logging held a world
of differences. The Douglas firs grew in dense stands and
with understories of hemlocks and hardwoods. They knew
winters of rain and fog and summers of showers. Their
timber was mainly cut for rough work and much of it was
shipped green, sometimes in lengths of more than a hundred
feet for bridges and other heavy construction.

The yellow and sugar pines of the gentle slopes of Swan
Creek in the Klamath were widely spaced. They grew as
in a park, with little brush. Winters brought them snow and
clear freezes. The summers were sunny and dry. The lumber from the pines was used by factories that made their
articles from wood; it went into boxes and home building.
The pine sawmills called mainly for sixteen-foot logs.

Where the long logs of the Douglas fir were skidded by
great bullteams at first, and then by heaviest machinery,
the short logs of the pines on the east side of the Cascades
made light and easy logging through the park-like forests.

On Swan Creek in 1910 one outfit was yet working the
stiff-tongued type of big wheels that had been developed
in the Lake States pineries. Back there, the old proposition
of moving logs from woods to mill by log-sleigh and river
drive had given way to the logging railroad and the big
wheels which permitted summer logging.

The usual set of two wheels was ten feet high, but sometimes a set would tower twelve feet. A heavy chain dangled
from the right of a set's axle, inside the wheel, and a toggle
rig from the left. Each hung from over the axle's top when
the tongue was down, level for hauling. A thick springboard was ring-bolted to the axle, its end jutting out behind

for six feet. A peavey handle stuck straight up from the axle by the springboard. When the teamster went out to the woods from the landing with his wheels empty, his two horses were hitched astraddle the tongue, which had its front end carried up in a neck yoke, as with a wagon tongue. The route was over rough roads which swampers had cleared to places where bunch-teamsters had built big-wheel loads of logs, each with a chain-hole under it. The teamster backed his wheels over a load to which the two wheel-loaders directed him, until the axle was above the chain-hole. Then the teamster unloosed the doubletrees and the team was driven out ahead of the tongue, to which one end of a long, light chain was secured. One loader mounted the springboard, grabbed the peavey handle, then hauled with all his strength while driving his legs down on the springboard with all his weight. This would tilt the tongue upward as the end of the springboard was borne down and rammed into the ground, to prop the now towering tongue. When the heavy chain was snaked under the load and toggled, then the team out in front pulled the tongue down forward with the light chain. The axle would turn forward with the descent of the tongue and the loading chain would begin to wind on it. When the tongue was brought to a level with the top log of the load, the winding would have lifted the load enough to ride in its sling under the axles. It was a mighty, mighty clever outfit, and millions upon millions of acres of pine forest were logged off with big wheels.

Soon slip-tongue wheels for four-horse teams succeeded the old-time stiff-tongues. Steep logging could be done with the new wheels, for they would let the load slip and drag when it would begin to run up on the horses. Eventually they were pulled by tractors.

The logging that men and oxen carried on in the long log country and the logging that horses and men did with short logs in the pines was hard on all, and in our fair modern day of peace and good will it might well be forgotten. But you cannot forget it if you ever handled horses on a big-wheel trail. . . .

Down the hill, with a load too close to a balance. The big wheels running up on the horses, hitched out at the end of the tongue, with no breeching, no brakes. On down the rough, swamped road that twists among stumps, brush, and blowdowns. Windrows of swamped brush along the trail-road. The trick is to zigzag the big wheels from one brush pile to another, slowing down the wild load of logs. Swing to the left, now! Haw, Bullet! Back to the right! Yo! Hup! Gee, there, Snorter, gee! Tight line, keep a tight line, teamster, and don't trip your calks on rimrock as that load of logs swings at you and a wheel shatters brush. Tight line pulls panic out of the horses; let go and it's a runaway. There she wheels, back to the left again, haw her true, gee back, and on. Then it's a straight pitch down ahead. Got to run for this one. The horses have to outrun the load. Hanging to the lines, you have to keep up, making seventeen feet at a jump; you are between horses and load, alongside the tongue that could bat your head off your neck in one of its wild swipes, so that as high wheel and logs rolled over you they'd bother you never, worry you not at all. You duck the tongue, you keep your feet, you hold a tight line to the end of the run and the level land to the landing. Other men have been doing it season after season for twenty years. You can do it, too. You are a pinetop likewise, by the holy old mackinaw, a handler of horses from away back on the big-wheel trail. Now we're logging. Big-wheel men.

LOGGING DYNAMITER

In 1910 Jim Hill built a railroad up one side of Deschutes River canyon and E. H. Harriman built one up the other side. It was a race of giants from the Columbia River main lines to the pine wealth of Oregon on the east slopes of the Cascades, and for a route to the Klamath country and California.

Bunch Horn was a boss dynamiter in one of the hill camps. His job was the digging and charging of a coyote hole—a toy tunnel in which men had to work on hands and knees—in the shoulder of a great cliff above the river. The job called for a load of seventy-five hundred cans of black powder and fifteen hundred cases of dynamite. Bunch put the job through in record time. Then he pulled the switch and watched the side of a mountain canyon split off with hellish roar and smoke, belching thousands of cubic yards of shattered rimrock down to choke a raging river for a day.

Bunch was old enough to have dynamited log jams on the Muskegon and the Manistee.* He liked to look solemn and tell the young hard-rock men, "Why, this coyote was no shooting. Paul Bunyan would set off the like with only one of his fulminating caps."

"Why, Paul Bunyan," Bunch Horn went on one time, "he took only seventeen charges to shoot all the timber, stumps to boot, in Dakoty off the scenery. The only item

* Rivers famous in Michigan lumbering.

of scenery he missed there in that monster foray of land clearing was a mountain that was h'isted whole by one of his shots.
Yes, sir, it stuck right with its timber and rocks, all in one
piece.

"Up and up that blasted mountain went," declared Bunch
Horn. "Up she blew, then she done a flip-flop over the clouds
and, still solid, still sticking, that mountain dropped down
to light on her head. And there she stood, quivering for a
spell, but not enough to shake off her upside-down trees.
The pines on the slope just stood, hung on their roots, crowns
pointing to the earth far below.

"There she'd still be, except for the fight of Paul Bunyan
and Hels Helson—the same Hels who muddied the Mis-
souri River forever with one spring bath. They clumb atop
the bottom of that upside-down mountain and fought 'er
out, so's to be sure and hurt nobody else. They did, though.
A teeny boulder blew so far it hit poor Pewee Wilkins, the
runt of Paul's crew, and broke his leg three feet below the
knee. Well, Paul and Hels tore that mountain to pieces
before Paul could win. You still see the pieces, scattered
all over. The Bad Lands, folks call 'em nowadays. . . ."

Summer's end, Bunch went up to Tacoma and shipped
to Ohop as a high-climber. The work was to trim and top
giant Douglas firs and rig them up for high-lead logging.
With climbing harness and "irons," life rope circling a tree,
ax and saw dangling from ropes at the back of the heavy
belt, Bunch Horn would climb and trim his way up a tree
blazed to serve as a spar for high-lead log skidding.

At a height of one hundred and fifty or more feet, with
a sixty-foot bush of boughs and crown above him, Bunch
Horn would saw and hew a shelf around the trunk, then

tie in dynamite sticks, fuse, and blasting cap. These explosive tools were drawn up by a passline which Bunch had carried along in a coil on his belt.

His gentle job went on this way: Lighting the fuse, Bunch drove downward with his legs, planted the spurs of his leg irons in bark and grain, flipped the circle of his life rope down the tree a way and held to it hard as he drove swiftly down with spurs again. So he would go in rapid motion to the ground.

It was Bunch's pride to time a fuse so that he would have only scant seconds to reach shelter after hitting the grit. On the ground he walked in all his gear, never hustling, always just stepping out of harm's way as the giant tree "blew its top." (That's where the slang term originated.)

The work went on with Bunch Horn climbing again to receive a larger block and line by passline to start rigging up the spar tree. This did not end until guy cables anchored to big stumps held the tree securely, and mainline, haulback, and loading-boom blocks were swinging from the top. Then the pull of a donkey engine below could be made to swing the ends of skidding logs over stumps and windfalls because it had a lifting pull from on high. The earliest donkeys that succeeded the bullteams were "ground-lead" affairs that simply snaked logs along the ground.

Bunch remained a high-climber in the Cascade Range woods until the topping of spar trees with dynamite lost favor to topping with saw and ax. But by that time logging roads were being run high in the mountains, costing ten thousand dollars a mile to blast out in some places. The last heard of him, Bunch was back in the hard-rock. He may

still be at it. "Dynos who are the real quill never die," he
used to say. "And they won't never quit powder."

CAT LOGGING COMES IN

The first logging in the Mamook Valley to make lumber
was in 1849. The trees that were felled then were at the
river's mouth and so close to water that they were rolled
by hand into rafting booms. The logging cleared a site for
the start of Illahee, a town of homes. More clearings up
the river bottoms were the start of farms. Logging went on,
slowly and steadily, spreading out to benches, then to hills.
The skidroad and the bullteam moved the timber from
stump to waterway. By 1899 the hoarse, chugging roar and
shrill whistle of the Dolbeer donkey echoed in the canyons.
The railroad came, and bigger and faster logging machines,
with high-lead and skyline skidding systems. They tore
through the timber in the twenties. Fire often rampaged
through the logging debris in the wake of the steam-driven
giants of the woods that had put Paul Bunyan and Babe
the Blue Ox in the shade.

Still there was timber. The Mamook area was roughly
one one-hundredth of the Douglas fir region—the land between the snow of the Cascades and the foam of the Pacific.
It had about two hundred and sixty thousand acres of "commercially available" forest land. About half of the acreage
and the sawtimber were publicly owned. Most of the sawtimber stands were on the uplands; rough country, tough
railroading.

By 1929 the type of tractor that took itself along on belts
of broad steel links, cleated outside and cogged inside, providing tremendous traction, was in the mountains that rose

from the headwaters of the Mamook. In front it carried a broad blade for trail-making—bulldozing. It pulled a trailer with a high A-frame rig that stood on crawlers, like the tractor itself. A cable ran from a drum at the tractor's rear up through the peak of the A-frame or fairlead arch. By this logs were snubbed up, their head ends were hoisted, and the tractor-puncher—heir of the bullpuncher and donkey-puncher—could yard timber down any old mountainside. The powerful logging truck was another development. Truck-and-tractor logging was the new giant of the forests of the Cascade mountains, in the pineries of the east as well as on the fir-bearing west slope. It was termed "cat logging," a derivation from the name of a popular tractor brand.

The development meant more than mechanical change. It was new promise for business in the timber. Young wage-earning loggers could not hope to save enough from their wages to build and equip a railroad outfit, but they could hope to finance a truck-and-tractor deal, and hundreds have done so.

Between 1929 and 1939 the depression hit the lumber industry harder than any other. Not until 1937, according to the U.S. Treasury, did the industry produce a profit—and in 1938 it slipped into the red again. In 1933 the Tillamook fire burned more sawtimber on two hundred and seventy-five thousand acres in Oregon than had been cut during the previous year from the nation's five hundred million and more commercial forest acres.

But also in 1933 a set of forest practice rules was accepted by the lumber industry as part of the Lumber Code of the National Recovery Act. When NRA was outlawed by the Supreme Court the industry voluntarily kept the forest prac-

tice section, and added to the organizations that had been
formed to make the rules effective. Pine loggers and fir
loggers of the Cascade country were leaders in this volun-
tary movement. In the Western Pine and the West Coast
Lumbermen's Associations forest conservation departments
were organized, with staffs of graduate foresters. The larger
timber companies began to hire foresters right and left. In
1941 a type of industrial forest management was agreed on
by private timber owners under the name of "tree farm."
This has come to represent the same things that "national
forest" represents in publicly owned commercial timber. The
logger whose land is certified by foresters as acceptable for
official registry as a tree farm must measure up to the highest practicable forestry standards.

So the lands of the loggers look good up the Mamook
nowadays. Most of the tracts that were torn up by oversized
and overfast railroad logging in the 1920's have come back
with thriving young forests. State laws of Washington and
Oregon now require the leaving of adequate stands of seed
trees on the logging cut-overs. The truck roads and tractor
trails serve to protect the new crops from fire. And the
tractor does not smash up the woods in the way of the great
skidders. These days, logging is less like mining and more
like an orderly farm harvest on the Mamook.

MAMOOK TREE FARM HARVEST

The Mamook Lumber Company and other timber people
of the area are the main supporters of a summer forestry
camp for members of the Boy Scouts, 4-H Clubs, the Future
Farmers of America, and for sons of forest industry employees. On a summer day after World War II sixty of the

campers were in the woods to see the logging, with Roy
Autry, forester of the Mamook Tree Farm, as their guide.
A federal forest ranger, a state fire warden, and a farm
forester were along. The trip was to be more than an outing;
it was to demonstrate how the whole two hundred and sixty
thousand commercial forest acres of the Mamook area were
coming under a plan of co-operation by all forestry agencies:
industrial, farm, state, and federal.

From a safe point the visitors watched two timber-fallers,
men of the same trade that Catty Dan and Nels pursued
fifty years earlier on the foothills of the Mamook. But for
the fallers of today there was no springboard-chopping that
would leave a ten-foot stump. The undercut to guide the
fall was sliced out with a motor-driven saw close to the
spread of the roots. The two men felled four times the trees
in a day that they could have brought down by chopping
and hand-sawing.

The standing timber hummed and droned with other
power saws. The big trees fell with a crashing thunder.
Down the hill the felled trees lay in packed windrows. There
single sawyers and axmen bucked the trees into logs and
chopped the limbs away.

"Too much wood in treetops, big boughs, dead snags,
broken and crooked small trees, are still logging leftovers,"
Forester Roy Autry told the young people. "Look up the
slope in the standing timber," he went on, swinging a hand
that way. "You see small stumps in the big trees there, with
tractor trails and brush piles. The usable small hemlocks
and other understory trees have been felled and snaked out.
Now they won't be smashed by the big operation that's to
come. Roads have been cleared through windfalls, also. We

call that *pre-logging*. There are machines made for it, little ones."

He waved a big brown hand down the slope. "Now look on out and away, down on the cut-overs of the log harvests of twenty to thirty years ago. Salvage logging going on. Hemlock trees were left then. Now we can sell hemlock lumber and there's a market for hemlock as pulpwood. And we also have crews with light machines gleaning after the main operation that goes on now. This leaves a cleaner stubble field, one in good shape for natural reseeding and for protection from fire. Douglas firs want clean, clear-cut land for reproduction.

"Foresters like to think of timber in terms of wheat or corn. It takes a tree crop longer to grow and ripen, of course. But it is a harvest with both timber and wheat. The tree logs are run through the sawmill as the wheat heads and stems go through the threshing machine. Then, just as wheat is made into flour, bread, and other food products, so is lumber worked up and applied in houses and other building construction. Then, ideally, we grow new food crops on wheat land and new building crops on tree land. The ideal is hard to achieve, of course. Floods may erode and damage the wheat land and fires may damage the tree land. Poor management in both cases can also impoverish the land.

"There is a good forestry management plan in effect here, on Mamook Tree Farm. There is another on the lands of the national forest. Foresters are in control of state lands, too. There are state laws that provide for reseeding on small forest ownerships, on farms and the like. But all this is not enough. Foresters need the support, the help of everybody; most of all to stop forest fires. This is why we show and tell the forestry story. This is why we have you young folks up in the woods to see the logging."

The visitors' trail led on down through the log harvest. The machine was king all the way. Below the buckers, crawler tractors were bulldozing trails and skidding large sawlogs among stumps and rotten windfalls to a landing pile.

Farther down was the truck-loading works, on a road along the mountainside that had been blasted and bulldozed out at tremendous cost. Here a compact steam skidder and loader pulled in giant timbers from the tractors' pile to a spar tree and swung them on motor trucks.

These trucks were traveling powerhouses. Roy Autry pointed to a new one that had twelve speeds ahead and four in reverse. It had the power and the brakes to wheel sixty tons of timber down to the railhead. The common unit was packed into a pair of front wheels, motor cab, a short frame, two rear axles and eight rear wheels, with an eight-wheel trailer that could be coupled out for any length of log load.

Unloaded trucks carried the trailer bunks and wheels behind their cabs on return trips. The truck roads were deeply ballasted, much more staunchly built than ordinary highways to bear the enormous loads. When one was braked to a stop at the railhead a transfer crane would lift its load from the truck and trailer bunks and set it on the bunks of a railroad log car.

"Tomorrow morning a trainload of logs will be dumped into the log pond or booming grounds above the Illahee sawmill," Forester Roy Autry concluded, at the end of the trail. "A machine something like a steam shovel without a shovel will nudge each load of logs off its car and drop them into the water with the kind of splashing snort that Paul

Bunyan used to emit when he sneezed. The boom men sort the logs by species and grade. The biggest and best Douglas fir, for example, are sold to plywood mills as peelers. The best hemlock are kept for lumber and the rest boomed apart for the pulpwood market. Up in the sawmill the logs are run through a variety of sawing machines, with picking, choosing, sorting, and operating going on all the time to produce the best grades of lumber from each log and each piece of a log. The better the grade, the more the market pays for lumber.

"There are leftovers in the sawmill just as from the threshing of wheat. The latter leaves chaff. Sawing lumber leaves sawdust. Much of the slabs, trimmings, and edgings are slashed into fuel wood. The rest is the straw of the sawmill. It is ground up by a mechanical monster called the hog and mixed with sawdust for fuel uses or used as fuel alone. The smaller sawmills in the area, twenty or so of them—two thousand or more in the Cascade region—have to burn most of their leftovers. Forest products engineers are developing new marketable items that may be made from the logging leftovers of today and the scrap, the chaff of the sawmills. Alcohol can be made from sawdust, sugar too, and a yeast that will fatten cattle. Other new products are from Douglas fir bark. There are five thousand wood products in common use, and more are coming on the market every day. This is what pays for forestry. Public forestry is paid for by taxes, of course, but taxes come in the first place from production and sales.

"Lumber is the thing, though," said the forester. "The sawlog is still the main product of logging here in the Cascades, as in all other forest regions. The pulp log, the ply-

Giant Douglas firs near the entrance to Mount Rainier National Park

Clouds hugging Mount Shasta

The open snow fields at Timberline on Mount Hood

wood peeler log, the fuel log, and all the other grades are on the side. Building lumber comes from sawlogs, and building is to logging and tree growing what bread baking is to wheat harvesting and growing. There's the meal ticket of the forester and his work on the land."

Thus the logger and the industrial forester go to the public with their story of forestry progress and of co-operation with the government forestry men. To repeat, a main reason for such effort with the public, and particularly with young people, is the need for all hands to keep at work on forest fire prevention. In 1940, "Keep Washington Green" and "Keep Oregon Green" committees were formed with representatives of various groups—the American Legion, women's clubs, etc., as well as forestry organizations—for forest fire prevention work. Success has been so great that there are now "Keep Maine Green," "Keep Florida Green," and "Keep California Green" organizations, with seventeen other state groups of the kind.

Forestry practices in logging on the piney eastern slopes of the Cascades have progressed there as well as on the Douglas fir side. It does our hearts good, it is a sight for sore eyes among all of us old pinetops and firconks of these parts. It looks to us as though the foresters are becoming well fixed to keep the Cascade Range green forever. So let us pray.

SHORT NOTE ON MINING

The mill of the Holden Mine, of the Howe Sound Company, is a thing of beauty on a mountainside of the Cascades. There it stands, or reclines, rather, a practical affair that was designed and built for utility only. Yet somehow its planes hold the gaze as a work of art—a prime example of modern-istic art. Looking at it, you may be surprised to find yourself thinking of the mill as the real picture, with the titanic scenery as a material frame only. The Holden copper mine is, however, the largest single metallic mining operation in the Pacific Northwest. In 1937 the entire state of Washing-ton brought forth only one hundred and twenty-eight thou-sand pounds of copper. Then the Holden mine started up. In 1938 the state's copper production was more than twelve million pounds.

The Cascade mountains have few other single operations in the mining field, whether in metals, clay, cement, or coal, that the people of the region can point to with pride. While Oregon and Washington are the two leading lumber-pro-ducing states, Oregon in 1946 was fortieth in rank and Washington was thirty-first among the states in terms of mineral output.

The first white people in the region were on the prowl for furs; then came the land-seekers in the early 1840's and after them the gold-rushers. In 1857 wild-eyed men stormed from California to the Fraser River in British Columbia, drawn by a gold discovery. Gold in Idaho, gold in the Blue Mountains, and gold in rich pockets in the Cascade moun-tains of southern Oregon, brought swarms of fortune-seekers at various periods of pioneer times. A tethered mule kicked the dirt from silver in Idaho's Coeur d'Alenes; there were strikes in Nevada. John D. Rockefeller invested in a mine called Monte Cristo, with its diggings in a scenic glory of the Cascades.

But even Mr. Rockefeller's investment, according to some, failed to pan out. The rough country and dense timber, par-

ticularly on the west side, made the Cascades poor prospecting country. When a man would cruise through and stake
a promising claim, its development commonly had to wait
upon the building of logging roads. Many an investment
went to smash on veins of promise which slipped away in
the characteristic faults in Cascade Range rock forma-
tions. Coal, cement, sand, and gravel have been the most
valuable products of mining in the Washington half of the
Cascade Range. Coal production hit its peak in 1918, with
4,138,424 tons valued at $14,564,445. In 1946 production
had dropped to 990,000 tons valued at $5,465,000.

In the 1850's there were great dreams in Oregon of a
gold-mining industry in the southern Cascades. One pocket
yielded $400,000 in a year; another, $350,000. Prospectors
combed the region, finding no more mineral wealth worth
mentioning, but leaving campfires behind them to burn
forest wealth. The Blue Mountains hold the mineral riches
of Oregon today. The Cascades hold the timber.

THE CASCADE FOREST

by Walter F. McCulloch

The powerful drumming of diesel donkey engines, the clanking of tractor treads, the solid thump of ax and whine of saw, mark the Cascade forest. For this is a production forest, and were it not for the steady processing of lumber, many men in Washington, Oregon, and northern California would not eat. The timber is not only their forest, it is their very existence.

In addition to its famed lumber production, the greatest in America, the Cascade forest has other unique characteristics. It is distinctly a linear forest, running north and south in long thin belts on both sides of the mountains. Above all, it is a fir forest. Here is the home of the Douglas fir, foremost timber species in the world, and here live all but three of the balsam firs in North America. West of the Cascade summit, regardless of local dominance of other trees, the forest is collectively known as the Douglas fir region; and east of the mountains as the ponderosa pine region.

Through Washington, Oregon, and in northern California, the Cascade Range is inland, walled off from the sea by the Coast Range. As a result the inland mountain forest is strongly dependent upon rainfall and local geography.

Its distribution is determined by competition among species, and is warped by fire.

RAIN, THE TREE MAKER

Moisture is the critical factor throughout the range. Very little falls during the growing season, and there is always a ruthless struggle among species for water. Slight changes in site, soil, or weather cycles cause marked shifts in tree distribution. Along the Pacific Coast, moisture-bearing winds sweep in off the ocean and in the first impact against the Coast Range spill a good deal of water. Up to 130 inches of rain is not uncommon; moss-covered natives claim even more. The eastbound weather slides down the inner side of the Coast Range into the Puget trough of Washington, the Willamette Valley of Oregon, and the Sacramento Valley of California. In these areas it is more miserly with its rain, averaging roughly 40 inches. Then commences the ascent of the rugged Cascades, with increased rain falling at higher elevations. The upper reaches are soaked with more than 80 inches, and in many places along the backbone of the mountains snow will be so deep as to hamper tree growth. On the east side of the range the clouds expand over the desert, drying up both weather and forest with astonishing rapidity. Where high ground east of the mountains carries the Cascade rain-shadow out into the dry belt, a pine forest follows it, as in the Horse Heaven Hills of southern Washington and the Klamath plateau of southern Oregon.

At the Cascade summit there is one of the sharpest vegetational breaks on the continent, for this forest is in reality two forests, east side and west side. The twain do meet on top, but the change in rainfall is so sharp that the transition from pure type to pure type is very marked. In less than half an hour's drive across the Snoqualmie, Santiam, or other mountain passes, it is possible to run completely out of the west-side fir-hemlock type and into the east-side pine type. One of the most interesting examples of the influence of rain on the forest is the unceasing wrangle between ponderosa pine and sagebrush in the tension zone between forest and brushland along the eastern foothills of the Cascades. During wet cycles, pine reproduction reaches east into the desert and becomes well established. It strikes root down to the permanent water table, and is able to hang on through the following drier years during which it could not have started. As these trees mature, their enlarging crowns demand more and more water, and the thirsty root systems expand accordingly. Hence the soil dries out, and smaller plants such as sagebrush are forced back to the outer edge of the forest fringing the desert. Small seedlings, too, are killed off or beaten back to openings in the stand where competition from the large trees is not so severe. During a very dry period, however, even larger seedlings cannot keep pace with the rapidly retreating water table, and they die; the older timber too is weakened by lack of adequate moisture; pine beetles attack, and many trees are killed. With the timber competition thus decreased the sagebrush revives and invades westward areas, once the province of the pine.

The ponderosa pine forest holds to a narrower band along the eastern Cascades in Washington than it does farther south, for in southern Oregon and northern California there is lower rainfall, which encourages western extension of the species. Here too, the Trinity and Siskiyou mountains intervene between the Cascades and the Coast Range to cause

climatic and biologic confusion; the southern Cascades and
Siskiyou cross ranges hence support an alley-cat complex of
species. These vary from the extremely dry-site mountain
mahogany to the normally wet-belt hemlock. The pine type
spills on over into the west side in the Umpqua, Rogue,
Klamath, and Sacramento drainages. It persists in the Sacramento, but gives way to redwoods in the fog-belt lower
Klamath, and to Douglas fir in the lower Rogue and
Umpqua valleys.

In one instance water has forever fixed the location of a
fir forest. This is in the lava country along the Cascade summit, between the south Santiam and the McKenzie passes
in central Oregon. A long time back, a viscous black lava
flow choked off a mountain stream, backing up its waters to
flood a small wooded valley. The body of water is now
known as Clear Lake and is noted for three things: won-
drously clear water, making the bottom of the lake readily
visible at considerable depths; water temperature so low that
immersed wood rots slowly if at all; and hence, and down-
right awe-inspiring, a cadaverous forest still standing upright on the bottom of the lake. Rainbow trout swim among
stout branches where eagles should perch, and men look
down, not up, to take the measure of a tall tree.

The bizarre forest of Clear Lake has one great advantage
over the neighboring woods—it will not be consumed by fire.

FIRE: SCOURGE OF THE FOREST

From the Puget Sound foothills to the brush-field plateaus in the Shasta-Lassen area, fire is a part of all forest
history. The degree to which fire upsets normal conditions
varies as those conditions were critical or nominal to begin

with. Fires change critical soil-moisture relationships, remove shade, and alter seedbed characteristics to favor one species over another. All the normal processes of competition and succession which govern the development of forests are grossly distorted by fire.

The influence of fire is illustrated by the competition between oak and fir along the western Cascade foothills in Washington and Oregon. Oak sprouts vigorously after fire, and so renews itself, phoenix-like; but young fir trees are killed by fire.

At the present time Douglas fir and grand fir are rapidly burrowing from beneath to pirate the oak stands. The needle-like tip of a fast-growing conifer drills its way through the forest canopy where the rounded crown of the slow-growing oak cannot gain headroom for itself. As a result, in all but the very driest sites oak is now losing ground as the firs march out of the mountain forest into the foothills. The question arises, why not before? why the conquest of the oak now, when in earlier days it withstood encroachment from the mountains?

The answer probably lies in the game-getting habits of northwest Indian tribes. It was their custom to fire the valley grass and brush cover in a great horseshoe. Deer and other game trapped by the blaze charged back and forth inside the narrowing circle of fire, frantically searching for an outlet. Sooner or later the fear-crazed animals would find and pour through the narrow throat of the horseshoe, only to meet two long parallel lines of hunters desperately at work with bow and spear. The killing over, the Indians proceeded with the business of slaughter and meat-curing while the fire, dismissed from attention, rampaged on to destroy young conifers and take great bites out of the west-side Cascade forest.

The result of the valley-generated fires was to make a patchwork quilt of age classes in the bordering mountain forest. In dry years the Indian grass fire might leap into the crowns of the trees in the timber and go uphill for miles, but in wet years it would snuff out under the first thicket of saplings. Thus a many-aged young forest arose on the lower slopes of the mountains. This has proven to be a saving grace during periods of heavy cutting; the difference in ages means that many blocks of small timber are scattered among older timber and cannot be logged. They will stand as seed sources for adjacent cut-over areas until they in turn become merchantable.

Fires arising from a different cause have mixed the age classes on the upper reaches of the Cascades. Here lightning is the scourge of the forest. The severity of lightning destruction increases from west to east and from north to south in the mountain range. The south and east portions are higher and receive more strikes; they are drier, which means that more inflammable fuels are present and that fires will start more readily; and finally, rain is a less frequent accompaniment to the lightning. All these things affect the distribution of timber species.

Toward the Cascade summit and over the east-side plateaus, a severe fire drastically changes the forest, for Douglas fir, Engelmann spruce, balsam fir, hemlock, cedar, white pine, and ponderosa pine are all replaced by lodgepole pine. This species is exceedingly vigorous in its youth. The small stony cones survive fire well, some in fact appearing not to open except by fire. In contrast, the papery cones and contained seeds of competing species are readily burned. Then too, the juvenile seedling of lodgepole pine is very hardy. It scoffs at frost, it makes light of moisture deficiency, it pioneers adverse sites with ease. Lodgepole is particularly effective in revegetating hard burns, pumice-dust areas, and other barren soils. This should earn it a better reward, but the very fact of reclaiming and enriching these sites makes it possible for other species to revive under lodgepole protection. Eventually the longer-lived, larger species will take all but the poorest areas from the lodgepole, leaving it to a country-cousin existence on the infertile fringes of the forest proper.

Toward the south-central and eastern parts of the Cascades the same kind of story is true, although the species differ. Ponderosa and sugar pine are the larger and much more valuable species in the overstory. Their seedlings start best under very light shade. Beneath the considerable shade of a mature pine-fir forest, the less valuable balsam firs, particularly Abies grandis (grand fir), Abies magnifica (red fir), and Abies concolor (white fir) will grow slowly, but persistently, like hemlock under Douglas fir. In the past, logging was concentrated on the big pines, which opened up the stand, permitted accelerated growth of the established young firs, and threatened to replace the valuable pines with then relatively worthless firs. Lately the changing economics of the lumber industry have made it profitable to cut a good deal of the balsam fir. This not only reduces the fir seed supply but makes more slash. Consequently there has been more slash burning, which decreases the quantity of established fir seedlings and equalizes competition between new pine and new fir seedlings.

There is one ghostly pine forest, across the Deschutes
River from the eastern Cascade foothills, that never again
will be concerned with firs or fires. This is the lava-cast forest southeast of Bend. In the most recent period of volcanic
activity, Newberry Crater broke out with splay-footed
streams of lava which romped over the stricken countryside.
The flow was very thin, and in several areas the fluid lava
washed up the trunks of ponderosa pines and congealed. As
the green trees charred and burned to ash, the lava hardened, and the basaltic casts of the trees remain. Now the
lava layer is twenty feet or more deep, full of holes which
were once tree trunks. The casts often extend four or five
feet above the surface of the main flow where the soupy lava
splashed up against the tree. The volcanic rock here is so
black that summer surface temperatures are unbelievably
high. In consequence little vegetation has been able to re-
establish, and the well-defined casts are markedly clear on
the landscape.

Farther south, in the lower part of the Cascades, scanty
rainfall and high summer temperatures work together to the
great disadvantage of the forest. Ponderosa pine and associated fir species here move across the summit and dominate
the west side. That is, where fire permits; for the flame-tor-
tured slopes around Mount Shasta show that fire has mas-
tered the forest in this region. The inflammability of the
species, the normally low humidity, the frequent lightning,
and the boulder-strewn terrain, all make this an exceedingly
difficult area to protect against fire. The soil is generally
thin, and drastic changes follow a hot blaze. Trees are easily
killed and humus is burned out of the earth. As a result,

rain and snow evaporate faster from the bared ground, less
water is absorbed, and runoff increases. This tears off more
of the precious topsoil. Minor flash floods along the little
creeks gouge deeply into the stream bed and lower the water
table of adjacent land. All these things dry out the ground
and make it inhospitable for trees. The fire-resulting vegetation which follows is a variant of that botanical complex
known as "the chaparral." In the southern Cascades this
consists chiefly of broad-leaved species such as manzanita, a
small evergreen bush with red bark and berries, bright
green and yellow leaves. It is the most widely distributed
plant in these brush fields; others are sticky-leaf laurel,
currants, ceanothus, and a whole host of shrubby species
called buckbrush and snowbrush. (Throughout the West it
is customary to designate many known and all unknown
brush species as buckbrush or snowbrush. There is no reason
to it, nor is there intended to be; buckbrush in one locality
will be snowbrush in another, and vice versa.) These shrubby
plants are worthless except for watershed protection and
game cover. In the aggregate they spread over several hundred square miles, most spectacularly in the brush fields of
the Shasta region. This is similar to the rolling hills of brush
in the Sierra Nevada east of Lake Tahoe.

Forest restoration in brush regions is no simple task. Even
where the soil is not wholly impoverished, many problems
remain. Some years ago enterprising federal foresters in
northern California devised the "Plumas brush-buster," a
heavy plow with which to bulldoze a path through the chaparral by main strength and sweat. The plan was to plant trees
in the cleared-off strips. Despite unreasonable odds, some

fairly satisfactory strips were cleared but this did not guarantee success. In the unholy underbrush lurked great numbers of rabbits which chomped down young trees as fast as the foresters could plant them. What the rabbits missed the deer virtually wore down, using the cleared lanes as convenient runways. The net result of all this adversity is that artificial re-establishment of forests has proceeded very slowly in the brush fields. In some parts the soil may be so drastically beaten that only nature can restore the fire-banished pine and fir. This will probably require several hundred years of incredibly slow advance of trees as they move in from the nearest forest fringe, shading out and killing one manzanita at a time and replacing it with a tree seedling which, if it lives, may finally reach over the edge of the brush field and lop off one or two more bushes.

This is the process of competition and succession, a quietly furious and continuous struggle between forest species. The various stages in the fight are less clearly marked than in tension zones where species contend for water; they are not so boldly outlined as where lodgepole pine triumphantly marches in to pre-empt an Engelmann spruce stand following a burn. But far more widespread, more intrinsic a part of the forest growing cycle, is the bitter, unremitting tug-of-war among species all through the Cascades. It is well illustrated by the perpetual competition between the light-requiring Douglas fir and the shade-enduring hemlock.

COMPETITION: DOG-EAT-DOG

After a fire in the Douglas fir region, seedlings of this tree generally swarm over the area in a short time if there is a seed source nearby. At first they compete only among themselves, and an even-aged, pure stand develops. As the stand thickens the forest floor is shaded, competition increases, and no new Douglas firs establish under the dark canopy; but balsam fir, western red cedar, and western hemlock seedlings begin to invade the site. Now begins a dog-eat-dog struggle. Hemlock seedlings will persevere longer than most other species despite both shade and competition from larger hemlocks and rival species. When the canopy closes overhead, the previously established young Douglas firs become thin and spindly and are finally choked off, but young hemlocks persist. As the Douglas firs mature their growth and vigor begin to decline, and trees are killed by the intense competition of the overstory. The tough hemlocks still hang on beneath the canopy. Eventually an old fir dies. With neither seedlings nor saplings of Douglas fir left beneath the stand, death of the veteran merely yields growing space to the hemlocks and their shady associates. Released from competition, active growth of hemlocks takes place in the understory, and with continued mortality of the old Douglas firs, more and more hemlocks attain position in the main canopy of the forest. Thus more hemlock seed source is provided, more seedlings arise, and the cycle from Douglas fir to hemlock is well along toward completion.

In the end the result is an uneven-aged old hemlock forest with a typically jagged canopy. Seen in profile it is saw-toothed, as mature trees alternate with the immature. This contrasts with a typically flat-topped even-aged forest which is still developing, still in the pre-climax stage. Left alone, the chances are that much of the wetter Douglas fir forest in the Cascades would revert to hemlock, the true climax type.

Fire interrupts this sequence. It kills young coniferous seedlings as well as the thin-barked older hemlocks and white firs, but frequently the thick-barked older Douglas firs will survive, to remain the only seed trees in the area. On newly burned ground the Douglas fir seedlings are hardier and will persist. The shade-loving hemlock and balsam fir seedlings germinate but do not survive the exposure and heat. As a result, the normal ecological cycle is broken, and the even-aged fir stand becomes dominant for long periods. Eventually the hemlock begins the time-consuming task all over again, only to lose out if fire sweeps the forest. Almost all pure fir stands show signs of old burns where fires have beaten down hemlock and maintained Douglas fir. Logging, and slash-burning fires do the same thing today. One exception is the so-called selective logging where only a small portion of the timber is cut, and normal forest conditions are not greatly disturbed. Here the slash is often left unburned. Under these conditions hemlock will continue to work toward eventual dominance of the stands. The exception to this sequence is found in the fringes of the valleys in Washington and Oregon, in southern Oregon and northern California, where the sites are too dry for hemlock, and Douglas fir is frequently the true climax species. On still more arid sites, fir in turn loses to the pines.

Over the Cascade forest as a whole, where hardwoods occur in the stand they enjoy a transient dominance following fire because their vigorous sprout growth greatly exceeds the slow growth of coniferous seedlings. Eventually the conifers regain command, and the hardwoods are pushed back to a few favored spots where additional moisture permits them to compete on even terms with the conifers.

THE HARDWOODS

The Cascade Range is not particularly hospitable to hard-woods. The summer growing season is normally marked by a long dry spell, and in consequence the moisture-demanding hardwoods are subordinated to the less thirsty conifers. The broad-leaved trees are limited mostly to the valleys, coves, meadows, and other well-watered areas.

An exception is the Oregon white oak, probably the most widely distributed hardwood in the Cascades. It is a slow-growing, leathery-leaved tree, persisting on thin-soiled hills which conifers disdain. Ironically, after the oak has pioneered an area and has enriched the soil, faster growing conifers move in under its protection and eventually poach the site away. Young fir forests along the fringes of the Cascades contain the gnarled and whitened carcasses of many veteran oaks smothered under the dense canopy lifted by the conifers—an ill return for oaken assistance in giving them a start. Not so large nor so useful as the eastern white oaks, this Oregon oak nonetheless has some local utility for furniture and flooring. One use is unique. It is made into wedges which timber fallers drive into the cut to keep the weight of the tree from binding their saw as they work.

Where the Siskiyous intersect the Cascades in southern Oregon, and on down into the Shasta-Lassen country, the Cascade forest in many places becomes a pine-oak woodland. Along with the Oregon white oak, another important species in this territory is the California black oak, a valuable timber tree in local areas. The term "black" refers to the bark rather than to the wood, for black oak lumber is by no means objectionably dark. On the contrary it is very attractive, has pleasing figure, and is as acceptable as white oak for commercial uses.

Other hardwoods include canyon live oak and the odd little huckleberry oaks, some of them scarcely more than bushes. The canyon live oak is especially interesting because of its foliage variation—half of the leaf margins may be sharply toothed and holly-like, the remaining leaf margins being entire.

One of the minor species in the Cascades foothills along the Sacramento River is the breath-taking, magnificent redbud. This small tree brightens a March day all along the dark canyon with its brilliant masses of tiny purple-red flowers. These appear before the leaves, and are so strikingly beautiful that callous travelers maim the tree, breaking off branches in such numbers that many a tree is horticulturally browsed back to a bush each year.

Associated with the northern California oaks in the Sacramento Valley, and scattered all the way to British Columbia in the Cascade foothills is madrone, a beautiful tree which the early settlers mistook for magnolia—hence Magnolia Point on Puget Sound near Seattle. The large dark-green glossy leaves persist for several seasons, but on young trunks the bark is cast annually. The papery-thin brick-red old bark cracks frequently in almost geometric pattern, to reveal the delicately apple-green new bark beneath—one of the rare sights of the southern Cascades.

More common than the oaks, especially in the northern part of the range, is bigleaf maple, the largest of the western maples. It is found as an understory tree in the lower levels of the mountains and in valley bottoms. There is not enough maple in single stands to support a large hardwood industry,

but it is used locally for furniture. Some bird's-eye is found
in this species, and it is noted for its prodigious burls, which
are exported in considerable numbers to France and other
western European countries. In the Oregon Forestry Board
headquarters at Salem each room is finished with a different
native species in a different pattern. The bigleaf maple room
is probably the finest of all these magnificent examples of
wood craftsmanship; the walls are sections of burls, so beautiful as to defy description. The traveler who drives through
Oregon without seeing this room has wasted his time and
gasoline. The bigleaf maple does not belie its name. Leaves
have been recorded up to twenty-two inches across, which
should be a record for maples if not for other hardwoods
as well.

From a medicinal standpoint, the most important hardwood in the Cascades is cascara. To date, the laxative principle in cascara bark has not been synthesized successfully
and there is a heavy demand for the bark. As settlement
and logging encroach more and more upon the haunts of the
cascara, the search for new trees becomes ever more frantic.
One Oregonian had two fine large trees flanking the walk
in front of his home in a small town. Upon return from a
late Sunday afternoon drive he was horrified to find that
someone had taken advantage of the early fall dusk to strip
both his trees—right in town. The ultimate purpose for
which cascara is intended frequently affects those who work
with the raw product. In consequence stevedores and other
freight handlers are somewhat wary of loading big cargoes
of cascara bark.

The largest Cascade broadleaf is the black cottonwood,
confined to major stream bottoms such as the Cowlitz, Wil-

lamette, and others, mostly on the west side of the range in Washington and Oregon. Diameters of four to five feet are not uncommon, and growing in the rich river-bottom silt the tree may add rings up to an inch wide for several years in succession. The chief uses are for fruit-box veneers, pulp, and excelsior.

There is probably more alder than any other hardwood in the Cascades. Minor botanical differences mark the red and white alder but the woods are mixed indiscriminately in the trade. Alder is light, easily worked, takes a good finish, but has no reputation of its own. Hence alder boards go in the back door of furniture factories and come out the front as chairs and tables with mahogany, maple, and walnut finishes.

Among the less important hardwoods is Oregon ash, which is more properly a valley species, reaching into the Cascades only in thin fingers along the wider streams. Rhododendron becomes a small tree in parts of the Cascades, and is a good-sized shrub toward the upper reaches of the mountains. In June and July its pink blossoms splash against the green conifers in festive air. Dogwood is the only other flowering tree of consequence. In spring the large, showy, white flowers lighten the dark-green forest, and in fall the bright red berries do the same. Dogwood has an extraordinary and most appreciated habit: part of the time the trees will flower a second time in the autumn. The white flowers, red berries, and green leaves make a festive mass of color, totally unexpected and hence more appreciated. An inconspicuous little dry-belt tree is the gnarled, gray-green mountain mahogany, Cercocarpus. Actually there are two species distinguished chiefly by variation in leaf form. They fringe the openings in the ponderosa pine forest and form dense thickets along the lava breaks, giving excellent deer cover. The genus is not even closely related to mahogany, its chief claim to fame being the exceedingly great hardness of the wood. You might as well go to breaking rocks with your ax as to try to chop seasoned mountain mahogany. Another minor tree is golden chinquapin, often a dense, compactly foliated tree, especially when young. This little-known species is fairly common in the Coast Range, not so prevalent in the Cascades. It deserves attention, for the wood is beautifully grained and colored and is most appealing for interior paneling and flooring. The evergreen leaves are attractive, for the bright, glossy, green upper surface contrasts sharply with the yellow underside.

The word yellow brings to mind trembling aspen, an unimportant "hardwood" but a major contribution to the beauty of the east-side Cascade forest. In summer the light-green leaves and chalky trunks relieve the somber hues of the unpretentious conifers; and in fall the rich yellow of the aspen gilds the landscape and warms the heart wherever it is seen.

The Cascade broadleaves as a whole display none of the superb coloring of the eastern hardwoods in the fall. Oak and cascara leaves usually turn a dingy brown, become discouraged, and fall off. Alder does not even go that far— the leaves casually drop off while still green. Aspen, ash, cottonwood, and at times bigleaf maple, become yellow beacons vividly resplendent amid the somber conifers. Dogwood works in soft pastels, part of the leaves ranging from a gentle red to delicate pink, while others stay light green. One small broadleaf is left to retrieve the honor of the western hardwoods in a brief moment of glory. This is the vine maple, either a small inconspicuous tree beneath the forest canopy or a big bush out in the cut-over areas. Most of the year it is just another poor-relation kind of tree like lesser alder species, elderberry, and similar modest hardwoods. In the fall, though, it makes a great effort to do for all the hardwoods what they cannot do for themselves—transform the forest to a painter's palette of color. Old burns blaze again, not with searing flame but with the joyous march of the vine maple in all the reds and yellows ever seen. There is so much beauty in this little tree that it offsets the lack in other Cascade hardwoods. At higher elevations and on the east slopes of the mountains the Douglas or mountain maple, in similarly brilliant colors, takes up the task and spreads riotous color where the vine maple does not grow.

One other hardwood must be mentioned, even though it is not a major component of the Cascade forest. This is the California laurel, according to California chambers of commerce and curio dealers; or Oregon myrtle, according to Oregon chambers of commerce and curio dealers.

A number of attributes mark the myrtle (or laurel). It is an evergreen with rich dark leaves and is strongly aromatic. Younger trees form dense compact green pyramids, older trees spread out into a wide rounded crown in the open but are more compressed in forest stands. The wood is a great prize. It is a bewilderingly beautiful assortment of grays, greens, and bronzes, combining and yet contrasting so that the figure at times is almost iridescent. It lends itself joyously to the lathe, and in skilled hands, products of breath-catching beauty emerge. The wood, especially from older trees, is magnificent beyond compare in all the endless variety of lamps, plates, platters, book ends and similar gewgaws in which it is pressed upon the wayfarer. In both states, innocents abroad are assured that laurel (or myrtle) "grows only here and in the Holy Land." Perchance it is hoped with this ecclesiastical aid to make a sale which might not come off if conducted on the grubby plane of ordinary commerce; but there is no virtue in this biblical association. It is botanical nonsense of the first order. Actually the tree grows only in the Coast Range and on the west side of the Cascades. This rare species will be preserved in spite of the tremendous demand for novelty uses. A "Save-the-Myrtle-woods" campaign in Oregon succeeded in 1948 in setting aside one of the finest groves along the Chetco River as a state forest.

There is undeniable appeal in the broadleaf trees as they change foliage with the shifting seasons. But the average hardwood is a sorry sight in midwinter, naked against a cold December sky in penance for its brief but gaudy fling in the fall. The conifers remain steadfastly somber year around; no turncoat change of color in a momentary flame of glory, for theirs is the workaday chore of just growing wood. This humble role serves well the people of the Cascade mountains, and the great Plains, and New England, and other centers of lumber consumption.

The Cascade hardwoods contribute less than one per cent by volume of the total lumber cut in the range, for the Cascade production forest is uniquely a coniferous forest.

THE CONIFERS

The conifer forest is composed of few species, for in most of the Cascades the growing conditions are so severe as to exclude all but a few types from each locality. The most widely distributed, and the tree which towers over all in sheer volume, is that which keeps green the memory of the Scottish botanist David Douglas. The Cascade forest is chiefly Douglas fir on the west side north of the Rogue River. Hemlock, red cedar, and true firs come in beneath the older fir stands here. This type gives way in the well-watered upper reaches to a forest composed chiefly of hemlock, with quantities of noble and silver fir at times forming almost pure stands in small areas. On the summit there is quite a mixture: the firs named above, plus alpine fir, mountain hemlock, white pine, white-bark pine, lodgepole pine, and Engelmann spruce. Going down the east side the forest is rapidly reduced to fewer species. The usual pattern is a ponderosa pine overstory with grand fir and white fir in the understory. As the forest flattens out on the eastern foothills, junipers first replace the fir and then the pine. In Washington quite a little Douglas fir occurs in the east-side forest.

In the southern part of the range, California red fir and Shasta red fir reach north out of California to the Crater Lake region. Another California tree, the sugar pine, is fairly common in the southern Cascades in Oregon, and one hardy specimen has been verified from the Warm Springs Indian reservation, close to Mount Hood. California incense cedar is a helter-skelter component of mixed forests as far north as the McKenzie River in central Oregon.

Except for the pine-oak woodland which tentatively appears in the Rogue country and southward, conifers are king. In the Shasta-Lassen area the pine is ascendant in the pine-oak type, and were it not for recurring fires it would probably crowd the oaks out of extensive areas which these hardwoods are now homesteading.

Conifers are protected against the Cascadian summer drought by their smaller leaf area and thicker bark, both of which cut down water loss. These characteristics permit evergreens to survive where hardwoods fail, and explain the prevalence of the coniferous forest, particularly the fir forest, throughout the Cascades.

DOUGLAS FIR

It is impossible to speak of the Cascade forest without thinking of much of it as the Douglas fir forest. This tree ranges from British Columbia to Mexico, but its best growth is in a moist climate where winters are not too severe—the Pacific Northwest. Considerable quantities are cut in northern California, but like southern Oregon the climate is too arid for the best growth of the tree. Where conditions are optimum, it will produce as much as 1,500 board feet of wood per acre every year. This is the best; the average is half that much. Though the redwood is intrinsically a more vast tree,* more long lived, and though some trees are even individually renowned, redwoods as a group are commercially insignificant compared to the Douglas fir. The latter is cut in such tremendous quantities that in total it is

* The two largest Douglas firs, one each in Washington and Oregon, are over 15½ feet in diameter, mere pipsqueaks compared to even adolescent redwoods.

a veritable Paul Bunyan of trees. More Douglas fir wood is used than that of any other tree, despite the fact that many species have greater virtue for certain uses. Sitka spruce is a better ladder material, but there are more fir ladders; hemlock makes better flooring, but there are more fir floors; and so on. There is just more fir in almost everything.

The most widespread use is for structural purposes such as plywood, dimension lumber, or timbers. With modern milling machinery it is readily worked, it is strong; and it has been produced for every conceivable kind of specification from mousetrap stock to mammoth timbers four feet square and one hundred feet long. It shares the housing field to some extent with ponderosa pine and the four southern pines, but for heavier construction fir is supreme. New developments in metal connectors and in lamination of planks have opened a big field for timber structures such as arches, columns, and beams. Many of the Alcan highway bridges were prefabricated of Douglas fir. Other uses for this great tree are endless. Normally it furnishes most of the plywood and more than twenty per cent of the nation's lumber, enough to build at least 800,000 homes annually.

Douglas fir is an integral part of the life of every mountain community throughout the range. Though other species are logged in respectable quantity, the west side of the Cascades is almost wholly the empire of the fir, and its total annual production far overshadows the east-side pine.

Oddly enough, the fir is known as pine in some trade circles. A good deal is exported as Oregon pine, and from British Columbia it is still shipped to Europe as "Nootka" pine, from Nootka Sound, whence the first fir timbers were shipped, away back almost to the time of the Spaniard. This recalls a long-delayed tragedy in a sawmill up Nootka way some years ago. A big fir log was being chewed rapidly into planks when a horrendous metallic uproar broke out at the head saw. Chunks of bark, log, men, and metal thudded around the mill deck. When clamor was stilled and dust settled, remnants of the saw blade were found deeply bitten into a rusted cannon ball, embedded so far in the log that the bark had grown treacherously smooth over it. What history here? A bold threat from the Spaniard or doughty Captain Meares to send the aborigine scuttling back into the timbered Nootka shore? Whose shot bided its time, and, centuries after, killed not red men but white? The lads so quiet on the mill deck would never know.

Similar accidents were not uncommon a few years ago, but in modern mills a type of mine-detector on the log-haul locates hidden metal in the timber and saves men as well as saws. This mechanical improvement has been accompanied by many refinements in mill practice and in better utilization of Douglas fir. It is now used for pulp as well as for lumber and plywood, and the formerly waste liquors from pulp mills are made to yield valuable by-products. Progressive plants even process the bark, beating the Chicago packers who use all but the pig's squeal.

These improvements in utilization echo back to the Douglas fir forest. More intensive wood use means higher return from the forest, and more margin is available to maintain and improve that forest. Largely through improved utilization, forest industries in the Douglas fir region are now able to develop their properties for repeated harvesting of trees. The old-time policy of "cut out and get out" is being re-

placed by progressive management which will keep Douglas
fir lands productive. Throughout the Cascades (and else-
where) such a policy will enable this species to maintain its
position as the finest timber tree in the land.

THE PINES

The second most important timber tree in the Cascades
is ponderosa pine, the prevailing type on the east side in
Washington and most of Oregon, and on both sides of the
range in southern Oregon and northern California. There
is an irresistible appeal to the crisp pine woods. The bright
reddish-yellow trunks and green foliage are striking against
a blue sky. Unlike the dense redwoods or hemlocks, a lot
of sky can be seen through a pine forest. Open ponderosa
stands invite the woodsman, hiker, and hunter, for the park-
like forest permits easy entry and people can more readily
enjoy its beauty than in more densely stocked stands.

For the most part ponderosa pine grows on relatively flat
ground compared to the rough fir and hemlock forests.
There are authentic records of old-timers actually cruising
timber from horse and buggy. This somewhat casual approach would hardly do in the present period of high stump-
age prices, for ponderosa pine is exceedingly valuable today.
As with the Douglas fir, the pine forest of the Cascades is
primarily a production forest, providing employment for
men who are thus enabled to enjoy recreation, to use the
forest for pleasure as well as for work.

The smell of pine sawdust puts a resinous tang in the air
of Omak, Bend, Klamath Falls, Dorris, and Weed, to name
only a few of the pine mill towns. Pine is big business all
over the east side, and well it should be, pine lumber is one

of the most valuable woods in America, the economic mainstay of many communities. This is the best-known and most
used box material in the West, particularly for fruit boxes.
It works with ease and hence is preferred for sash, doors,
furniture, toys, and general shop purposes in addition to
housing construction. A new solvent drying process removes
objectionable pitch from the knots and now the wood can
be painted satisfactorily, which opens up still more uses for
this already universally used timber.

In addition to its great value as lumber, the pine forest
protects the watersheds which mean life or death to the irrigated farms in the valleys below; under the trees there is
nutritious summer range for sheep and chunky beef cattle;
and the forest provides an unsurpassed habitat for wildlife.

The Cascade ponderosa pine is cursed with a number of
insect enemies, chief among them the western pine beetle
which kills annually twenty to twenty-five times as much
timber as forest fires. Adult beetles lay eggs under the bark,
the larvae hatch and begin to gnaw tunnels in the vital
food-conducting tissues. If the larvae are so numerous that
their tunnels overlap, the tree is effectively girdled, and
dies. These beetles thrive on disaster. Following a terrific
blowdown which weakened whole forests of pine some years
ago, beetles moved in on the distressed trees and in one season took more timber than all pine loggers in the area. To
combat these epidemics, ponderosa foresters are now using
a system pioneered in northern California. Trees are classified according to beetle susceptibility and in a very light
cutting the most susceptible trees are removed, perhaps several years before the normal logging front would have
reached them. The trees which are left are sufficiently re-

sistent to withstand normal attacks. There are other beetles attacking ponderosa and other pines, but the western pine beetle is by far the worst. Its threat of epidemic is a constant sword held over western pine forestry.

A dreaded insect defoliator in the pine country is the large, showy pandora moth. Its big, fat larvae feed upon ponderosa needles and in serious epidemics may strip the trees. In earlier days the Klamath Indians considered the grubs a great delicacy, roasting them on a splinter over a pine-cone fire. There are other insect enemies of ponderosa and its associated Cascade pines, but these two exemplify the worst of the common types—bark beetles and leaf eaters.

Despite the inroads of pests and past heavy logging, ponderosa forests are now being managed on a long-term basis in most places, and increased protection from insects and fire should assure that this great tree will always be a mainstay of the east-side Cascade forest.

In the Lassen-Shasta region and in southern Oregon a close associate of ponderosa pine is its near relative the Jeffrey pine. Ponderosa overlaps the Jeffrey both north in the Cascades and south in the Sierra. Commercially they are all one; the lumber is cut and sold without discrimination. These two species hybridize and give taxonomists a headache which is not cured even by the reams of "identification literature" which allegedly make all things clear between the species. Extreme specimens are readily distinguished, but the characteristics are often so alike that any two similar trees will at once provoke a furious controversy. In the main, Jeffrey trunks are more reddish; the bark is broken into narrower, deeper plates; the needles are more bluish-green, and longer; and the cones are larger, often purple when young, and a very light chocolate-brown when mature. The Jeffrey seeds are large, and hence very attractive to squirrels, who clip off and destroy the cones to get at the seeds. This habit is particularly noticeable in the magnificent stand of Jeffrey pine around Manzanita Lake in Lassen Volcanic National Park. Red squirrels laboriously climb the big trees here, chop off the large green cones and drop them with an earth-shaking thump. Often as not a golden-mantled ground squirrel will pop out from a secluded den, seize the cone, and with considerable grunting lug it into a burrow before the red squirrel, in screaming indignation, can scuttle down the tree fast enough to retrieve his prize. The red squirrels never seem to learn; they climb, and cut, and grow thinner and thinner, while the golden-mantled squirrels sit, and eat, and grow fatter and fatter.

Sugar pine is the most valuable of the western pines but is much less a tree in the Cascades, both in quantity and distribution, than in the Sierra. However it is still a magnificent tree in the Cascades. The reddish or magenta bark points out the tall heavy trunks from all other species. In early fall the great cones are pendant from the tips of long straight branches, ornamenting the crown as though it were a giant Christmas tree. Sugar pine from a distance has stateliness, but close at hand the great trunks, the warm coloring of the bark, the noble crown, give it a grandeur almost unsurpassed.

It is limited to the southern end of the Cascades and in commercial quantities does not extend far north of Crater Lake. Here it is subject to disastrous frost injury. The thin bark is little protection, and sudden drops in temperature sometimes result in circular cracks in the wood. When placed on the saw carriage, logs may open up like leaves of a quickly riffled book, the wood separating into uselessness along lines of the annual rings. This represents a severe loss of valuable wood.

Another adversity besets sugar pine and its five-needled relatives, western white and white-bark pines. This is blister rust, the dread disease which has killed untold numbers of these trees and which perils their continued existence. Imported by accident in 1910, blister rust is now found all over the West (the East, too). It has jumped as much as two hundred miles in a year, making eradication both difficult and costly. The most common control measure used at present is the elimination of currants and gooseberries, upon which hosts the disease must spend half of its life cycle.

The western white pine is a sort of lesser sugar pine, with smaller cones, smaller trunk, and a gray bark heavily checked into small squarish plates. It is a fine lumber species, and were it not for the surpassing value of the bigger tree, it would be the best of western pines. This species is sparingly distributed in the Cascades, never attaining the fine stands that characterize white pine forests in Idaho.

Ponderosa, sugar, and western white pine have supplied the lumber market for generations. Lately a long-despised Cascades pine has also received some commercial notice. This is the lodgepole, previously classed as too small and scrubby to be of use. Now it is used as small poles, and minor quantities are being sawed. It makes good pulp too (but there is not enough water for pulp mills in most of the western pine country).

White-bark pine is of interest because it is a creature of the high places, a timber-line tree frequently associated with mountain hemlock. Small, often scrubby, but always a tenacious tree, it lives a rough and precarious existence between rock and snow. The five needles tend to cluster tightly, giving twigs a startled, bristly effect in contrast to the softer sprays of sugar pine or white pine.

Two other pines in the Cascades have little utility for the common purposes of man. Digger pine is restricted to the California section of the range. It is a small, spraddled-out tree, often with several trunks. The thin, bluish-gray foliage sets it off sharply from other vegetation along State Route 89 on the east-side foothills and in the upper Sacramento Valley on the west side. The large stony seeds of this tree were cherished as a food item by the Digger Indians. Knobcone pine is found in limited quantities in southern Oregon, and in California chiefly on the west side of the Cascades. Heavy, stony cones are borne in small clusters next to trunk and branch, frequently becoming completely encased by bark or wood. The cones are not readily consumed by forest fires, but often are opened by the heat. This gives knobcone a head start on burned areas and it becomes abundant where other species and their seeds are completely fire-killed.

THE HEMLOCKS

Western hemlock is the archetype species of the dark, dank forest. Chiefly it is an understory tree, hanging on, resisting competition, until it wears down some of its associates and gains an equal position in the canopy. The thin dark-brown bark is broken into long shallow ridges, and the trunk is clean and straight, often free of branches for many feet aboveground. The needles are not uniform as in the firs, but of all lengths, small and fine, giving the twigs a delicate lacy appearance. The tiny cones belie their seed-producing capacity, for hemlock usually produces large quantities of very small, light seeds. They travel far, and account for the wide dissemination of young trees wherever hemlock seed source exists.

One odd characteristic of this tree is worth mention. The seeds often light on top of an old stump or rotting tree. The inherent hardiness of hemlock frequently enables the young seedling to survive in such an unfavorable habitat; roots quickly push down through the rotting wood and strike a substantial footing into the solid ground. When the old trunk finally decays into a pile of rubble, the husky young hemlock will be found propped up in empty space by its tough-fibered roots. At times these air-borne hemlocks assume grotesque forms.

Western hemlock suffers from a black sheep in the family. Eastern hemlock is a poor timber tree—acceptable for casual local use, but not a commercial species of any consequence. When undiscerning loggers first hit Puget Sound they said "Oh, more of that worthless hemlock," and for years it was kicked around and cussed because it interfered with Douglas fir logging. Strenuous efforts were made to get rid of this so-called "weed tree." To the consternation of all hands, it was presently discovered that this was not eastern hemlock at all, but western hemlock, an entirely different species. In fact not only was it valuable, but in some places and for some uses, even more valuable than the favored Douglas fir. For example, it makes a more satisfactory pulp at less cost; and it is a harder, more durable flooring. It has also been found that in some local areas hemlock will produce more wood per acre than Douglas fir. For these various reasons this long-maligned tree has now come into its own and is one of the leading commercial species in the Cascades.

On more justifiable grounds the mountain hemlock is as yet unknown to the lumber trade. It is a smaller tree, though occasionally it stretches to four feet in diameter; and it is frequently bowed and gnarled from ceaseless struggle with the elements. The mountain hemlock is no sissy; it grows on the roof of the Cascades where life is a constant free-for-all against wind and stone and storm. It pioneers on lava flows and the pumice-dust high prairies; it battles the deep summit snows to push timber line just a little higher. Its heavily seamed gray bark is comparable to the wrinkled hide of the old homesteader who won't admit the severity of life on his rugged claim. The mountain hemlock deserves more recognition. There are substantial forests of this species on high ground close to the Cascades summit. In many areas it is the only tree, sometimes the only vegetation, and hence it is extremely valuable as a watershed protector.

For many years there was an infallible aid in identifying the hemlocks—the terminal lops over like a buggy whip. This easy era came to an abrupt end recently when an earnest freshman forester honestly inquired, "But what does a buggy whip look like?"

THE BALSAM FIRS

Noble fir is a tree of the clean mountain slopes ranging from elevations of 1,500 to 5,000 feet. The form of the tree is a delight to the lumberman as well as to the layman; tall and straight, it tapers but little until the very crown. Frequently the crown is concentrated on the upper portion of the stem, leaving a long clear trunk. The foliage varies from

deep green almost to a robin's-egg blue. Viewed from a
lookout tower as the afternoon sun slants across these vari-
colored rippling twigs, the branches seem almost fluores-
cent. To complete the virtues of the noble fir, it has a magnificent cone, probably largest of the genus except for that
of the California red fir. The spear-tipped papery bracts
of the bright-green cone completely wrap it, spiraling
around in precise rows which make it most attractive. As with
all balsam firs, the cones shatter while still on the tree, leaving the central stalks upright like Christmas candles.

In addition to these natural graces, noble fir has another.
Along with the Shasta and California red firs, it is a Christmas tree of incomparable beauty. In the young tree, branches
and twigs align themselves into patterns as geometrically
perfect as snowflakes. In this form it is such a majestic fir
that the most costly ornaments are shabbily synthetic compared to the intrinsic beauty of the tree.

Lumbermen have been guilty of a botanical libel in the
naming of noble fir. Years ago an enterprising lumber dealer
found that he could sell larch when he couldn't sell balsam
fir, so noble fir promptly became larch. It is still "larch" to
Northwest loggers, and the misnomer is perpetuated in
Larch Mountain, east of Portland. There are no larches
within many miles of the mountain, and the top is wholly
covered with noble fir.

During World War II there was a frantic scramble for
high-quality wood to be used in aircraft. Noble fir was found
to have the necessary qualities, almost identical to those of
Sitka spruce, and access roads were pushed all over the Cascades to reach the fir. The R.A.F. Mosquito bomber was
built of noble fir frames and birch wing covering. War uses

demonstrated that the fir was a versatile wood and it is now more widely used than ever before. Foresters have begun extensive plantations of noble fir in reforestation projects.

Close relatives of the noble fir in mountain habitat and in use are the California red fir, Abies magnifica, and its variety, Shasta red fir, Abies magnifica var. shastensis. Both these firs are more heavily represented in the Sierra than in the Cascades, but they reach into southern Oregon around Crater Lake and a little north. It is very difficult to distinguish between these two without the cones: that of magnifica is smooth on the surface, while in the Shasta variety the papery bracts project like little bookmarks. The Shasta red fir, in cone and in other characteristics, is intermediate between the California red and the noble firs, giving credence to the belief that these trees hybridize extensively. The species have so many similar characteristics, and there are such variations in form within one species, that throughout the Cascades the identification of the various firs is baffling to expert and amateur alike.

The red firs are highly prized for Christmas * trees under the name of silver-tips, and they fetch fantastic prices. One enterprising vendor takes pictures of individual trees in the forest, each tagged with a number. The pictures are then displayed with great showmanship to a "restricted clientele" in a gaudy metropolitan area. Patrons pay up to $25 to have specific trees reserved for future Christmas seasons.

The red firs are increasing in value as lumber species. For

* The Cascades yield other holiday decorations. Mistletoe, staghorn moss, and huge sugar-pine cones now go to Chicago and other eastern markets. Local favorites are chinquapin leaf and burr clusters, salal greens, and the attractive coral-red clumps of madrone berries.

many years the more favored trees such as sugar pine and ponderosa pine were cut almost to the exclusion of the red firs. Lately, decreasing quantities of the former species in accessible areas, plus high lumber demand, make red fir logging a profitable enterprise.

The Pacific silver fir does not appear in California but is an important tree in the Cascade forest in Oregon and Washington. It is cut along with noble fir, Douglas fir, and hemlock, and the wood is rarely distinguished from noble fir in trade circles. The silver fir gains its name in part from the whitish trunk of younger trees and from the strikingly silver underside of the leaves. These form a sharp contrast with the dark glossy green of the upper surfaces. The needles are blunt and closely appressed to the twigs, giving small branches a stubby appearance. The heavy purple cones are smooth, smaller than noble fir, but also very attractive against the heavy foliage.

Like the red fir, the grand fir, Abies grandis, and white fir, Abies concolor, are steadily advancing in economic importance. The former has been used by Northwest pulp mills for a good many years, but extensive milling of both species is a comparatively recent development. These trees are well distributed throughout the Cascades, although grandis is found sparingly in the California part of the range, and concolor is more concentrated there than to the north. Both species are marketed as white fir, and when properly dried are acceptable for most lumber purposes.

Alpine fir, the last of the balsam firs found in the Cascades, is the most widely distributed of the species, running from Alaska to New Mexico. It is more of a Rocky Mountain species than a Cascade mountain species, though it is found at many points throughout the range in Washington and Oregon. It has no commercial value as yet, but is beneficial in watershed protection. Every migrant to southern California depends in part on Colorado's alpine fir for his water supply; and Klamath potato growers are equally reliant on alpine fir in the southern Oregon Cascades. This is not a big tree, but it is an interesting one. It has by long odds the sharpest crown of the mountain species. At times the heavily foliated lower branches cluster thickly all the way down to the ground, where they ripple out and drape around the base of the tree like a heavy velvet dress, too long for its wearer. It is unique and very lovely. The alpine fir also does something for the soul as well as for the sight. The long, tapering, needle-like spires, steel-sharp against a pristine cloud, give the mountain dweller a cathedral of the joyous heart, a proof against the spiritually meager existence of the mean and money-grubbing town. No man who has stood on a rocky summit will question the worth of alpine fir.

THE CEDARS

The most extensive cedar in the Cascades is the California incense cedar, which runs up into Oregon almost to the Santiam country. At various times this species has been used for pencil-slat stock, but it is subject to severe heart rot, and the difficulty of cutting out clear material has forced abandonment of operations. Because of the indigenous rot the wood is not suitable for many other purposes, and it is frequently left in the woods when more valuable species are cut. This is gradually creating a serious problem in forest management: with so much seed source of incense cedar remaining, the young forest following cutting will run heavily to this ill-favored species.

Western red cedar does not reach into California in the Cascades, but in Oregon and more especially in Washington it is an important timber species for lumber, poles, and shingles. Most of the shingles made in the United States come from Washington. This tree was important in the Indian economy of the Northwest. It furnished war canoes and totem poles, logs for the lodges, bark strands for weaving clothing and baskets. Red cedar was most plentiful on the moist lowlands of Washington. Now that area has been turned to farms and pasture, and as logging progresses up the Cascade slopes there is less cedar in the forest; it begins to be a scarce commodity in some lumber markets.

The Alaska yellow cedar is less well known than the other cedars, for in the Northwest it is confined almost entirely to scattered areas in upper reaches of the Olympics and Cascades. Textbooks do not show the tree in California, but recently its presence has been authenticated in the extreme northwestern part of the state. The extremely stringy and pendulous branchlets on this tree give it a unique waterfall effect. The small globular cone is similar to that of Port Orford white cedar but it is six-segmented rather than eight, and there are little hooks on the cone scales. For certain identification, the wood just beneath the thin bark smells like a freshly cut potato. Alaska yellow cedar wood is beautiful material to work. Many years ago the writer and some friends built a two-story log cabin, roofing it with yellow cedar shakes, and what shakes! They were an inch thick, a foot and a half wide, and nearly four feet long, fully lapped to give a double roof. This rugged construction was needed to

bear up under the wet twenty-foot snows of the northern
Cascades. Another use of yellow cedar warrants mention.
Along the north Pacific Coast where the Cascades fringe the
sea, boats are as germane to daily life as are cars in California. Many local craftsmen in the little cannery towns lend
their skills to boat building. The Indian fishermen used to
be very handy in boat work, molding the wood to shape their
seaworthy craft with scarcely a nail. The wood they prefer
is Alaska yellow cedar. It is light and tough and works so
well that it is a joy to use. Too bad there is not more of it in
the southern Cascades.

THE LARCHES

There are two larches in the Washington Cascades, one
in Oregon, and none in California. The more common tree
is western larch, sparse throughout the Cascades in comparison to its extensive stands in the Rockies. Mature trees are
almost as large in diameter as ponderosa pine, and compare
favorably in height. The foliage is a soft green, the needles
clustered on little knobs along the branches. There is a delicate fern-like pattern to the twigs in their summer green, a
brief moment of bright yellow in autumn, and a forlorn
spider-web appearance against gray winter skies when the
needles have fallen—for the larch is deciduous. Western
larch ranges over widely differing territory. In northern
Oregon it is companion to ponderosa pine on pumice flats
along the Metolius River, and in Washington it is an associate of balsam firs and Douglas fir in the upper slopes.

Mountain larch is confined to northern Washington at
high elevations and is noteworthy for two reasons: few
people have seen it, and those who do may not believe their

eyes. The young branches are fuzzy with a white wool; when one of these dew-covered trees is silhouetted against a misty early morning sun, each twig apparently wears a halo, a very arresting sight.

ENGELMANN SPRUCE

The last major conifer in the Cascades is Engelmann spruce, more properly a Rocky Mountain tree and only sparingly found in the former range. However, since it is the only spruce in the Cascades, something should be said for it. This is a good tree, tall and clean, excellent for lumber purposes, though not occurring in stands large enough to support any extensive harvesting of the species. It is strictly an upper-slope type, and does not overlap the better-known Sitka spruce of the Coast Range. For purposes of identification the species are distinguished as follows: an unsuspecting citizen brashly seizing a Sitka spruce branch would be moved to yell "Blankety blank blank"; whereas the same man taking hold of Engelmann spruce would merely say "Ouch." In other respects they are much the same—small flaky plates scaling off the thin bark, which is essentially reddish purple, but darker in the Sitka and somewhat grayer in the Engelmann. In the Cascades, Engelmann spruce is a useful member of the watershed protection group of summit trees.

PACIFIC YEW

A minor tree, but common throughout the west-side Cascade forest is the yew, of archery renown. This is no lost art for there are public hunting grounds in the West reserved to archers. In local areas the processing of yew bolts into bows is quite an industry. Yew is an understory tree, generally found beneath the canopies of Douglas fir or hemlock. Needles are flat, dark green above, lighter beneath, and the twigs hence resemble redwood superficially. However, the fruit is a delicate pink berry instead of a cone, and the bark is not thick and stringy, but thin and red-plated over a smooth purple underbark. A curious habit of this species is to form dense jungles of a few to many acres. A notable example is near Lake of the Woods in southern Oregon.

The Cascade conifers have been reviewed roughly in order of diminishing importance. None of them is valueless; even those not yet turned into wood products, such as alpine fir and mountain hemlock, have considerable utility for watershed protection. However, all other forest values are relatively unimportant compared to the tremendous worth of the Cascade conifers in the lumber business. In northern California, lumbering is one of the most important industries, and in Washington it supports one-third of the people directly or indirectly. In Oregon the lumber business leads all industries, even including agriculture, and it has contributed a half-billion dollars to the state in a single year. The economic lifeblood of the Pacific Northwest is the forest, most of it the coniferous timber of the Cascade mountains.

THE FUTURE OF THE FOREST

The forest manager must utilize each species for its highest use, control the growing conditions so far as possible to produce the best timber crop, and conduct the harvest so that other forest values are not impaired. This kind of multiple-use forest management in the Cascades is of relatively recent origin, but it has come a long way in a short time.

The beginning of private forestry in the Cascades properly dates back to a stormy summer afternoon nearly forty-five years ago. Thunder rolled ominously and lightning stabbed the forest. Marvin Nye propped himself in the doorway of the old moss-grown toll station at Cascadia, watching anxiously. Not only keeper of the tollgate on the Willamette Valley and Cascades Mountain Wagon Road, he was also custodian of the valuable forest grant through which the road worked its rugged passage. Electrical storms in the arid summer were a constant cause for worry and for watching. There it was! A thin plume of blue smoke rose slowly, raggedly, above the green firs on the distant mountain across the rough Santiam Valley. Nye hastily summoned a crew and they plunged into the woods with ax and mattock to subdue the fire. The year was 1904. The date is important because it marked the first organized effort of forest owners in the mid-Cascades to combat fire, their greatest enemy.

Pioneer Nye * lived until 1944, and witnessed in this period an incredible transformation of forestry in the Cascades. From his humble beginning—finding a small fire and putting it out—forest management in these mountains has grown to a complex enterprise employing thousands of men and requiring the investment of millions of dollars. To maintain the supply of raw material a number of companies and individuals have established "tree farms": forest properties pledged to permanent production. Tree farms must meet

* An interesting side light is Nye's reaction to the first automobile which appeared at the tollgate. The old tariff sign, about four by six feet in size, gave the rates for passage of everything from weaners to wagons. But no automobile. Nye was only momentarily nonplussed. In a decision worthy of Solomon, he charged the first car to pass through the gate three cents, the same rate charged for a hog

standards of good forest management established by foresters of the lumber industry. Under this program, coupled
with better utilization of wood, a large segment of the industry can stabilize its production, maintain employment, and
sustain communities.

Among the public forest owners, states and counties have
only minor holdings, but state forestry along the West Coast
has made a good beginning. State forest practice laws, better
protection standards, and more thorough reforestation, are
all helping to keep timberlands productive in the Cascade
mountains.

The federal government is the largest owner, public or
private, in the entire range. National Forests extend from
the Mount Baker at the Canadian boundary to the Lassen in
northern California. From a timber-production standpoint
these are the most important federal forests in the country.
They are managed by the U.S. Forest Service, the Bureau
of Land Management, and the Indian Service, for multiple-
use purposes. This means that considerations of recreation,
wildlife, grazing, and watershed protection are taken into
account in timber management planning. Under the multiple-use policy, some national forest lands will not be operated for timber production.* These include scenic road and
riverside strips, campgrounds and primitive regions, and
winter sports areas such as the Mount Hood and Mount
Baker "winter wonderlands."

On all these public timberlands, and on an increasing num-

* Of course no cutting is permitted on the exclusively recreational areas
administered by the National Park Service. Forests in the three National
Parks, Mount Rainier, Crater Lake, and Lassen Volcanic, have greater
esthetic value than lumber value and will be retained uncut.

ber of private operations, timber is being harvested on a sustained yield basis—that is to say, the quantity of timber cut in any period is limited to the quantity which the forest manager can grow in the same period. This necessitates protection of young timber during harvesting; the leaving of adequate seed sources or replanting, thorough protection against fire, insects, and disease; and research, especially in forest products, to make the best possible use of all the wood which is grown. Developments like these will give greater permanence to lumber towns and greater value to the Cascade forests.

CASCADE FORESTER

An account of Cascade mountain trees would be incomplete without acknowledgment of Oliver Matthews, the tree tramp of Salem, Oregon. He is the benevolent chronicler of the trees, a man devoted to the wildwood. He knows well the great forest, and in his quiet way strives to make it appreciated by the layman. Cascade timber to many people is chiefly a valuable commodity, but it is also ruggedly beautiful, and this aspect of the forest will live in the woods and in the pictures of Oliver Matthews.

The man himself is sharp nosed, sharp eyed, and long legged; agile as an antelope, too. His shock of wiry white hair belies the vigor with which he runs the legs off young woodsmen. He is neither a forester nor a botanist by profession, but he knows more about Northwest trees than either of them. In winter he labors long nights at a cannery, and in summer scours the forest untiringly in search of more tree information. Let there be even the faintest rumor of an odd tree, a big tree, an old tree, or a species growing off the reservation, and the crack of dawn will find Oliver en route. He will return triumphant with the facts, for he never quits until he has run the answer to ground. As a result of this unending capacity for hard work, this singleness of purpose, he has shamed armchair taxonomists by proving them conspicuously wrong in identification or distribution of certain species. He has extended the range of limber pine into Oregon, and Alaska yellow cedar into California; he has discovered the rare cut-leaf alder sport and the columnar white fir; he has found a new variety of Baker cypress now deservedly named for him; he has put more than 225,000 miles on his Model A, and has taken years off his life through exposure and adversity. The result of all this ardor? A gem of a tree book being worked upon with absorbing effort, regardless of health or cost or time.

THE FLOWERS IN OUR
BIT OF PARADISE

by Harry W. Hagen

Every man dreams of some peaceful, quiet place where he can go for recreation, a place that is entirely different from his everyday hurried existence. It may be the ocean beach, a dude ranch, a lake in the deep forest, a certain fishing hole, or any of a thousand and one places in this wonderful land of ours. Some years ago my wife and I found the place that fulfills our dreams, a place where we can "get away from it all," as it were, and forget all our cares and worries. We forget all these anxieties because our Bit of Paradise, as we call it, is so full of wonderful things to see and to do that there is no time or energy left for worrying. What appeals to us most about this place is the abundance of beautiful flowers that fills our paradise to overflowing. Where is this place? It is high up in the mountains in what the naturalists call the Hudsonian zone where the trees open up into beautiful meadows so full of flowers of every color that they excite the interest of everyone, be he flower lover or not.

Almost all mountain ranges rise high enough to contain this lovely Hudsonian zone. Perhaps you will say that we can go many, many places and find our paradise. In a sense this is true, as the mountain meadows of all ranges are generally

217

very much alike and are filled with quite the same types of flowers the world over. But when Maxine and I are in the alpine meadows of the Cascades, we feel as though we are at home and that these are our own meadows. Here are the flowers we love the best because we know them so well. Everyone is aware of the wonders and beauties of other places, but those he knows, those that are a part of him and of which he is a part, always seem a little better. I suppose it is the affection of intimacy that makes this so—the same deep feeling we have for old friends. So it is in any of the alpine regions of the lovely, friendly Cascades that Maxine and I have our Bit of Paradise.

Below and leading up to this Eden of ours, the slopes and ridges are covered with a magnificent forest of coniferous trees: fir, cedar, pine, and hemlock, with a sprinkling here and there of maple, alder, willow, cottonwood, and a few others. This forest, too, is filled with flowers, some large, others small, some very lovely and others with strange forms. In some parts it is dark and somber and in others it is open and sunny. Each place has its flowers: some need the light and others like shade, some seek dry slopes and some want it wet. Winding through this very fine forest are highways, roads, and trails of all sorts that will take us up to the alpine meadows with their sweeping views of timber-covered ridges, sharp high peaks, summer snow fields and gorgeous carpets of lupine, lilies, asters, phlox, paintbrush, and many other flowers. These highways and byways are what Maxine and I call the Trail to Paradise and a wonderful, flowery trail it is, exceeded in beauty only by the Paradise to which it leads. Since it is the flowers you want to hear about and just where and how to find them, Maxine and I are going to take you on a trip along this trail from beginning to end, through our Bit of Paradise and even up onto the high ridges and peaks above it. Then, after this simulated trip, perhaps you will want to come and take a real trip and see for yourself all the wonders that are waiting here for you. If once you make the acquaintance of a few of the flowers, you will never be satisfied until you know more and more of them. First, however, I want to tell you how we discovered our Bit of Paradise and came to learn that the paths we had trod so often before were a part of the wonderful Trail.

OUR FIRST ADVENTURE AMONG THE FLOWERS

It was on a wet mid-June day, on our honeymoon in the mountains, that the flower enthusiasm came over us. How completely we were taken we did not realize at the time, for we were climbers—lovers of the high peaks. There we felt the exhilaration of space and height that only the climber knows. On this wet June day we had planned to climb Boulder Peak, but the rain and fog tagged our heels as it had everywhere else we had gone. Breaking out of the wet forest we came to a high mountain lake surrounded by snowbanks, patches of bare ground and clumps of trees with everything engulfed in fog and drizzle. We built a small fire with the help of squaw-wood and pitch strips and warmed our cold fingers. As weather like this might last indefinitely, there was no use going farther. We started back. For want of anything more interesting to do we decided to see how many wild flowers we could find along the way and how many we knew. Having come from the East Coast just a few years before, Maxine knew almost none, and although I am a native of Seattle, I was of little help.

Our meager knowledge proved to be a challenge. A month
and a half later found us in the mountain meadows of Mount
Rainier National Park for a week This time we came
equipped with several books to help us with identification.
Armed with our slight knowledge and learned books we
started up the trail toward Pinnacle Peak. Each time we
found a new flower we sat down to see if we could discover
its identity. Words like hypogynous, glabrous, serrate, calyx,
were like a foreign language to us. A glossary helped but
it was slow going. One glen, which was carpeted with saxifrage, mimulus, shooting stars, and many other flowers unknown to us at the time, completely ensnared us, and we
just sat there for the rest of the afternoon.

The effects of our enthusiasm were beginning to appear.
We began to realize how many flowers there actually were
and how very little we knew of them. From then on our
trips have been planned with the primary object of learning
the flowers and their habits, and the climbing of the peaks
has become secondary. Many a mountain mile we had covered before and had seen only the scenic wonders. Now
we are accompanied by a host of new-found friends. They
had been quietly standing by all the time, but we had been
too eager to get along the trail, too eager to reach the summit of our peak to notice them. It takes longer now to make
a thousand feet of elevation, and when we reach the lovely
flowering alpine meadows they usually fascinate us so much
that the peaks above quite often have to wait until another
day. We still climb them, though, and are richly rewarded
because some of the loveliest and most charming blossoms
are found growing on the cliffs and among the rocks of the
high peaks far up in the Arctic-Alpine zone.

THE ROADS ARE LINED WITH FLOWERS

Now it is time to begin our trip, so let us get in our car and we shall be on our way. We shall have no itinerary, for who can tell how long we will be with each flower or where our wandering footsteps will take us. We only know that we must see as much of these wonderful Cascades as we can, see them in the spring, the summer, the fall, and spend some time in each of the different zones they contain. We shall travel from the Transition zone at their base and in the low river valleys, up through the lovely Canadian zone into the glorious Hudsonian zone (where our Bit of Paradise lies), and finally up to the high ridges and wonderful peaks of the Arctic-Alpine zone. These zones do not have a constant elevation throughout the range. They are lowest in the northern part, with a gradual upward trend from north to south.

As we speed along the highway and draw near to the mountains the flowers seem to come out to greet us. Buttercups cover the moist places with a golden-yellow and green carpet and spill through the fences into the meadows and pastures of the farms and ranches along the way. Large white daisies bob and nod their heads as we swish by, and the foxglove lifts its tall spire of white or deep-pink tubes for us to admire. Foxglove is a native of Europe but has become perfectly naturalized here in the Northwest, a fact that amazes many people. The drug digitalis is extracted from it, and therefore Digitalis purpurea is beneficial as well as handsome. Goat's beard, Aruncus sylvester, grows on moist banks and gets its name from the way its long thin panicle of small white flowers droops down. Rosy spireas

line some parts of the roads and in the open woods we see
ocean spray, elderberry, and the lovely, fragrant syringa
which some people call mock orange.

TALL, MAJESTIC TREES

Our car plunges into a canyon, a canyon of trees, tall and
majestic, for at last we have come to the virgin forest. The
major part of the Cascades is within National Forests and
so, fortunately, large tracts are barred to the logger. Three
National Parks: Mount Rainier, Crater Lake, and Lassen
Volcanic, are included within its far-flung reaches. Some
areas are designated as Primitive Areas and have no developments at all except trails and a few access roads. Here
we can find the forest primeval, unscathed by sharp ax or
rasping saw, and though we are here to find flowers, we
cannot help raising our eyes and admiring these wonderful
trees. This is the home of the huge Douglas fir which sometimes reaches a height of three hundred feet and is exceeded
in size only by the sequoias of California. Western hemlock is abundant here, growing to a great height though
not equaling the Douglas fir. Western red cedar frequents
the low, moist river valleys. Its wood is noted for weather-
resistant qualities and the Indians hollowed out the great
logs to make their canoes. Silver fir, noble fir, and grand
fir are scattered throughout the forest but never reach the
size or dominance of the Douglas fir and the western hemlock. At Crater Lake National Park and in the southern
end of the Cascades the Douglas fir is less abundant, and
here we find ponderosa pine, which is generally called yellow pine, and lodgepole pine. In valleys, along streams,

and in other favorable locations broadleaf maple, vine maple, alder, willow, and cottonwood are common.

Walking through a forest is like being in a different world entirely. Trees, large and small, stretch up and up to the life-giving sunlight, for you know they must have light to survive. The weaker, slower growing trees are gradually overshadowed by the strong, vigorous ones and sooner or later die for lack of sunlight. Lower branches die off, one by one, as the trees grow taller and taller to keep themselves in the sun. Thus the forest thins and prunes itself, and eventually great trunks are produced that stand like pillars in a temple, tall, straight, and awe-inspiring. Trees that measure 75, 100, and even 150 feet from base to the first branch are frequently encountered.

The ground is covered with shade-loving plants and shrubs that form a tangle of underbrush, while dead trees, leveled by age or the elements, sprawl upon the ground or lean against their neighbors—some newly fallen, others covered with mosses, and some in the last stages of decomposition.

WE START UP THE TRAIL

Somewhere in this wonderful forest we shall find a trail to our liking, and here we shall leave our car, for we must take to our two feet to see the flowers. It makes no difference just where we choose our trail—northern, middle, or southern part of the range—for every section has charm to spare.

Lovely little spring beauty, Montia sibirica, will be there to greet us with its small white or pinkish flowers veined with red. It is one of the very first to bloom, is quite common, and keeps blossoming well into the summer. Another species we shall see is the small-leaf spring beauty, Claytonia parvifolia. It grows on mossy banks and cliffs and along rocky stream banks. The small, single flower growing near the clump of spring beauty is star-flower, Trientalis latifolia. If you look closely you will see that its blossom is a perfect little six-pointed star which, like the spring beauty, is sometimes white and sometimes pinkish. A patch of yellow ahead catches our eye and when we get there we find it is the yellow woodland violet, Viola glabella. Most people call it Johnny-jump-up. Johnny-jump-up grows abundantly all along the trails and throughout the forests of the Cascades until we have climbed quite a bit higher where we will find a cousin that likes higher altitudes. His pretty yellow flowers and heart-shaped leaves will capture your heart as they have mine. Violets are one of my favorite flowers and I always delight in finding them.

Sometimes I hear a conversation like this, "Why look over there! There is some bleeding heart. What's it doing way out here? I've got some in my garden at home." This always amuses me because wild bleeding heart, Dicentra formosa, was here long before the white man ever came. Its home is in these forests and here for ages it has spread its lovely, lobed, fern-like foliage and held up its sweet little pink hearts. Its specific name, formosa, means beautiful and when you see it you will say that truly it is well named.

Now our wandering feet lead us near a boggy stream and a strong, unpleasant odor assails our noses. We follow it to a handsome yellow flower that looks something like a calla lily growing right in the mud. The flower appears first, and later the large, cabbage-like leaves will develop. The scientist calls it Lysichitum americanum, a few people call it swamp lily, but to everyone else it is skunk cabbage and our noses say this is right. It may have an offensive odor but its large yellow bloom brightens up gloomy, swampy places like a patch of golden sunlight. Now let us look around a little bit, for this is the home of another of Johnny-jump-up's cousins, one that is as shy as he is bold. Ah, there it is nestled down among the grasses and other plants, a little bit of pale violet or lilac. It is our pretty little swamp violet, Viola palustris, shy and inconspicuous, moisture-loving, short of stature, but a fine example of our wild violets. We will find it in bogs, along mossy stream banks, and in wet meadows from the foot of the mountains all the way up to the alpine meadows where it joins with myriads of other wild flowers in our Bit of Paradise.

But come, we must be on our way, for there are many treasures yet to be found as we make our way up the trail through deep forest and open glades, by rushing streams, murmuring brooks, and splashing waterfalls, and across occasional old burns. Each of "nature's darlings," as John Muir called them, demands that we stop and make its acquaintance, but there are so many hundreds of different flowers that in the short time we have together I can describe only a comparatively small number of them and tell you the names of a few others.

Trilliums like the shady forest and are unmistakable with their three white petals and three broad leaves at the top of a stout stem about six inches to a foot long. The flowers turn lovely shades of pink and purple just before they die. They are close relatives of the eastern wake-robin. The wild lily-of-the-valley, maianthemum, raises its stalk of tiny white blooms, and we see the small white stars of false solomon's seal, smilacina, and the dainty bells of the twisted stalk, streptopus. Now our trail leads through more open forests and here we see the fine tiger lily, Lilium columbianum, named in honor of the Columbia River on whose banks it was first discovered. Its beautiful petals are orange covered with brown-purple spots. Why it is called tiger lily instead of leopard lily I have never been able to find out, but people do many peculiar things, so tiger lily it is. If we happen to be in Oregon, we shall see the Washington lily, Lilium Washingtonianum, with its beautiful white blossoms finely dotted with purple. It seems unfortunate that the lily bearing the name of the state of Washington does not grow there and that Washingtonians must go to Oregon or California to admire it, but such are the vagaries of plant nomenclature. All plants have their northern and southern limits, as well as their altitudinal limits, but perhaps some day someone may undertake the fine task of gathering seeds of this beautiful lily and sowing them in various places in the Cascades of Washington. If they will not grow there, nothing will be lost, but if they do, then Washington will have gained a fine new inhabitant and all Washingtonians will be grateful to him who sowed so well. If we are lucky we may see a checker lily, Fritillaria lanceolata. This one has dark purplish flowers mottled with greenish yellow but unfortunately is not as common as the other two.

The tall shrub with magenta flowers and prickles which scratch our arms as we brush by is the salmonberry. It is so named for the color of its fruit, which ranges from shades of deep yellow and salmon to dark red and is shaped like an overgrown raspberry. The one with larger leaves and flat whitish flowers is the thimbleberry. It has a flattish, red fruit like a wide shallow thimble. The red elderberry is covered with sprays of creamy white, and just ahead we see a large bush with roundish leaves and showy white flowers. That is a serviceberry. The bush with the oval, dull green leaves that fills many places between the trees with a massive tangle and tumbles down over banks is salal. The small urn-shaped flowers all hang from the underside of the flower stalk and develop into black sweet berries that were gathered in great quantities by the Indians. The pioneers made pies and jams of them, but nowadays we very seldom hear of anyone gathering them. Salal is related to the eastern wintergreens and, like those plants, it contains an oil which makes it an extreme fire hazard during dry spells. It then takes fire very readily and burns rapidly with an explosive, crackling sound.

See that smaller shrub with the glossy, holly-like leaves and loose spike of yellow flowers? That is the Oregon grape, Berberis Aquifolium, the state flower of Oregon. Well chosen it is, say I, for the whole plant is beautiful, not just the flowers. It is held in such high esteem that it and its varieties are used in multitudes of rock gardens as well as to line walks and driveways, not only in the Northwest, but in many other parts of the country. It is not really a grape at all but is a member of the barberry family and brings forth dark-blue, tart berries. When I was a boy, my brother and I used to pick them as well as salal and my mother made an excellent jelly by combining sweet salal and tart Oregon grape. Wild strawberries are frequently found in these open forests and if we have time to look around, we shall surely find some. The berries are much smaller than the cultivated varieties but they are also just as much sweeter as they are smaller. If you like your strawberries fresh from the vine without cream and sugar, there is a treat in store for you when you bite through a wild strawberry. Blackcaps are another real treat. We shall recognize them very easily because their stems are nearly white, have stout stickers, and are densely clustered at the base. The white flowers are small and inconspicuous but the black berries, shaped like little skullcaps, are delicious. A dish of blackcaps with cream, or better still ice cream, is a dish fit for the gods.

THE FOREST RECLAIMS ITS OWN

A forest fire is like a demon let loose and leaves in its wake only destruction and desolation. If the fire is a large one, it consumes everything. The very fertility is burned out of the soil. Some of the older logging operations were nearly as bad. The slashings were left on the ground and soon became as dry as tinder. Eventually they caught fire, and, just as with a regular forest fire, the aftermath was desolation. So much is taken out of the soil that practically nothing will grow in it and the area presents an unvarying bleak, wasted appearance year after year. Mother Nature, however, being wise in all things, has designed plants that will flourish even in these burned-out places.

Our trail leads through one of these old burns and the first thing we see is giant fireweed, Epilobium angustifolium. It is generally about two to three feet high but on occasion grows much taller; it has long, narrow, alternate leaves and is topped with a long loose cluster of deep-pink or rose-purple flowers. It is very abundant in dry places like this, and though a single plant is not overly beautiful, large masses of it make a very pleasing sight.

I remember one trip where our road crossed a place that had been logged off a long time before. Enough time had passed so that the ground was generally covered with a little green, and patches of alders, four or five feet high, grew here and there. But what made us stop the car was the fireweed. We were on a gently rolling plateau and the whole area was covered with deep-pink fireweed like a sea of color swelling, rolling, and sweeping away from us for miles in every direction. High spots that caught the sun's direct rays were pink, slopes were a deeper pink, and the hollows were rose-purple. Nearly every degree of shading was there, and we just sat and drank it in until Bs-s-s-t! a bee went right through the car, in one open window and out the other. Then we noticed that there were swarms of bees buzzing around in every direction. The explanation was simple. Fireweed makes excellent honey. A beekeeper, taking advantage of the hundreds of acres of nectar-filled blossoms, was parked a short distance from us with his truck, trailer, and portable beehives. We closed the car windows and lingered a little while before driving on our way. The Indians gave this plant its name of fireweed because when it is in bloom, it makes the hills look as though they are on fire. Later the seeds blow away in masses like clouds of smoke.

Now let us drop our eyes and see what some of this green is that sparsely covers the ground. There is a vine with stickers and plain white flowers. We call them wild blackberries, although there are other blackberries that grow wild

here. The latter are just called blackberries. Wild blackberries straggle along the ground and grow over old logs
and stumps. They are the hardest ones to pick, but also have
the finest flavor. They make the best preserves and when
baked in a pie, are in a class by themselves.

These old burns are favorites of the brake fern, or bracken
as some call it. We have seen it in practically all dry, waste
places but it has a great liking for logged-off or burned-off
land. Brake fern is anywhere from two to six feet tall and
has rather plain, coarse fronds in contrast to the beautiful,
delicate, feathery fronds of some of the forest ferns. Brake
fern, though, does serve a very definite purpose. Underneath the large fields of it are last year's plants, dead and
dry, and beneath them are countless others decaying and
gradually adding a little humus to the burned-out soil. The
fireweed grows, blooms, and dies. Wild blackberry leaves
unfurl, grow larger, wither, and drop to the ground. Brake
ferns poke up tight little fists, reach toward the sun, cast
their spores, then shrivel and die. The cycle of life goes
on and on year after year. Slowly, very slowly, a little richness is gradually added to the poor soil until finally a tiny
winged seed, blown from the forest, comes to rest and finds
enough good earth to sprout and grow. A seedling is born
and as it grows it sheds needles which, decomposing, add
their tiny bit to the soil. More seeds find favorable spots,
become young trees, and by shedding add still a little more
richness. Nature has at last reclaimed the land laid waste
by the fire demon and if it is left undisturbed, a mighty
forest of giant, stately trees will cover this spot a few hundred years after we, while eating juicy blackberries, admire
a sea of deep-pink fireweed.

COMMON FLOWERS, SAPROPHYTES, AND ORCHIDS

How cool and shady it is for us to be in the forest again. Here is a good place to sit and rest while we have some lunch by this little stream tumbling down the hillside. See that mass of wide, leathery, heart-shaped leaves trailing over the ground? Look under the leaves near the ground. Ah, there it is, an exotic, brownish-purple little jug with three long, thin appendages. It is the blossom of the wild ginger, Asarum caudatum. Notice the faint ginger-like odor which accounts for its common name.

One of our constant companions as we climb up the Trail to Paradise is foamflower, whose loose raceme of very small white flowers is like a bit of airy fluff. In the lower woods its leaves are divided into three leaflets and it is called Tiarella trifoliata. Higher up, in the Canadian zone, the leaves are not divided but are merely lobed, and it is called Tiarella unifoliata. All intermediate leaf forms can be found. Fringe-cups are common all along the way, and the plant with three large, fan-shaped leaflets and a compact spike of small white flowers at the end of a long slender stalk is vanilla-leaf, so named for its odor. When dried, the leaves are even more fragrant and because of this some people call them sweet-after-death. The pioneers and settlers called them smelling-leaves. They used to dry them and hang them in bunches to perfume their cabins and log houses. The little shrub that brightens so many spots among the trees with its four to six creamy-white, petal-like bracts surrounding a head of tiny greenish flowers is Canadian dogwood, Cornus canadensis. The leaves are four in number and are strongly veined like those of its cousins, the flowering dogwood trees.

In the fall it is conspicuous with its bunch of bright red berries which give it another common name, bunchberry.

Do you notice a delicate, sweet fragrance in the air? Let us get around this turn in the trail and see what it is. It is twin-flower, lovely, dainty twin-flower. Small, pink, tubular bells swing on the ends of short slender stems and are always in pairs, hence its name. It is a prostrate trailing vine that covers the forest floor in places, spreads over rocks and rotting logs, climbs old stumps, and hangs over banks. The leaves are evergreen, small and shiny, and above them is the thick covering of sweet-scented, pendant bells. Beloved it is of naturalists, for they named it Linnaea borealis in honor of Linnaeus himself, the great Swedish botanist, doctor, and teacher who laid the foundation for the study of modern botany. His systems of plant nomenclature and of classification, though not followed today, were the means of systematizing all botanical study and paved the way for present methods.

In the deep, moist forests where branches of the dense trees interlace overhead to form an evergreen canopy and where, even on bright summer days, a condition of semi-twilight exists, live a small group of very strange plants. They have lost all green coloring matter, which is necessary for self-support, and live on dead and decaying matter. The best known of these strange, saprophytic denizens of the forest is the Indian pipe or ghost plant, Monotropa uniflora. Its stout stems are from four to ten inches tall, usually occurring in clusters, and bear a solitary small, bell-like, drooping flower at each tip. The whole plant is waxy or pearly white, which accounts for the name ghost plant. The name Indian pipe comes from its fancied resemblance to an

ordinary clay pipe. The many-flowered Indian pipe, Monotropa Hypopitys, is similar to the Indian pipe but instead
of being dead white it is yellowish to reddish and has a number of flowers near the top of the stem. Occasionally it is
called pine-sap.

The most striking member of this group is the barber's
pole or sugar-stick, Allotropa virgata. Numerous scale-like
leaves clothe the bottom of a distinctive red-and-white
striped stalk about six to twelve inches high topped with a
short, crowded spike of flowers that lack petals. Pine-drops
is the largest of this group, growing from one to three feet
high. It has a reddish-brown, sticky stalk with globular
flowers arranged along the upper part. Its scientific name is
Pterospora andromedea. Two other members of this saprophytic group occur in the Cascades: Newberrya congesta,
a flesh-colored plant with a crowded or congested mass of
flowers at the end of a short stalk; and Pleuricospora fim-
briolata, an erect, white or yellowish fleshy plant about six
inches high with flowers in a dense raceme. If our Bit of
Paradise did not have such an irresistible attraction, we
would take some time to hunt for these odd members of
the heath family, for the best way to find and to see wild
flowers is to leave the trail and scour through the forests or
the fields and meadows where they are unmolested. But as
we have only a comparatively short time to see many, many
more flowers we must keep going up the trail, remembering
always to "make haste slowly."

Do you see that little plant with two opposite, broad
leaves in the middle of its stalk? If you look closer you will
see, near the top of the stem, some very small green flowers
that look like little orchids. They are orchids, for this plant

is a listera, a member of the orchid family of which a number are native to our Cascade Range. Three species of
listera grow here and are very similar, all of them being
called twayblades from their characteristic pair of opposite
leaves borne about midway on the stem. Another kind of
orchid is the coral-root, corallorhiza. Coral-roots get their
name from their coral-like, branching roots. Generally they
have pinkish or purplish stalks and lovely little orchids on
short stems.

Aha! I have found a hidden beauty behind this large
tree. It is a lady's slipper, Cypripedium montanum, one of
our showiest wild flowers. It has a white slipper-shaped lip,
veined with purple, and brown or purplish petals that are
wavy or sometimes twisted. If fortune smiles upon us, we
may see the queen of them all, the rare, beautiful calypso,
holding her solitary court in a shady temple whose columns
are towering tree trunks which support a roof of lacy
branches through which sunlight filters as it does through
the windows of a great cathedral. Calypso's petals are light
purple and her slipper-like lip is a delicate rose or pink
mottled with maroon or purple. Inside is a tuft of yellow
hairs. Truly we would have to search a long time to find
another single flower to match the delicate, fragile beauty
of this queen of our orchids. Like many another fair plant it
has been gathered extensively by a thoughtless public, and
though formerly common it is now quite rare.

WE ENTER THE CANADIAN ZONE

Do you notice how much smaller the trees are up here
than they were where we left the car, and that the forest
is less dense and shady? We are entering a different life

zone—the Canadian zone. There is no sharp line of demarcation, but a gradual transition from one zone to another within a few hundred feet of elevation. Although the western hemlock and Douglas fir are still common, they no longer dominate the forests. White pine, which we saw occasionally below, is common now along with silver fir, grand fir, noble fir, and Alaska cedar. In the southern part of the range we will find red fir, Shasta fir, lodgepole pine, and white pine. The undergrowth of bushes and shrubs is less dense, and the forest floor is open in many places. The slopes are generally steeper now. Rocky outcroppings, deep canyons, and narrow valleys are frequent. Numerous streams tumble down the mountainsides, and in this region we will find many small bogs, lakes, wet cliffs, and waterfalls. In many places the tree trunks and branches are clothed with drooping, thread-like, pendant lichens that give them a light gray color. How different is the aspect of the forest here, clothed in its light gray garb, from the majestic trees of the lower forests with their luxuriant masses of undergrowth.

Many of the shrubs and herbaceous plants of the Transition zone continue on up into the Canadian zone. Foamflower is still with us and has completed the change of its leaf from compound to simple. Johnny-jump-up is smaller in size and we do not see his bright yellow face as often, but right by your feet is his cousin the round-leaf violet, Viola orbiculata. Its flower is also bright golden yellow but its leaves are evergreen, nearly round, and usually lie flat on the ground. The Canadian dogwood shows to even better advantage here than it does lower down. That pretty little shrub, vying with it for our attention, is pipsissewa or prince's pine, Chimaphila umbellata. It has narrow, toothed, leathery leaves and four to eight nodding pink flowers in a loose terminal cluster. When very young the blossoms are like little pink globes, but when in full bloom the flowers open up and the petals become concave. It stands anywhere from six to twelve inches tall. Another species, Menzies' pipsissewa, Chimaphila Menziesii, grows here also but it is much smaller, only four to six inches high, and has only one to three white to pinkish flowers. We might not see it, though, as it is not very plentiful. The beautiful white star that mixes with the Canadian dogwood and the pipsissewa is alpine beauty, Clintonia uniflora. Between the two or three tulip-like leaves it bears a single, pure white star which is truly an alpine beauty. On occasion I have heard it called Queen's cup, but I much prefer the other more common name.

The large bushes, literally covered with clusters of rose-pink blossoms, that fill the open place just ahead of us, are rhododendron. Each bright corolla is a jewel, a single cluster is enchanting, and to see a rhododendron bush in full bloom, glowing with color, is a thrilling sight. They are quite generally distributed, in open parts of the forests at low and middle altitudes, in the southern Washington Cascades, throughout all of the Oregon Cascades, and on into California. Purple ones are sometimes found and, on rare occasions, a white specimen is seen. The superb rhododendron has been chosen by my home state of Washington as its state flower.

Those bits of scarlet flame dancing about in the breeze are columbine. Their faces are bright lemon-yellow while their backs and five long spurs are scarlet. Each flower, borne on the end of a slender stem, nods and sways with every little bit of wind. There, in that moist spot beside the trail, is something I have been looking for—an old friend, the monkey-flower, Mimulus guttatus. We will find it in wet and moist places, by streams and on river bars all through the mountains at low and moderate elevations. Sometimes the plants are few, but in favorable places they grow in masses from two to three feet high and are covered with large yellow flowers. They owe their common name, monkey-flower, to a very slight resemblance to a monkey's grinning face. I once heard a lady say that they looked like some kind of a wild snapdragon; but no pampered, cultivated snapdragon, fine as it is, ever has the carefree, jaunty air of a monkey-flower.

The pink flower we see just a little farther along prefers moist ground too. It is Corydalis Scouleri, the first plant we have encountered for which I can find no common name. I suppose there are mountain folk who have named it, but I have yet to meet them, and the people who do know what it is just call it corydalis. The lack of a common name is a little difficult to understand because it is one of the most delightful flowers of this part of the forests, and though it is not profuse we will see it often. It grows in masses about three or four feet high and has, in my opinion, the most beautiful foliage of all, even more pleasing than the ferns. The soft, delicate leaves are divided into many round or oblong lobes and are a wonderful shade of blue-green on top and lighter gray-green underneath. The flowers are borne on terminal racemes, and each blossom, with its long spur, looks like a little pink, long-tailed bird. They perch, one above the other, on the flower stem with a very sprightly air and seem about to hop off, one after the other, and fly away in formation.

Let us hurry along up the trail to that deep shady place, for there we shall find some shade-loving flowers. On that bank is one of the best of them, the ethereal forest anemone, Anemone deltoidea. It generally grows in patches or groups and has a fragile white flower, about the size of a silver dollar, on the end of a very slender stem. Near the middle of this stem are three broad, toothed leaves. Anemones have no petals, as do most flowers. The parts that appear to be petals are the sepals. They are among my favorite wild flowers, not the forest anemones alone, but all species of them. We have several species, as you will see, each liking a different locality and each with its own special charm.

The little trailing plant with small, strawberry-like flowers is a rubus, a member of the same genus as the blackberry. There are two of them; one, Rubus pedatus, with three to five leaflets, and the other, Rubus lasiococcus, with lobed leaves. They are usually called trailing raspberry, and the former is sometimes called bird's-foot bramble. In the late summer and fall they both have a small, irregular red berry that looks like a few segments of a raspberry.

Here is a peculiar little plant with its flowers all growing from one side of the stem. It is the one-sided pyrola, Pyrola secunda. It has a stalk from five to ten inches tall that curves over slightly, and the small, greenish-white flowers are all attached on the inside of the curve. The leaves are nearly all basal and resemble the leaves of a pear tree, thus giving it its name of pyrola which means a little pear. There, by that old log, see the stalk about a foot high with pink flowers and long-stemmed, basal leaves? That is Pyrola bracteata.

A few other species of pyrola are found in our Cascade forests but probably we shall not see them for they are found only occasionally.

Some of the shrubs encountered most frequently in this region are the huckleberries. There are three or four different species and they all like the open forests where they sometimes form thickets among the trees, around the edges of boggy meadows, and along lake shores. They grow from three to six feet high and bear small round or urn-shaped white or pinkish flowers. They are not, however, noted for their flowers, which, though pretty, are small and inconspicuous, but for their delicious berries. They make wonderful jelly and jam and are delicious eaten fresh in any way you like fresh berries. Huckleberry pie just melts in your mouth. When Maxine and I are in the mountains during berry season, we have them with nearly every meal and always take some home with us. They start to ripen in August and the peak of the season is around Labor Day. Then large numbers of people come to the mountainsides and reap a fine harvest. Some folks pick just for themselves, but others gather large quantities which they sell at roadside stands or in the cities and towns.

Many of the pickers we see are Indians. In the old days, before the white man came and changed their life, a large part of the Indian's diet consisted of berries of all sorts including the delicious huckleberry. They gathered huge quantities of huckleberries to be dried and pressed into a kind of cake for use during the fall and winter. On the eastern slopes leading up to Mount Adams, in the southern part of Washington, is a vast open area where huckleberries grow in great profusion—many, many acres of them. These

were and still are the favorite berry fields of all the Indians
for miles around in every direction. Formerly they came by
foot and on horseback with their whole families and pitched
their tepees in the same places where their ancestors had
camped before them. Along with the picking and preparing
of the berries, foot races and horse races were held, games
were played, and at night huge campfires were enjoyed with
story-telling and dancing. The Indians still come but no
longer on horseback or on foot. Now they come in cars of
all sorts, large and small, but mostly old jalopies loaded
with men, women, children, dogs, and belongings.

Our trail crosses a small trickle of water and the ground
all around is boggy. Nestled down among the other plants
is an old friend from below, the shy swamp violet. All those
stalks with the green flowers are green bog orchids, Habenaria saccata. Out there in the middle of the bog that very
handsome one is a fine rein-orchid, Habenaria leucostachys,
generally called white bog orchid. Its stout hollow stem
stands from ten to thirty inches tall, has narrow leaves at
the bottom, and bears numerous fragrant white orchids about
a half-inch long, in a terminal spike. Come over here to the
little rivulet itself and see this patch of lovely grass of
Parnassus—attractive white, shallow cups at the ends of
slender erect stems. Clustered at the base are succulent, kidney-shaped leaves about one to one and one-half inches
broad, truly a fitting flower for the delightful name grass
of Parnassus. It is, however, not a grass at all but a member
of the saxifrage family called Parnassia fimbriata. Its name
comes from Mount Parnassus in Greece where it was first
discovered a very long time ago.

We must leave this wet place now, for time presses hard

on our heels, as it always does when we are in the mountains.
Each flower is so interesting or lovely and there are so many
other things to see and do that minutes and hours fly swiftly
by and days, even weeks, slip pleasantly, dreamily away, always leaving some places unvisited and some flowers to
bloom unseen.

As we swing up the trail again we see more trilliums, and
that reddish-purple flower is one we missed in the lower
forests. It is a penstemon, Penstemon nemorosus. It prefers
these rocky, open slopes we are crossing now. The tube-
shaped blossoms, about an inch or more long, are in a loose
cluster at the end of a long leafy stem. They are called
beardtongue in the eastern part of America and in Europe,
but here in the Northwest we usually call them penstemon.
On these rocky, open, sometimes dry slopes we shall find
different types of wild flowers from those in the forests and
wet places. You no doubt will recognize the yarrow. It is
very common in dry ground at sea level and occurs all
through most of the Cascades from their foot to the flowering meadows. The loose sprays of small white flowers, scattered over the slope, are rusty saxifrage. Up on those rocks
is something we have not seen before, a sedum, member of
the stonecrop family which is a very durable tribe of plants
that has the faculty of enduring long periods of drought.
Stonecrops always grow on rocks and cliffs where they are
exposed to the sun's full withering force and where water
is not held very long. The stems are short and tufted with
light-green, small leaves that are always thick and fleshy,
and if you were to cut through one, you would find it filled
with moisture. In some species they are egg-shaped or
rounded like little barrels filled with water to keep the

plants fresh when others around are dried up and withered. At the ends of the flowering stems are tight clusters of bright yellow, five-pointed stars.

That place where water is seeping over the rocks should be interesting. It is indeed, for here is our first harebell, the beautiful Campanula rotundifolia. Lovely blue bells, swinging on slender, delicate stems, nodding and dancing, hardly ever still, are rung by the slightest bit of breeze. We shall find them on rocky cliffs, talus slopes, gravelly stream banks, and in the high meadows of our Bit of Paradise. They are known to many people by the name of bluebells or mountain bluebells.

Let us follow the trickle of water a little way down the slope and see what we shall find. Here is another saxifrage, one with long-stemmed, broad, basal leaves. The small bushy plant with light-yellow flowers is yellow willow-weed, Epilobium luteum, cousin of the giant fireweed. There is something that looks like a violet. Let us take a closer look at it because, although its deep violet-blue flower looks like a violet, it is, instead, the butterwort with the very odd name of Pinguicula vulgaris. The plant itself is not at all like the violets, with their heart-shaped leaves, but has a basal rosette of flat fleshy leaves with slightly rolled-up margins. The strange thing about them is the slimy, sticky secretion with which they are covered. This viscid substance catches and holds any small insects that are unfortunate enough to come in contact with it, and the plant proceeds to digest them. From the center of the rosette arises a single bare stalk topped with a violet-blue flower—a lovely lure, beckoning unwary mites to their destruction.

Let us take a moment here to enjoy another kind of

beauty. These open spots give us wonderful, sweeping panoramas. We can see the forests flowing down the mountainsides to the river valleys below, covering nearly everything
with a mighty host of trees. The roar of the river, now far
below us, has become a faint murmur, and we have the feeling of being really high in the mountains. Tall ridges, glistening snow fields, and lofty peaks that were hidden from
our view before, are revealed in ever-increasing numbers
as we travel upward on the Trail to Paradise. Across the
valleys we can see rocky cliffs, rock slides, and an occasional
avalanche chute making a bright green streak in the dark
green of the forests. Not very far above us on some of those
ridges, do you see where the solid forests end and small
openings begin that soon become larger and larger, with
clumps and patches of slender spire-like trees? Those are
the meadows that are our Bit of Paradise. We know now
that we are nearing the end of our trail, that soon we shall
be reveling in the fields of flowers, drinking in all the beauty
that is there.

THE CASCADES ARE VERY DIVERSIFIED

While we are sitting here enjoying the views spread out
before us I think this is an appropriate time for me to tell
you a little about some of the other parts of the Cascades
that are very different from those that we have seen and
are going to see. The trail we have been following is on the
western slope of the range, which is supplied with a copious
amount of rainfall and snow by the moist westerly winds
that blow in from the Pacific Ocean. The eastern slope receives much less precipitation, and as one travels eastward
the amount of rainfall becomes smaller and smaller until

at the eastern base of the mountains semi-arid conditions prevail. In these dry places sagebrush is common and there are very few trees. On a journey into the mountains from the east, you would find the few trees gradually gathering their forces until they form a fine forest. This forest is made up almost exclusively of ponderosa pine, a very handsome tree up to two hundred feet in height. The older specimens, especially, have clean-cut appearing trunks and rich cinnamon-colored bark. This yellow pine forest is very different from the luxuriant coniferous forests of the western slope. The trees stand farther apart and there is an almost total lack of undergrowth. This continues for quite a long way into the mountains, until, with the advent of more moisture, a few firs and hemlocks put in their appearance. These become more and more numerous until they are the dominant trees and the forest is similar to that which clothes the west side.

I must take time to tell you of one group of flowers that grow throughout these drier regions. They are the splendid lewisias, named in honor of Captain Meriwether Lewis of Lewis and Clark fame. Their rosettes of flat or narrow succulent leaves and delicately tinted flowers are usually found in rocky locations. The finest species, and one that is considered by many people to be unexcelled as a rockery plant, is Lewisia Tweedyi. It has wide green leaves and sprays of large flowers which are the most delicate tint of apricot or salmon pink. It flourishes in Washington in a comparatively small area bounded on the north by the upper end of Lake Chelan and on the south by Blewett Pass. Fortunately for me this area is fairly close to my home.

Another very interesting part of the Cascades is the southern end of the range where it crosses from Oregon into California and marches on down to Lassen Volcanic National Park. Here you will find a delightful blending of northern or Cascade types of flowers with southern or Sierran types. One very characteristic plant of this region is the bright red snow plant, Sarcodes sanguinea, which appears soon after the snow has melted. It is a fleshy plant about a foot high, and is related to the Indian pipe, barber's pole, and other saprophytes.

The picturesque Columbia Gorge, by which the mighty Columbia River penetrates the range and through which its waters pour relentlessly on toward the sea, has a flora that is unique as well as beautiful. In range of altitude the region is almost wholly within the Transition zone, but the flora of that zone is scarcely represented at all. Through some phenomenon of nature the flowers are mainly Canadian and Hudsonian types. Shooting stars and saxifrage, among many others, will be found there. Arabis furcata, which I have found at seven thousand feet on Mount Adams, also grows on the rocky banks of the gorge at elevations of only a few hundred feet.

There are many, many more of these fascinating, beautiful, and different places in the Cascades, each having a flora to fit its own peculiarities. Perhaps among my readers there will be those who feel that their favorite parts of the mountains have been slighted or overlooked. All I can say is that on such a short trip as we are having I can give only a few glimpses of this diversified range. From its southern end, just a few miles south of Lassen Volcanic National Park, it stretches more than six hundred miles in a straight line to the Canadian border and then continues on into British

Columbia where it bends to the west and merges with the
Coast Range It is truly a tremendous range, one in which
a person could spend a lifetime and not know it completely.
A whole volume could be written on just the wild flowers
alone that are to be found within its far-flung reaches.

BACK TO THE TRAIL

We must be on our way now, so it is back to the trail and
up toward the meadows for us. The leafy plant about three
feet high growing right beside the trail is Mertensia pani-
culata borealis. Its attractive, tubular, light-blue flowers,
about one-half inch long, are borne in loose clusters. It is
generally called mertensia, though one of our books says
it is western bluebell and another calls it lungwort. The tall
shrubs covered with large flat bunches of small white flowers are mountain ash. They are common in open places and
along the borders of woods all through this zone and in the
alpine regions above. They reach a height of six to fifteen
feet and have compound leaves made up of many small, oblong, toothed leaflets. In the fall brilliant clusters of scarlet
berries hang on these shrubs for a long time and make a feast
for the mountain birds including the Clark's crow and our
bold friend the camp robber. Now we see some bright golden
heads of arnica—yellow disks surrounded by bright yellow
rays. They are members of the composite or sunflower family which is the largest in the plant kingdom. There are a
dozen or more species of arnica in the Cascades and they are
all so much alike that it takes some botanical training to tell
them apart. I am, therefore, not going to try to describe any
for you except to say that they have opposite leaves. Any

similar flowers which we find with leaves arranged alternately on the stems will probably be senecios.

As we follow the trail into the woods again we find a handsome shrub about six feet high with showy, creamy-white blossoms that occur in twos and threes. Some of the glossy leaves are splotched with yellow as if they had a blight. This is mountain rhododendron or white rhododendron, Rhododendron albiflorum. Over there, in that shady spot, I see some small deep-purple flowers which cannot be pinguicula because the ground is not wet enough. Let us have a closer look. They are violets, the loveliest ones we have in our mountains and the only ones with the color generally associated with violets. These shy sprites hide away in shady spots of the forests and snuggle down among the grasses, sedges, and other taller plants of the alpine meadows. Because they are inconspicuous they have no common name, so we shall just have to call them purple violets or Viola adunca.

There, growing almost in the trail itself, is a fine clump of many-flowered Indian pipe. We might mistake them for the drippings of some giant fairy candle. In that open sunny spot ahead, stands a tall plant drawing every eye like a shining white beacon. It is squaw-grass, a plant which attracts perhaps more attention than any other. It has a thick mat of coarse, grass-like leaves and a flower stalk about three feet tall topped with a large, dense, club-like bunch of beautiful creamy-white flowers. It is a member of the lily family, as you will see by examining one of the small, fragrant, starry blossoms, and has the tongue-twisting name of Xerophyllum tenax. In days gone by the Indians used its tough leaves in making their baskets, which accounts for its common names of squaw-grass and Indian basket-grass. It is so conspicuous and attractive that it has a number of other popular names, some of which are bear-grass, elk-grass, pine lily, and mountain lily. In the open forests, especially where the trees are small, we shall find it growing sparsely in some places and in others very abundantly. Some parts of our Bit of Paradise are brilliant with the massed, shining beacons of squaw-grass.

Our trail now leads across a small bench through which flows a tinkling, laughing brook. Growing in all the wet places and even right in the water itself are our first marsh marigolds. Lovely white blossoms are held up by erect stems for us to admire. Like the anemones, to which they are related, they have no petals, but instead have petal-like sepals. The two species we have in the Cascades are very much alike, differing mainly in the shape of their succulent leaves, which are mostly basal. One, Caltha leptosepala, has large heart-shaped leaves, and the other, Caltha biflora, has broader, kidney-shaped leaves. Just a little farther along is a group of uniquely shaped flowers, our gorgeous shooting stars, Dodecatheon Jeffreyi. They have large clumps of upright, broad, basal leaves about six or eight inches long and numerous erect stems bearing at their ends wonderful light-magenta to rose-purple blossoms. The petals are bent back and give them a shooting-star effect. They are sometimes called birdbill but shooting star is the most popular and appropriate name.

The small, white, airy clusters are another kind of saxifrage, one that likes wet places, and it adorns all the streams and rills we shall encounter from now on until we have climbed to the very highest meadows. The tall stout-stemmed plants with broad divided leaves, large flat clumps of white flowers, and a covering of fine silky hairs is cow parsnip. It is from two to five feet tall and is abundant in moist soils throughout the higher forests and some of the meadows. Large size and a robust appearance, not beauty, are what make it a notable plant. In the wetter places are more stalks of green bog orchids and on sloping, sunny banks are purple asters and yellow senecios.

Again I call your attention to the trees. The western hemlock has been replaced by the mountain hemlock, Douglas fir has been left far down the mountainside, and the first alpine firs now make their appearance. We have entered a most interesting region, the place where the upper part of the Canadian zone meets and intermingles with the lower part of the Hudsonian zone. Here we shall find flowers and shrubs of both regions growing side by side. In the shade of trees are twayblades, Canadian dogwood, pyrolas, and mountain rhododendron, and right next to them in sunny, open spots are asters, arnicas, shooting stars, and marsh marigolds. Yellow monkey-flowers are joined here by their cousin, the bright pink monkey-flower, Mimulus Lewisii. Scarlet columbines dance in the wind, yellow violets lie close to the ground, and we shall even find a few trilliums. Seemingly coming down to meet them are a few clumps of blue sweet-scented lupine, while here and there are patches of pink heather, a scattering of phlox, and delicate white stars of avalanche lilies. The low shrubby plant forming patches on the dry rocky banks is shrubby penstemon, Penstemon fruticosus. Its tubular, purple flowers are about one to one and one-half inches long and are borne in small clusters above the rest of the plant. Eager as we are to reach the open fields of flowers, we must stop a moment to examine the strange shaped blossoms of the common lousewort, Pedicularis racemosa. It forms tufts with the stems nearly always leaning out, away from the center. The white or pinkish flowers have a peculiar twisted appearance but still are quite pretty. Lousewort will be our constant companion from now on and will delight us with the different odd shapes of the various species.

OUR BIT OF PARADISE

As we climb steadily upward our trail crosses the little dashing brook again, and its banks are lined with bright masses of pink mimulus, purple asters, and tall white valerian. Any feeling of fatigue we might have is now forgotten and we swing along the trail with renewed vigor. We come to a small side-hill meadow filled with sweet-smelling lupine and dotted with brilliant red paintbrush, white tufts of mountain dock, tiger lilies, and valerian. We hurry across it, into and up through a thicket of alpine fir, Alaska cedar, and mountain hemlock, scarcely taking time to notice the flowers. The slope eases off and then suddenly the trees open up and, as if stepping through a doorway, we are in a gently sloping meadow covered with a carpet of wonderful flowers. It is like being in a different world and indeed this is true, for here is a different world, the world of mountain meadows, with scattered groups and clumps of alpine trees. We have reached the end of the Trail to Paradise. The loveliest part of the mountains now lies before us.

"Above the forests there is a zone of the loveliest flowers . . . so closely planted and luxurious that it seems as if nature, glad to make an open space between woods so dense and ice so deep, were economizing the precious ground and trying to see how many of her darlings she can get together in one mountain wreath—daisies, anemones, columbine, erythroniums, larkspurs, etc., among which we wade knee deep and waist deep, the bright corollas in myriads touching petal to petal. Altogether this is the richest subalpine garden I have ever found, a perfect flower elysium."

Thus wrote John Muir,* the famous geologist, explorer, naturalist, and conservationist. From a Californian by adoption, whose favorite mountains were the Sierra Nevada of California, such words were a very great tribute to the flowering meadows of our beloved Cascades. It so happens that the area of which he wrote is now Mount Rainier National Park, but the same words are true of the regions around any of the old, dead volcanoes of the Northwest from Garibaldi in British Columbia to Lassen Peak in California. Change a word here and there and you have a description of almost any Cascade mountain meadow. Here in these marvelous subalpine regions we shall find masses of flowers of every hue, veritable gardens to delight us. The best time to see them is in the last two weeks of July and the first two weeks of August. It is during this period that the most flowers are in bloom, but the flower season starts much earlier—some time in mid-June when the drifts of snow are rapidly melting away, leaving more and more ground to be warmed by the bright sun.

*From *Our National Parks*, by John Muir Copyright, 1901, by John Muir. Published by Houghton Mifflin Company, Boston.

THE WHITE AND GOLD OF SPRING

Most of the slopes and swales are soon white again, not with snow, but with lovely, fragile avalanche lilies. They cover large areas with dense fields of nodding, white, starry flowers. A single blossom, silhouetted against a deep-blue sky, is a regal beauty with its white, recurved segments and yellow center. In other places glacier lilies hold sway, turning the banks and hollows to gold with their bright golden-yellow corollas. Both kinds bloom right next to the snowbanks and even thrust their leaves up through the edge of the snow in their eagerness to feel the warmth of the sun after so many long months in the icy grip of winter.

To watch one of these seas of golden or creamy-white blossoms rippling in the wind is a sight that will linger long in your memory. The beauty of these flowers has gained each of them a number of other common names. The white avalanche lily, Erythronium montanum, is sometimes called deertongue, adder's-tongue, and dogtooth violet, while the yellow glacier lily, Erythronium grandiflorum, is called fawn lily and lamb's-tongue. Avalanche lilies seem to prefer the western side of the Cascade crest and the glacier lilies prefer the eastern side. In some situations this holds true right up to the very divide itself, as was delightfully illustrated to Maxine and me on a short trip to Chinook Pass early last season. On the west side, around Tipsoo Lake and above, the slopes were white with masses of avalanche lilies, flecked here and there with the gold of glacier lilies. The trail crossed over the divide and followed the eastern slope for some way and here were golden-yellow fields of glacier lilies with an occasional avalanche lily. We chose a branch of the trail that led us to a pair of lovely twin jewels named Deadwood Lakes. In doing so we recrossed the ridge to the west side and here again we found fields of white avalanche lilies. Somewhere south of the Mount Baker–Harts Pass region, in the northern end of the range, no one knows just exactly where, the avalanche lily reaches its northern limit and then the glacier lilies take over both sides of the mountains.

The mountain buttercup, Ranunculus Eschscholtzii (another tongue-twister), is a companion of the lilies. Soon after the snow has melted its small plant blooms, but its glossy yellow flowers, though commonplace, are never seen in such profusion as the lilies. Along with these early spring flowers appears another hardy pioneer, the western anemone, Anemone occidentalis, whose silky-haired, feathery foliage and fragile appearing blossoms seem to belie its hardy nature. Shortly after the snowbanks have receded, up pop tight little fists which soon develop into short hairy stalks topped with paper-thin, whitish flowers. The backs of the petal-like sepals are tinged with blue and covered with fine hairs. The leaves stay tightly rolled up in their buds until the stalks have grown taller and the sepals have dropped. Then the fine, feathery leaves unfold and the handsome gray-green, plume-like heads develop. They grow about eighteen inches tall and last all through the summer and early fall, waving their fuzzy plumes at every passer-by. Later in the season you will sometimes come across the following very pleasing sight. About a foot from the edge of a late snowdrift are little fists of western anemones poking through the ground, five feet away they are in the glory of full bloom, a few feet farther are taller stalks with ragged and drooping flowers, and still farther away are the soft, feathery leaves and fuzzy plumes of fully developed plants. A few people call them pasqueflowers and more than a few call the seed heads little dish mops.

THE GLORY OF SUMMER

Spring lasts a few short weeks and then summer bursts forth in all its glory, filling the meadows with a wealth of beautiful flowers of nearly every color, size, and shape. This, then, is the time we shall want most of all to be in our Bit of Paradise, to inhale deeply of the indescribable fragrance that fills the air, and to feast our eyes on the enchanting fields of flowers. We can wander wherever our fancy takes us in these open park-like places Finding a likely spot we can sit down and admire the magnificent sweeping views of forested ridges rolling away into the distance and rugged peaks thrusting their rocky summits high into the clear air. Snow fields on the higher mountains shimmer in the sunlight and quite often we shall see one or more of the great old volcanoes rearing their mighty heads far above all the rest, their flanks clad with snow and gouged by streams of glacier ice. Our Bit of Paradise has a background of rugged mountain scenery and a foreground of tender flowers.

Probably what will catch your eye first are the paintbrush, because of their brilliant coloring, and the lupines, because of their wonderful fragrance and profusion. The paintbrush, castilleja, are clustered, erect plants that look as if they had been dipped in a paint pot. The whole tops are bright with color ranging from orange through shades of red, scarlet, and deep crimson. Their brilliant clusters are scattered throughout this region in large and small patches and occasionally they form large groups. There was one of these groups near our camp last summer at Mystic Lake, in Mount Rainier National Park, and from the slopes and ridges above it looked like a deep crimson pool. The lupines are about the most abundant flower in the fields, filling some of them with a multitude of blue to blue-purple blossoms. They are leafy plants with palm-like, divided leaves above which rise many long racemes of flowers which fill the air with their sweet scent. Vying with paintbrush and lupine for your attention will be mountain dock, Polygonum bistortoides, and valerian, Valeriana sitchensis, a pair of long-stemmed white flowers. Valerian is usually the tallest plant in these flower gardens and bears at the end of its stalk a convex clump of very small white blossoms. The leaves are mostly basal and have a strong odor, while the flowers have a pleasing heliotrope-like scent which accounts for its also being called mountain heliotrope. Actually there is no relationship between the two plants. Mountain dock has a dense, oblong, white cluster at the end of a slender jointed stem. Because this stem is so slender they appear, from a little distance, to be small blobs of white floating among the other flowers.

Yellow is added to the other colors by a number of plants. The mountain dandelion, Agoseris alpestris, is quite like the common dandelion. Arnica and senecios add their bit, and the fanleaf potentilla, Potentilla flabellifolia, is common. It resembles the buttercup and has fan-shaped leaves that are divided into three parts. It is a larger plant than the buttercup, though, and the flowers are a deeper yellow and not as glossy. No matter whether you call it a buttercup or not, it is very pretty and in some places it covers large areas with a carpet of green and gold. Potentillas are also called cinquefoils, a name that originated in Europe.

Light shades of purple are added to the color scheme by asters and erigerons, one of the latter being the common mountain daisy. Almost everywhere are the heathers, low shrubby plants literally covered with small pink or white bells. Pink heather, Phyllodoce empetriformis, with its bushy stems and pretty pink bells will be encountered first, but after our wanderings have taken us a few hundred feet higher, it is joined by white heather, Cassiope Mertensiana. White heather is a little shorter than pink heather and has tiny leaves that press flat against the stems, giving them a four-sided appearance. Near the ends of these square stems are the lovely, pure-white, nodding bells. To see these two, phyllodoce and cassiope, growing side by side surrounded by other flowers, is a wonderful sight.

Stalks of lousewort are scattered here and there among the other plants and in favorable situations they form thicker groups. Each of the several species has its own distinctive, strangely shaped flowers. One in particular, the elephant's head lousewort, Pedicularis surrecta, is sure to catch your eye. It grows in moist soil and boggy places and each of its red-purple blossoms is shaped just like an elephant's head— large ears, long trunk and all.

ALPINE LANDSCAPE

Our Bit of Paradise is not an uninterrupted expanse of meadow, but rather a blending of open subalpine forests and colorful flower-filled meadows. The first openings reached are small and are generally encircled by the forests, but as we climb upward the trees give way more and more to open fields that soon become park-like with an exquisitely haphazard arrangement of trees in groups of various sizes and even an occasional rugged individual going it alone. Over most of the range the groups are usually made up of alpine fir, mountain hemlock, and to a lesser extent Alaska cedar and white-bark pine. Toward southern Oregon and over the southern part of the range the Alaska cedar disappears, alpine fir is less prevalent, and here we shall find Shasta fir, lodgepole pine, and western white pine along with the mountain hemlock. All of these species form pure stands in some locations but more often they grow in association with one another.

My favorite tree is the alpine fir, Abies lasiocarpa, which is considered our most beautiful conifer by many persons. It is tall, slender, spire-like, and clothed with luxuriant dark, blue-green foliage. The lower branches are drooping, often hiding the short trunk. On the topmost branches are borne the cones which, from a distance, appear to be little owls perched in the top of the tree. It has a pleasing habit of forming "family groups" with the large trees in the center and seedlings around the outside, like children clustered around their parents. A small single tree with seedlings around it has been likened to a hen with her brood of chicks huddled under her body and wings.

The meadows themselves are not all alike, but are composed of a variety of terrains that are mixed together in every possible way. In each location Mother Nature has planted a different kind of garden with its particular type of flowers, and we will find flowering meadow gardens, wet gardens, and rock gardens. Each has its own special charm but combines with all the rest to form a whole of infinite beauty.

The flowering fields are a riot of color with their lupine,

paintbrush, mountain dock, valerian, potentillas, and heathers both pink and white. Light-purple mountain daisies and purple asters are sprinkled throughout the other flowers, and in some spots the ground is covered with them, swaying in unison with each breath of the breeze. Arnica, senecios, mountain dandelions, hawkweeds are scattered everywhere. We shall see alpine forms of pearly everlasting, yarrow, and goldenrod. The list of flowers belonging to the composite family is long indeed, too long for me to point them all out to you at this time. It includes even the prickly leaves and purple heads of the Indian thistle. Cusick's veronica is a small plant that adds deep blue to the color scheme, and purple violets will be found here, but your eyes must be sharp to see them since they grow very close to the ground. In contrast to these small plants is the green or giant hellebore, Veratrum viride. It has large, strongly veined, pleated leaves, rises from three to five feet high, and has small greenish flowers arranged in a drooping panicle like the tassels of a cornstalk. Its size and robustness, among other plants so slender and highly colored, is what attracts attention.

Wherever there is dry ground we shall find the spreading phlox, Phlox diffusa, an attractive plant with numerous lilac to white flowers and clustered, sharp-pointed, very narrow leaves. As its name suggests, it spreads over the ground and has a habit of covering little hummocks with a mass of blooms. Contorted lousewort and bracted lousewort raise their clustered stalks of peculiar flowers here. Alaskan spirea, Lutkea pectinata, is common in these meadow gardens, sometimes forming thick mats of sharply cleft, bright-green, small leaves topped with dense racemes of small creamy-white flowers The tall beacons of squaw-grass will be found in these same dry locations and the mountain blueberry, Vaccinium deliciosum, a low twiggy shrub, frequents them also. As its specific name implies, its fruit is a very delicious berry much sought after by birds, bears, and people.

The groves and clumps of trees are full of flowers and flowering shrubs; each sunny glade within them is like a miniature meadow. Dwarf mountain ash, mountain rhododendron, and rosy spirea bloom among and around the edges of the trees. It is around their margins, too, that we shall find mertensia's baby-blue bells and the loosely tufted plants and clustered blue cups, each with a yellow center, of Jacob's-ladder, polemonium.

The lily family gives us some of our most exquisite wild flowers. One of the fairest of these is the calochortus that adorns many of our mountain meadows. Its creamy blossom has on the inside a dark purplish spot and long soft hairs like those in a cat's ear. It is endowed with a wonderful, delicate beauty, and this winsome charm has given it a number of names including Mariposa lily, sego lily, mountain tulip, and cat's ear. I shall never forget the memorable trip on which Maxine and I saw our first calochortus. We were camped with our club, the Mountaineers of Seattle, at Chambers Lake and made the fortunate decision, with a few friends, to visit a place called Snowgrass Flats, an area of fine alpine meadows. We hiked for some time through high open forests, down to and across a rushing stream, and up the ridge on the other side. Presently we came to the first small glades and very open forests just below the flats themselves. Our trail followed up the course of a brook, and just before we reached the meadows we heard a waterfall. Going to the brook to investigate, we discovered twin waterfalls with merry, colorful flowers crowding their margins. They were not high, roaring falls, but, rather, small intimate streams of water tumbling, side by side, over a short rocky cliff—the most beautiful falls I have ever seen. We feasted our eyes on them for a long time and then continued on the short distance to the open fields. There we found our calochortus. There were many of them and our hearts were full.

Often in the summer there are places where shade or a sheltered location has retarded the melting of a snowbank. Here will be an island of spring flowers—avalanche lilies or glacier lilies, buttercups and western anemones—surrounded by the more highly colored summer flowers. Spring and summer are here joined together in the same marvelous garden.

Boggy places, lakes, tarns, streams, and rills abound in our Bit of Paradise, providing us with many delightful wet gardens. The banks of creeks and rivulets are gay, in many places, with the bright rose-pink of Lewis' monkey-flower. As we approach closer we shall see gorgeous shooting stars, pure-white marsh marigolds, and occasionally the wonderful deep blue of delphinium. Small white stars of saxifrage, in loose airy clusters, are scattered along these watercourses. Alpine veronica, a little smaller and a lighter blue than Cusick's veronica, grows here too, as do a number of dwarf fireweeds which have small pink to light-purple flowers. The lovely white cups of grass of Parnassus follow these streams up from the forests below, but are not seen as frequently as most of the other flowers. Finest of all the monkey-flowers, and in my opinion the most beautiful yellow flower we have, is the alpine or tufted monkey-flower, Mim-

Squaw-grass sometimes called bear-grass

Indian pipe, often called ghost plant

Seed pods of western anemone
Called "old men or the mountains"

Glacier lily

Western anemone, picture taken at 6,000 feet
in Mount Rainier National Park

ulus Tilingii, variety caespitosus. It is found along water-courses, especially in the upper meadows, where it forms dense masses that are covered with bright-yellow blooms like particles of concentrated sunlight. Sometimes right in the middle of a brook you will find it growing on rocks, changing them into tiny islands of gold.

Marshy lake shores and boggy places are the home of ele-phant's head lousewort, marsh marigolds, shooting stars, and rosy spirea. If we look closely we may find pale swamp violets hiding among the grasses and sedges. Another incon-spicuous flower in these swampy situations, one that most people overlook, is the alpine swamp laurel, Kalmia poli-folia, variety microphylla. It is diminutive, hugs the ground, and its blossoms are lovely deep-pink, shallow cups. The cotton grass or cotton sedge, Eriophorum angustifolium, grows abundantly here and sometimes seems to take com-plete control of small areas. Each slender stalk holds aloft a little tuft of cotton.

In these wet places we shall find the deep-blue gentian, Gentiana calycosa, usually growing in clumps with each stem ending in an upright tubular bell that is colored a fine deep blue. It was first discovered near Mount Rainier by Dr. William Fraser Tolmie, one of the first white men to pene-trate the wilderness of the Cascades. On September 2, in the year 1833, he made a collection of plants on a mountain in the northwest corner of what is now Mount Rainier Na-tional Park. This mountain has since been named Tolmie Peak in his honor.

Some of the most fascinating parts of our Bit of Paradise are the charming rock gardens we shall find on every cliff, ledge, and outcropping of rock. Each crack, fissure, niche, or cranny that will allow a plant to gain a foothold has its flowers. This is the home of the shrubby cinquefoil, Potentilla fruticosa, and the cliff or rock paintbrush, Castilleja rupicola. Dainty blue bells of campanula, small starry saxifrage, and the little bulbous leaves and yellow blossoms of stonecrops adorn these rocks. The dwarf mountain daisy, Erigeron compositus, is occasionally found on rocky ledges where it forms cushion-like tufts and bears white to pinkish short-stemmed little daisies. Small patches of phlox and Alaskan spirea grow on these ledges, too, sometimes trailing over their edges and blurring the harsh contours of the rocks. The rocks are also softened in many places by the prostrate, creeping mats of mountain juniper and kinnikinnick. Kinnikinnick, or bear-berry, has small bunches of pinkish, urn-shaped flowers that develop into bright-red berries. It also has the jaw-breaking scientific name of Arctostaphylos uva-ursi. Bears are extremely fond of these berries and go to great lengths to find them.

Here in the rock gardens are fine displays of rock penstemon. The commonest is Menzies' penstemon which is low, bushy, has small leathery leaves and purple flowers. Less abundant, but more than making up for it in brilliance, is the best one of them all, the cliff penstemon, Penstemon rupicola. It has rounder, gray-green leaves and brilliant rose-crimson flowers. Once in a while you will find the rare sight of both kinds growing in the same place. Wherever the rocks are wet we shall see mist-maiden, a succulent plant with slender stems, thin kidney-shaped leaves, and airy sprays of small white blossoms. We might even see Drummond's anemone tucked into a rocky crevice. The delicate creamy-white flowers will be washed with a faint bluish tinge.

As I tell you of these flowers that seem to spring from the very rocks themselves, a verse comes to my mind just as it did to Maxine and me one time in the mountains. It is Tennyson's poem:

"Flower in the crannied wall,
I pluck you out of the crannies;
I hold you here, root and all, in my hand,
Little flower—but if I could understand
What you are, root and all, and all in all,
I should know what God and man is."

Equaling or perhaps surpassing the cliff gardens in charm and beauty are the rocky slopes that are characteristic of many parts of our Bit of Paradise. Mother Nature has planted some of them with rock gardens so exquisite in their apparently haphazard arrangement that a mere human gardener will either exclaim with joy or weep from frustration on seeing them. The rock penstemon, paintbrush, shrubby cinquefoil, harebells, saxifrage, stonecrop, etc., are as much at home here as they are on the cliffs and ledges. Thick mats of phlox and Alaskan spirea spread around and over many of the rocks, and Cusick's veronica makes spots of blue here and there. In the lower parts of the Hudsonian zone we shall see the tall stalks and clustered blue-purple flowers of Penstemon serrulatus and a little higher are two shorter, dainty ones with very small flowers, a half inch or less in length. The more common, Penstemon procerus, is bright blue and the other, Penstemon confertus, is a delicate, creamy yellow. Sandwort, arenaria, is generally distributed over these slopes, and here too are the small pink or light-purple flowers of rock cress, arabis, and the lobed white petals and bladder-like capsules of silenes. In the northern half of the range are two very pretty rockery plants, the bright-yellow mountain wallflower, erysimum, and the mountain primrose, douglasia, which is low, tufted, and has small clusters of rose-colored, primrose-like blossoms.

Many more rockery flowers grace these marvelous rock gardens. In some places the heather, asters, daisies, lupine, lousewort, and other plants of the meadow gardens grow among them and join with them to create a picture that is complete in every detail.

This open, park-like terrain through which we have been roaming is very limited in area when compared to the vast extent of the forested regions. But the wonderful panoramas of rugged mountain scenery, the soft, verdant beauty of the slopes and fields themselves, and the marvelous arrays of flowers combine to give it a charm and beauty surpassing that of any other part of the mountains.

In this fairyland of mountain meadows, so full of flowers, Maxine and I have found our Bit of Paradise and we know that you, too, will react as we did to the magic of its spell. A few hours spent hiking along the forest trails and wandering at will through the alpine meadows will create a desire to spend days and weeks of happy, leisurely relaxation in this wonderful Cascade mountain playground.

By various means the alpine regions have been made accessible to everyone. A way can be found for you to reach your Bit of Paradise too. If you are addicted to hiking—and in my opinion this is the best mode of mountain travel—there are innumerable trails, all a part of the Trail to Paradise, that will take you there. In some places rough Forest Service roads reach this region, and if you are limited by time or by physical ability to traveling on paved highways, it is still attainable. Fine smooth highways give access to the flowering meadows of Mount Baker, Mount Rainier National Park, Mount Hood, Crater Lake National Park, and Lassen Volcanic National Park.

TIMBER LINE AND THE ARCTIC-ALPINE ZONE

Even more restricted in extent than the Hudsonian zone is the Arctic-Alpine zone for it is limited to the upper slopes of the dormant volcanoes and other high peaks that rise above the limit of tree growth. It is a region of rocky peaks and ridges, scree slides, high barren slopes, snow fields, glaciers, and severe weather conditions. You might assume, as most people do, that surely no plant life can exist in these barren, inhospitable places, exposed as they are to all extremes of weather and where winter lasts eight, nine, and sometimes ten months of the year. Such is not the case, however, as quite a few flowering plants inhabit this highest of our zones. All of them are interesting and some are very beautiful. It is something of a thrill to find a lovely little tuft blooming in a rocky crevice and to realize that it also grows, near sea level, in Alaska, in Greenland, and around the Arctic. A few of our species are also native to the high Alps of Europe.

Our trip includes a short jaunt into this interesting region where we will find flowers blooming above the snow and ice. The easiest and best way to get there is on the slopes of one of the sleeping volcanoes, but before we reach it we must climb through the upper part of the Hudsonian zone. As we gain elevation the trees become ever smaller and fewer until at timber line they are reduced to gnarled, prostrate specimens. There is also a gradual change in the flowers; a few carry over into the upper regions, becoming smaller and dwarfed as they go, and some new ones make their appearance.

In the higher meadows we shall find the alpine aster, Aster alpigenus; yellow heather is added to the white and pink varieties; saxifrage takes to the rocks and now includes Tolmie's saxifrage, the most attractive of them all. As we approach timber line we shall begin to see Lyall's lupine, a dwarf species that forms rosettes of small silvery leaves and short, tight bunches of brilliant blue-purple flowers. The golden aster, Erigeron aureus, a dainty, tufted plant with bright golden heads, enters the picture here too. I remember one time when Maxine and I were climbing the trail on Burroughs Mountain, a broad-topped, bleak old mass, and as we neared the summit a sweet fragrance that could only come from lupine filled the air. When we poked our heads over the top, we saw a field of Lyall's lupine and golden asters like a wonderful carpet of blue and gold. It was breath-taking.

All of the plants we see now are small, grow in tufts, cushion-like clumps or mats, and generally are thickly covered with some kind of hair. The purple and crimson rock penstemon make fine displays here, and the dwarf mountain daisy is seen more often in these higher rocky places than it is lower down. Eriogonum pyrolaefolium, variety coryphaeum, a member of the buckwheat family, is common in very dry or sandy soils. It has a cluster of small oval leaves and dense, rounded umbels of whitish flowers on stout stalks. Growing with it, but not as common, we shall find pussy's-paws, Spraguea caudicifera. Its leaves are

darker green and more densely crowded, and the pretty little flower heads are pinkish to rose-red.

As we pass beyond the last trees the ground becomes
more barren and rocky, and we are in a world that is bleak
indeed, the Arctic-Alpine zone. The flowers still continue
the struggle, and though their foliage is greatly reduced in
size and they have fewer blossoms, each blossom is just as
large and brilliant as those of the lower elevations. Smelowskia, a member of the mustard family with finely divided, gray-green leaves and tiny white flowers, is seen to
good advantage here, and the mountain sorrel, Oxyria
digyna, haunts the sheltered nooks and crannies. Drummond's anemone is encountered infrequently, but it will be
worth our while to search for these fragile appearing flowers, tinged on the backs with lovely shades of blue. Vying
with Lyall's lupine for first place in beauty is the silky
phacelia, Phacelia sericea, an elegant little plant of the
waterleaf family. It has silky silver-green, divided leaves
and dense head-like clusters of deep violet-blue. Forms of
mountain dandelions, Agoseris alpestris, Agoseris villosa,
and Hulsea nana, make occasional spots of bright yellow.
Here we will find Suksdorf's silene, a short-stemmed
variety, and alpine Jacob's-ladder, Polemonium elegans,
with its tiny leaflets and showy clusters of blue-violet flowers with yellow centers. It also has an unpleasant, skunk-like
odor. This inhospitable region is the home of the exquisite
moss campion, Silene acaulis. It grows in cracks and on
ledges of cliffs and outcroppings of solid rock where it forms
pincushion mats, like patches of moss, that are literally
covered with lovely deep-pink flowers.

If we were to continue climbing higher and higher into

the Arctic-Alpine regions the flowers would drop out, one by one, and become very scarce. We would have to climb quite high, though, before they disappeared entirely, for smelowskia and Draba aureola, another member of the mustard family, have been found at an altitude of ten thousand feet.

A short description of part of a climb we made to the summit of Columbia Peak, elevation 7,134 feet, will serve, I think, to give you some small idea of what might be encountered on a rock peak extending up into the Arctic-Alpine zone. We left our camp at the old ghost mining town of Monte Cristo quite early in the morning and swiftly passed through the Canadian zone on the trail to Poodledog Pass. From the pass we took a branch trail that leads to Twin Lakes through the lovely Hudsonian zone. Shortly before reaching the lakes we left the trail and took to the west ridge of the peak itself. Trees gradually became fewer and smaller and the views grander as we climbed higher and higher. At last, on a high shoulder of the ridge, we passed the last trees. Above us were only rocky slopes, bare rocks, and a few snow fields.

We continued doggedly upward expecting to see few, if any, flowers. Close above us a mountain goat, monarch of all mountain climbers, trotted across a snow slope and soon disappeared from view. We scrambled on, seeing a number of flowers scattered here and there. One slope held quite a garden of bush penstemon, phlox, saxifrage, stonecrop, harebells, and other flowers. Presently we came to a ledge about fifty feet below the summit and here, at an elevation of 7,100 feet, we found Drummond's lovely fragile anemone, beautiful, deep violet-blue silky phacelia, and cushions of exquisite deep-pink moss campion. This alone was worth the hours of hiking and climbing we had already put in, but we were not yet finished with surprises. We made the interesting climb of the last few rocks, and as we gained the summit, the very highest point itself, lo and behold, what was there to greet us but the pretty yellow blossoms of the shrubby cinquefoil. We were amazed to find it in such a place, exposed to every mountain storm and to all extremes of weather. Though the leaves were very small and the plants stunted, each flower was as large as any we had seen far down the mountainside. The combination of an exhilarating climb, magnificent views, and beautiful flowers trembling in the wind, sent us happily on our way home, tired in body but recreated in spirit.

ALPENGLOW

Time is running out on us, the sun hangs low in the western sky, and our trip, as all trips do, is rapidly nearing its end. We must retrace our steps swiftly lest darkness overtake us before we reach our car. Down we go to our Bit of Paradise, where we linger for a few last moments to fill our beings with all the beauty that is there. Then into the forest and down, down the trail until at last we reach the place from which we started.

As we roll along the highway toward home, the sun sinks behind the Coast Range to the west and we stop to see the Cascades flushed with the gorgeous alpenglow. Then we wish that we were back in the high places, in our Bit of Paradise, where we can best see the first delicate shades of pink turn darker and darker as the shadow of night swiftly creeps out of the valleys and up the sides of the mountains until everything is engulfed in darkness. We might be fortunate enough to be there when the valleys below are filled with clouds, like a vast sea that stretches to the horizon. It was in such a lovely setting that my friend Clark Schurman saw a rare occurrence that inspired him to write:

> "Into the cloud-sea far below
> I, lonely, watched the red sun go.
> Then, turning, miracle of glad surprise,
> Enchanted, saw the full moon rise."

THE BIRDS OF THE CASCADES
by Ellsworth D. Lumley

The Cascade Range is a natural barrier which effectively separates most of the birds of the eastern slope from those of the coast. Birds from both sides move up and down the mountains but few cross over. The Cascades offer a wide variety of bird habitats, for they extend from the low foothills with logged-off and burned-over areas, through sections of uncut virgin forests, up to the mountain meadows with their islands of alpine fir, and beyond to the snow-capped rocky peaks. The number of different bird habitats is further increased by the many rivers, ravines, lakes, and swamps found throughout the range.

The rise from slightly above sea level to an elevation of several thousand feet places sections of the Cascades in four life zones. Because of their ease of movement birds cannot definitely be placed in discrete life zones. Most birds show a decided preference for one habitat and may be found with more success in a specific place. However, in their search for food and during migration they may wander or deliberately move into habitats and zones in which they are not customarily seen. The bird watcher in the mountains may therefore have a number of pleasant surprises as he finds bird friends in unexpected places.

Low valleys cutting through the foothills at the base of the Cascades lie in the Transition zone. Practically all of these valleys have been logged off and many of them have been burned over a number of times. Typical birds to be seen in the open country are the Lewis woodpecker, California quail, Oregon ruffed grouse, and Pacific nighthawk.

Just above the Transition zone lies the Canadian zone. Here the fauna and flora are similar to that of the lower Canadian provinces. The great forests which have not been logged are made up of the giant Douglas fir, western hemlock, and red cedar. Such flowers as trilliums, Canadian dogwood, and twin-flowers are common. In this zone one may expect to find the varied thrush, winter wren, pileated and Harris woodpecker, sooty grouse, Steller's jay, Oregon jay, kinglet, nuthatch, and chestnut-backed chickadee.

The Hudsonian zone lies above the deep forests. Here the Douglas fir, red cedar, and western hemlock have given way to the tall slender alpine fir, the Alaska cedar, and the mountain hemlock. These trees appear in islands scattered about the great alpine meadows. During the short summers the meadows are blanketed with a mass of brilliantly colored flowers. The moist clouds blowing in from the Pacific cover these meadows with many feet of snow during the winter. The trees are tall and spire-like with their branches all growing downward to shed the snow. This part of the mountains attracts many bird watchers for here are to be seen birds not often encountered in other places. A few of the many birds to be observed are the mountain bluebird,

Clark's nutcracker, hermit thrush, calliope hummingbird, Grinnell's chickadee, and slate-colored fox sparrow.

Many peaks and ridges of the Cascades rise above the 6,500-foot elevation and thus leave behind the Hudsonian zone. Except where heavy winds prevail, these high elevations are covered with perpetual snow and ice. During the short summer the sun's heat melts exposed lower surfaces, where a few hardy plants are able to survive. A few birds find the rocky ground and bare cliffs suitable homesites. The pallid horned lark, white-tailed ptarmigan, Hepburn's rosy finch, and pipit are to be found beyond the tree line in the Arctic-Alpine zone.

The smell of the trees, flowers, and forest floor; the feel of the moss, the soft spongy earth, and the rough bark of trees; the sound of running water, hum of insects, and the songs of birds, all are as pleasure giving and soul satisfying as the beauty of the mountains, the color of the flowers, and the sight of flying birds. The truth is, many songs are heard where one bird is seen, so that the ability to identify a few bird songs brings more pleasure to the mountain climber than the ability to identify a few birds by sight. Many of the songs have an emotional appeal similar to the soft music of a pipe organ or the gay music of the violin. Bird watchers time many of their mountain visits to the song season just to hear the morning and evening songs of some of the mountain birds.

The deep gloom of the Douglas fir forests that skirt the base of the Cascades creates a mood altogether fitting for the melancholy song of the varied thrush. To the naturalist, the single note repeated over and over, seldom on the same pitch, is as much a part of the forests in spring and early summer as are the Canadian dogwood, Queen's cup, and trillium. The varied thrush, often called the winter robin and Alaska robin, migrates vertically, therefore during the winter months many are seen about the cities of Puget Sound. With the coming of spring they slowly move up the mountains singing their weird song during most of the day. The guttural single note is so easily imitated that it is possible, by whistling the note, to coax several of the birds to answer the song and to flit through the branches overhead. After the song season is over the varied thrush becomes a ghost bird which silently moves through the trees, giving the bird watcher only an occasional glimpse of a fleeting shadow.

The rapid bubbling song of the winter wren entirely changes the somber mood of the forests, for this cheerful songster seems to bring rays of sunshine to the forest floor. The winter wren buoys up your spirit and makes you want to sing with the tiny sprite. And oh! how tiny he is. You get but a glimpse of him as he hops and flits through the tangled roots of the fallen giants. His movements are decidedly mouse-like until he mounts some half-hidden root where, with his tail standing straight up on his back, he pours forth his long gurgling song. You stand amazed that such a tiny creature can sing so long a melody.

The joyous song of the winter wren is sometimes changed to one of alarm and fear. While hiking up a narrow ravine with its small stream crossed and crisscrossed by old moss- and fern-covered logs, I was attracted to a pair of winter wrens by their rather loud and persistent calls of distress. At first I suspected it was my presence near their nest that was causing so much alarm, but as I moved away I noted that the two continued to dart about a small log a few feet from the trail. I quietly retraced my steps and climbed upon the end of the log to see what was causing so much alarm. I was startled by the sight of what appeared to be a snake with a feather headdress, coiled in a small patch of sunshine. When I stepped near to examine the strange sight I found it to be a garter snake with a partially swallowed young wren. Unable to move away with the wing and tail feathers widely protruding from its mouth, the snake quietly continued to engulf the bird as I watched. This was tragedy for the parent wrens and my first impulse was to kill the snake and liberate the dead bird. Yet I knew that I was witnessing a part of the normal activities of nature, a part that few people are privileged to see. I watched for a short time, filled with the urge to stop this sad event, yet realizing that whatever I might do would only make a double tragedy and be a real offense against nature.

While only a few musical songs are heard in the dense forests, there are a number of calls which serve as the song of certain birds. Once recognized, they are thoroughly enjoyed by the bird student for they are like the off-key whistling of the little boy who saunters down the street. Such musical ability cannot be compared with that of a Lily Pons, yet recognizing the cheerful whistle brings as much joy and happiness as hearing a real artist.

So while the nasal "yank-yank-yank" of the red-breasted nuthatch is not musical, it brings the same joy to the heart of the outdoor person as does the bubbling song of the winter wren. A song not heard unless the ear is attuned to bird notes is the high-pitched call of the pileated woodpecker.

This handsome black bird with his flaming red crest is admired by all who are fortunate enough to get a good look at him, yet few people have ever heard him sing. The "pee-ist" call of the western flycatcher is repeated monotonously from some shadowy branch in the forests. When he chooses to sing, his effort produces four metallic notes that sound as though they were produced by an insect rather than a bird. Yet there is something pleasing to this as you watch the little fellow cheer up his gloomy habitat. High overhead one often hears the call of the crossbills as they search for food in the tops of the trees or quickly pass by in flight. Their song is no more musical than the notes of the chickadees and kinglets, yet it is a tantalizing song for you never get a good look at these birds except in more open woods near some stream or lake where they often come to drink.

Where the forests have been cleared away for roads, camps, or small farms, and upon rocky slopes where the forests are thin, the Townsend solitaire pours forth a melodious song from some high tree or snag. This truly western bird is looked for by almost every bird lover who visits the mountains, not because of his beauty or his song, but solely for the deep satisfaction of seeing him. His feeding habits are so similar to those of the flycatchers that he is often referred to as a flycatcher.

Fortunately for the bird watcher, the Townsend warbler prefers to remain in the open forests where he can be seen more easily. His wheezy song, lisped over and over again from the treetops, keeps the observer peering through the openings in the trees in hopes of a glimpse of this striking bird. Patience is usually rewarded, for this warbler's actions are somewhat leisurely and when he does come into view on some branch tip he remains long enough to present a good view of his bright yellow and black markings.

Only a part of the Canadian zone of the Cascades remains blanketed with great forests. Man has moved into the mountains with powerful logging equipment and has stripped much of the land, leaving behind stumps and scarred earth. Nature soon covers the scars with a thick growth of fireweed, willows, alders, maples, and evergreens. In places where the logging was done many years ago, there is now a large stand of second-growth forest. Where the logging is more recent the country is more open. This open brushy country is the home of many birds that love the shelter of brush and the bright sun overhead. The songs of these brush-loving birds are now common.

The warbling vireo's song is heard continuously throughout the day along the streams and river beds. The joyful and varied notes of the song sparrow and the high trilled song of the towhee are common in the brushy logged-off land. Both birds gather much of their food from the ground where they are often seen scratching among the leaves. Where man has cleared small tracts of land for homes and small gardens, the towhee is somewhat of a menace to sprouting peas. A pair will go down a row pulling up every seed just to enjoy the tender sprout.

Warblers enjoy the deciduous trees which quickly take over logged-off land. During the spring and early summer the songs of the yellow warbler, lutescent warbler, Audubon warbler, Macgillivray warbler, and pileolated warbler are common. Their songs are distinctive enough to provide identification for each bird.

The "chickadee-dee-dee" of the Oregon chickadee is a

common song of the lower mountains where second growth is again making the earth green. This song always invites me to a little game with the birds. By stepping among the branches of a bush or tree and whistling the "phoebe" song of the chickadee I can soon have several of the males excitedly fluttering about my head, scarcely giving me my turn to whistle the little song. On two occasions they landed on me. Once one sat on my shoulder and continued to sing his phoebe call, and another time one clung to the rim of my hat and looked down and answered my whistle. These little talks with chickadees during a hike are as refreshing as a cool drink from a mountain spring.

The loud "what! three cheers" of the olive-sided flycatcher is one of the most common songs heard on the open mountainsides. From his favorite perch high atop some tall tree or old snag he repeats his song during most of the day. When not loudly whistling his song, this large flycatcher monotonously utters a soft call of two notes which betrays his whereabouts to the hiker.

Probably the best friends of our forests are the woodpeckers. These birds work the year around in the destruction of insects and larvae which they find in the cracks of bark, under the bark, and deep in the trees. Nature has provided the woodpecker with specialized tools for removing wood-boring beetles, which are said to destroy more trees in Washington than are destroyed by fire. The woodpecker's tail feathers are stiff and pointed, so he appears to sit on his tail while he digs for the insects. His beak is sharp and chisel-like for digging into either soft or hard wood, and his tongue is long with a bony, barbed tip for spearing the hidden wood borer. Such labor-saving devices materially aid woodpeckers in holding in check the destructive forest insects.

At least eight woodpeckers are to be seen in the Cascades. The northwestern flicker is probably the most common, for this bird quickly moves into an area after the old forests have been logged and replaced by second growth. The flicker is also common in the alpine country.

The green and pinkish Lewis woodpecker lives in the lower sections of logged-off and burned-over foothills, particularly where red elderberries are common. He varies his insect diet with different fruits.

The most brilliant of the woodpeckers is the northern red-breasted sapsucker. These birds love cedars, and the great series of holes drilled into the bark of the trees is evidence of their activity. They have not much fear of man and will permit rather close observation.

The Gairdner woodpecker is a form of the downy, and is well known to all bird lovers. This little woodpecker prefers the lower elevations where he can find willows in which to search for food. His larger cousin, the Harris woodpecker, is more common. The latter enjoys not the burned-over areas only, but also the deeper woods, and is occasionally seen in the alpine firs of the Hudsonian zone.

As was mentioned earlier, we usually find the pileated woodpecker in the deep forests. This is the largest woodpecker in the mountains; it is a flashy black bird with a brilliant red crest. Another species common to the forests is the Alaskan three-toed woodpecker. He is not so devoted to the large trees as the pileated, and so may be encountered in the trees in the alpine meadows.

Wide river valleys reach back in the Cascades until they

become narrow gorges with rushing tumbling white water. Where the rivers flow lazily in wide valleys between distant peaks the evening twilight comes early. While the upper part of the mountains still glows in the setting sun, the russet-backed thrush begins its evening song. Picnickers and campers whose ears are never tuned to the robin's song, stop and listen to the twilight song of the russet-back as he sings from some dense thicket. To become personally acquainted with this thrush requires patience and a little know-how, for the bird is so shy that he seldom comes into the open. The most common note of the bird is a low "whit" which is easily imitated. I have stepped into a large bush and whistled this note when russet-backs were singing near-by. In just a few seconds the note was answered, first by one bird then by another. Gradually the birds moved about, getting closer and closer, until I had a quick glimpse of them as they flitted from branch to branch. Once the thrushes see the source of the strange whistle they stop their calling and quietly disappear. However, there is an exhilarating thrill in the fleeting glimpse one gets of the birds as they cautiously move through the bushes.

It comes as a surprise to many mountain visitors to see ducks on the rivers and lakes. Apparently most people never associate waterfowl with the mountains. Yet probably the most beautiful, and certainly the most striking, of all ducks are seen in the mountains.

Flocks of the American merganser are often encountered where the rivers are deep and not too swift. Higher in the mountains where the rivers have narrowed, the smaller and more distinctive hooded merganser is seen. This bird prefers some lake hidden in the woods, however, and makes its home there as soon as the ice and snow melt away. It nests in a hollow of some nearby tree and is most difficult to find. Authorities claim that its eggshell is harder and tougher than that of any other native North American bird.

The harlequin duck is the most gaudily marked of the waterfowl. Hikers who are fortunate enough to get a good look at a group of harlequins ask many questions about this species of the first "bird man" they meet. The bizarre and fantastic spots and patches on the head and body make the bird one to be remembered. Harlequins love swift and turbulent waters where they swim and dive with the ease of grebes. They usually nest on some small island in a river or stream. After the family is reared they move down the rivers to the salt water where they spend the winter.

Visitors to mountains, rivers, and streams also get a surprising shock when they first see the water ouzel calmly walk off a flat rock and disappear under the water. It looks as though the bird were trying to drown itself. But in just a few seconds the ouzel walks out of the water onto another rock and bobs its body up and down several times. The ouzel, probably better known as the dipper, is a true songbird with no aquatic characteristics, yet it is as much at home in the water as is a duck. The ouzel will plunge into swiftly running water where you would expect to find it dashed to pieces, search for food in this strange environment, then suddenly appear upon another rock to continue its bobbing and dipping.

The dipper is an accomplished songster, his song being similar to that of the winter wren. An attractive moss nest is usually built so near water that it is dripping wet from spray most of the time. Severe winters do not drive this

bird from the mountains. He merely moves to lower elevations where he finds sufficient food in the icy rivers.

The many mountain lakes dotting the Cascades from the
Canadian border to the Columbia River offer a home and
resting place to a good many waterfowl. Barrow's golden-
eye, unlike the American golden-eye which migrates north
to breed, moves up into the mountain lakes to make its
summer home. Here the birds find ample food and excellent
nesting sites in hollow trees. During the autumn, mallards,
pintails, and green-winged teal may be seen on many of the
mountain lakes. These migrating birds find a welcome sanc-
tuary on these small isolated bodies of water during their
fall flight. With the ducks may be seen the western grebe
and the pied-billed grebe. Loons, which once were common
on many lakes, have now become rare summer visitors, possibly due to potshots often taken at them by unthinking
hunters.

Bird trips to the mountain lakes in the fall will usually
result in the finding of such shore birds as the semi-palmated
sandpiper, killdeer, western solitary sandpiper, Wilson's
snipe, and the spotted sandpiper. Many of the latter are
mountain birds for they build their nests in the high alpine
meadows or when possible on a sandy shore near water.
Summer campers on mountain lakes often hear the "peet-
weet" call of this bird as it flies out over the water.

Another fall visitor to the mountain lakes is the blue
heron. To the person whose heart is not filled with prejudice
against all creatures that take fish, the blue heron is as much
a part of our lakes as are the reeds and half-sunken logs
about the water's edge. The heron gives life to the lake and
makes it a living part of the wilderness.

Many of the mountain lakes are shining jewels in a setting of evergreen trees. The bird watcher sees and hears the many birds that make this majestic setting their home. Late one afternoon as I sat resting on the shore of one of these beauty spots, a flock of evening grosbeaks dropped almost at my feet from the trees above. They hopped about the narrow beach for a few moments, satisfied their curiosity as to what I was, then, softly whistling their chirp and high trill, flew back into the trees. Since they are seen all during the summer in the high timbered sections, they undoubtedly breed in the Cascades.

On another occasion a flock of crossbills drank and bathed within a few feet of where I was sitting on a half-sunken log. After they had gone it was hard to realize that I had been watching crossbills without the use of glasses and without acquiring a stiff neck from looking upward.

No mountain bird demands and gets the attention of hikers and picnickers as does the Oregon jay or camp robber. Like a genie this bird appears as soon as lunch sacks are opened, whether it be in deep forests or in alpine meadows. Lacking the fear which most wild creatures have for man, the camp robbers soar down from the trees to within a few feet of the picnickers, then hop up and take food from the hand. This show of confidence has earned the birds many full meals, for most people are more than generous with such friendly birds. Campers often find the jays a nuisance after the first day or two. The fun of feeding them disappears when every piece of unguarded food is carried away. I have watched the birds fly off with food from a camper's plate while he was tending to the fire or getting hot coffee. Camp robbers are a real joy to the hundreds of people who spend a part of their summer in a mountain cabin. They are certain to form a reception committee within a few minutes after the cabin is opened and to come flying up to the porch with a whistled greeting. From then on the birds may be expected at any time for their handout of food.

One summer a pair regularly entered our cabin at mealtime and ate from the table. Our hospitality caused the death of one of the birds. It was necessary to keep a number of mousetraps set on the cupboard to keep down the number of deer mice that made our nights sleepless by rustling through paper sacks and food boxes. One morning just as it was getting light I was awakened by the snap of one of the traps and by considerable noise as the trap was banged about on the floor. I investigated, to find that one of the jays had entered through the window and had been caught in the trap. We were careful after that to hide the traps where only mice could get at them.

I might say that we always felt regretful about catching the mice, for they were dainty creatures with their large eyes and ears. Many evenings we sat quietly and watched one of the mice come in through the window, run across the table, jump to the cupboard, and then snoop into every sack. However after a hard day in the field there is nothing more irritating than the sound of a mouse rattling cellophane and paper sacks in search of food. Regardless of how cute the little fellows look in the glare of a flashlight, it becomes necessary to control their numbers if you are to eat and sleep.

The attractive Steller's jay is found from sea level to timber line. Though not as common as the Oregon jay, this black-headed fellow with the deep-blue body is to be seen on almost every trip to the mountains. His saucy habits and warning notes given when hunters are stalking game, together with the fact that he does steal the eggs from a few nests, have placed him on the predatory list. While it is true that he will occasionally pilfer other birds' nests, there is very little evidence to show that any great harm is done. The joy and pleasure he gives with his beauty and interesting habits more than pay for the slight damage he may do.

Numbers of bird voices heard by hikers and campers are voices of mystery, for they are so unbird-like that they are often associated with other creatures. People unused to the woods and mountains often allow their imaginations to run wild when they encounter sights and sounds to which they are unaccustomed. I once met a group of boys on a mountain trail who excitedly told me of the "cougar" that had awakened them the night before with its screaming. After listening to their story I was convinced that what they had heard was simply the call of some owl. Another time a man and his family excitedly told me of hearing a bear grunt and growl at them as they walked along a trail. After getting them to repeat the noise as closely as they could, I knew they had been frightened by the hooting of a sooty grouse.

Several owls are to be seen and heard in the Cascades. The Kennicott screech owl enjoys the fir woods about the base of the mountains, where his diet consists of small rodents, birds, insects, amphibians, fish, and worms. His song —if such it may be called—is not a screech, as his name would indicate, but more a series of whistled "woo's." A somewhat smaller owl which may be encountered in almost any place in the mountains is the saw-whet owl. He gives a number of calls, one sound being enough like the filing of a saw to give him his name.

For about ten days during August a pair of northern spotted owls hooted back and forth across a canyon at about three o'clock every morning. The song was most irritating to my companion for it invariably awakened us, yet to me there was something pleasant in hearing these strange birds calling to one another in the night. The dusky horned owl is also a resident of the Cascades, where, like the other owls, he carries on a valuable service in holding the many rodents in check.

Summer is short in the Hudsonian zone. The heavy snows melt slowly at this altitude, so that many of the alpine meadows are under snow through the first week of July. The flowering season is therefore rapid; one week the fields are white with snow, the next they are white with avalanche lilies, western anemones, and marsh marigolds. The next week these white flowers are almost gone and the lupine, red paintbrush, giant hellebore, and many other brightly colored flowers have taken their place.

During June, while the snow is still several feet deep, the singing of birds becomes common over the open mountain slopes. The urge to nest is so great that many of the birds raise their first families in what must look to the young like a world of white.

It is in this zone of flower-covered meadows and clear exhilarating panoramas that some of the most beautiful bird songs are to be heard. Bird enthusiasts often make special trips to the alpine country for the sheer joy and pleasure of hearing the songs of these avian mountaineers.

Two sparrow vocalists that are enjoyed by all who take

a few moments to listen are the slate-colored fox sparrow and the smaller Lincoln sparrow. The fox sparrow arrives quite early and sings his full rich song all during June and the first of July. Though often heard, the fox sparrow is not so often seen, for he enjoys seclusion in the thick alpine firs. The sly and elusive Lincoln sparrow darts and creeps about the underbrush so that only glimpses can be had of this retiring bird. When the male sings, however, he pours his soul into his beautiful bubbling joyous song.

Two other sparrows that make their homes in the mountains are the chipping sparrow and the Shufeldt junco. Both birds enjoy a wide range, being found from the foothills to the tree line. The song of these two birds is so similar that it is often confused, for it consists of a single high trill.

If a prize could be awarded the family of birds whose songs have the greatest appeal to the public, the thrush family would win hands down. The robin's cheerful, rollicking song welcomes in the day just as light is breaking. The weird song of the varied thrush in the forest gloom is melancholic yet appealing. With the setting of the sun the charming song of the russet-back in the valley strikes a pensive chord with a tinge of sadness. It is the evening song of the hermit thrush, however, as he sings from the rim of the canyon, that makes one stand quietly, with hat removed, as though a prayer were being said. The song is inspiring and reverent. The notes are so pure you hesitate to speak above a whisper while the hermit chorus sings. The Sierra hermit thrush reaches the high altitudes during May, while winter still rules. The bird is so shy and retiring that most mountaineers never see him, but his flute-like song which makes the mountains seem sacred is payment enough for the hike to high country.

The most beautiful bird of the thrush family to be seen in the Cascades is the mountain bluebird. Dr. D. L. Serventy, noted ornithologist of Australia, considered this bird the most beautiful in the United States. It ranges eastward from the Cascades; very rarely does one wander down the west side to Puget Sound. The bright azure-blue back of the male shades to a light bluish gray on the breast. The female is a bluish gray with the lower back a light blue.

That the mountain bluebird is a singer does not seem to be generally known, even by those authorities who have spent some time studying the bird. My first experience with its song came at six o'clock on the morning of March 25, 1934, in Montana. It was still quite dark, but I soon found the bird on the roof of a house. After singing for five minutes it flew away, passing so near me that I could make a positive identification. From that morning on I watched and listened for the bird, and often heard the song early in the morning twilight. The singing habits of the mountain bluebirds that spend their summers in the Cascades are similar to those of Montana. Their song is usually a flight song given while it is still quite dark, although on two different occasions I have heard the mountain bluebirds sing from an alpine fir in the middle of the morning. The song is comparatively simple, consisting chiefly of descending warbles which invariably begin on the same pitch. One song follows another so closely that it is difficult to determine when one stops and another begins. I found the voice of the bluebird impossible to imitate and almost impossible to describe. It is low in comparison with other bird voices and carries several undertones which make it extremely difficult to find the exact pitch.

Cavities in old snags and dead trees are used as nesting sites by the bluebirds. After the families are reared and the birds are ready to migrate they have the peculiar custom of migrating with Audubon warblers. Mixed groups of the two birds are often observed during the fall.

The western bluebird is attractive, with his deep-blue back and chestnut or reddish breast. He fails to excite the admiration that the mountain bluebird does; however, this may be due partially to the fact that the western bluebird is seen in the lower foothills with a deep evergreen background, while the mountain bluebird is observed in the bright sunshine of the high meadows.

The most amusing bird of the Hudsonian zone is the Clark's nutcracker or Clark's crow. First recorded in the journals of Lewis and Clark and named after Clark, the bird has interested and entertained mountain visitors ever since. Daring, saucy, boisterous, this gray crow begs and steals what food he can, while at the same time driving off the chipmunks and ground squirrels that come for their handout. He is often mistaken for the camp robber by people who are not too well acquainted with the mountain birds. He is much larger in size, is gray except for the black wings and black central tail feathers, and his voice is loud and raucous.

The cone of the white-bark pine is hard, and to extract the seed requires much work. Yet this cone is a choice item of food for the nutcrackers. They will spend considerable time pecking and prying to get to the kernel. One summer one of the nutcrackers had the misfortune to poke his lower

mandible into a hollow chicken bone some picnickers had
thrown away. I watched this bird during the summer as he
attempted to remove the bone by hammering it against tree
trunks and the roof of the cabin. This seemed only to drive
it on more firmly. By turning his head sideways he was able
to pick up enough food from the ground to survive the
summer. Several attempts were made to catch the bird and
remove the bone but he could not be lured into a trap. The
following summer he was not seen with the bone, so he had
either rid himself of the cruel handicap or had died of starva-
tion during the winter.

Nutcrackers nest while the mountains are still in the grip
of winter, building their nests in the sheltering evergreen
trees. The young are dependent upon the parents for a long
period after they leave the nest. I have watched adults feeding their young by regurgitation during July when the young
were fully as large as the adults.

Cassin's purple finch, like the mountain bluebird, is an
eastern Washington bird which moves as far west as the
crest of the Cascades. During the summer months, sunshine
or fog, its clear warbled song is often heard from the alpine
firs. So few of the mountain birds have more than a patch
of red on them that it is a delight to watch this finch with
his crimson-red head, pink throat, and reddish-brown back.

Singing from the same trees with the purple finch is sometimes heard the Grinnell chickadee. His "chickadee-dee-dee"
song is like that of the Oregon chickadee but his phoebe call
is quite different. It is whistled at a higher pitch and usually
consists of four instead of three notes. For some unknown
reason the birds have shown only a mild interest when I

Mountain bluebird

Clark's nutcracker

White-tailed ptarmigan

Townsend solitaire

Cooper's hawk

Western grebe

Eagle Creek Punch Bowl

Granite Falls in Stillaguamish River

have whistled to them, never coming as do the Oregon chickadees.

To my knowledge the chestnut-backed chickadee found in the wooded sections of the mountains never gives a phoebe call; its only song is the one common to all chickadees. When I have whistled to them they have shown no interest.

Above the tree line lies a land of rocks and snow. The few plants that can live in this environment are small and scattered. It is little wonder that few birds choose this habitat in which to raise their families.

One of my most pleasant bird experiences occurred in this Arctic-Alpine zone. During the first week in August I was hiking along a high ridge when a soft chirping, like that of a baby chick, attracted my attention. I thought it might be a young ptarmigan so I began looking about. I could find nothing and was about to give up when it occurred to me that possibly the mother was nearby and might come if I whistled the distress notes of a little chicken. After about the third chirp I heard a soft cluck to one side and saw an adult white-tailed ptarmigan slowly moving toward me. When she was within a few feet she stopped, then began to circle me slowly. When she moved I could see her plainly, but when she stopped her mottled coloring was so much like the ground that she almost disappeared. In a few minutes she quieted down, began clucking, and walked away. To my surprise six little ptarmigans came hurrying to her from among the stones. They had been so perfectly marked that I hadn't seen one of them, although they were all in plain view. This species of ptarmigan has little fear of man. Many times groups of people have walked within a few feet of the bird without anyone's seeing it until it began to walk slowly away. The bird depends upon its coloring rather than upon flight for escaping any possible harm.

In the fall, first the under parts, then the upper parts turn white, so that during the winter when the mountains are covered with snow the ptarmigan again is invisible against its white background. During the winter the bird feeds upon the buds of willow, alder, and other deciduous plants that are not buried under the snow.

A bird that must truly love snow, cold, and storms is Hepburn's rosy finch. During the winter these birds are seen in eastern Washington where the winters are often severe; early in the spring they migrate up to the mountain's bare rocky cliffs where storms are common. Here they build their nests in cracks in the rocks. The buds and seeds of heather and other alpine vegetation, as well as insects that are found on the snow, make up their food. Fog seems to be the only element which can drive them down to open meadows during the summer.

The pipit is not such a rugged individualist that he chooses the bare rock cliffs for his summers. As the snow recedes and the ground becomes bare, the pipit builds his cup nest in the shelter of heather or under a small shelf of earth. The male sings a sweet song, often giving it while in flight.

The high mountain country also attracts the pallid horned lark. Its behavior is similar to that of the pipit, but the bird is easily identified by its larger, plumper body and the striking markings on its head and body.

For the person who enjoys an air circus the mountains have a special appeal, for here a number of birds can be witnessed putting on thrilling air maneuvers and air battles.

Close-formation flying, daring dives, and air-current glidings are all featured in the show.

During the fall migration many hawks take advantage of the Cascade air currents which aid them in their southern flight. Dozens may pass by in an afternoon, giving the watcher an excellent opportunity to study their flight characteristics. Occasionally one will seem to start from far below in the canyon and then be swiftly catapulted into view over the edge of a cliff. Few of the hawks ever seem in a hurry; they apparently prefer a slow easy soaring to a more rapid energetic flight. The western red-tailed and Swainson hawks are experts at taking advantage of every current of air which sweeps up the mountains. When hungry, they leave the migration route and soar in large circles over meadows from which they gather mice, ground squirrels, and small marmots.

The golden eagle with his large broad wings uses the upward movement of air for sailing. Although often accused of killing fawns and the kids of mountain goats, such killings are very rare. Rodents make up the bulk of this bird's diet. Our national bird, the southern bald eagle, follows the spawning salmon into the mountains where he is often seen soaring slowly up some river canyon. Being a fish eater, he seldom travels far from the waters which furnish him his food.

The three accipiters, the goshawk, Cooper's hawk, and sharp-shinned hawk, often amuse and entertain mountain visitors with their swift darting flight. The first two breed in the Cascades and are to be seen during the spring, summer, and fall. Both are sufficiently large that most birds fear them. When one comes into view a hush settles over the area as all the birds seek shelter in the trees and bushes.

The smaller sharp-shinned hawk migrates through the mountains during the late summer and fall. It is then that exciting aerial battles occur between these small hawks and the nutcrackers. Several nutcrackers will "gang up" on a passing sharp-shinned and attack him from all sides while simultaneously shrieking loudly at him. When the sharp-shinned turns to attack one of the nutcrackers, that bird streaks for the nearest tree while the other birds try to divert the hawk's attention by screaming even more loudly and attacking more viciously. Although I have witnessed a number of these battles, I have never seen the hawk catch a nutcracker. It almost appears to be a game with the birds as they dart about a passing hawk.

The kingfisher is a perfectionist in dive-bombing, for the amount of food he eats depends upon his accuracy in hitting the mark. Along most of the rivers and lakes this beautiful bird, with his peculiar rattling call, searches for his slippery prey. Two methods are used in locating the fish. One is to fly over the water until a likely fish is spotted, then hover a second or two lining up his sights, and finally dive swiftly into the water to spear his fish. The other method is to sit patiently on some branch or snag which overhangs the water, watching for any movement below. When a fish comes within range, the kingfisher plummets into the water and usually emerges with his prey in his beak. Fish culturalists tell us that while the kingfisher will take any fish he can catch, the coarse scrap fish make up the most of his diet. By thus removing the competitive fish, more food and shelter remain for the game fish. This attractive bird which is so much a part of our waterways thus becomes an aid to the fisherman —a fact which is too seldom appreciated.

One of the most amazing aerial displays to be seen in the mountains is exhibited by the rufous hummingbird. The female will sit indifferently on the branch of a small bush or will sip nectar from a flower while the male flies in front of her in a great arc. He darts up twenty or thirty feet like a small jet rocket, then heads straight for the earth, levels off and zooms by the little lady, "buzzing" her as he passes, again to flash straight into the sky. Back and forth the male swings while the female calmly preens her feathers or gathers her food. While this aerial show thrills human eyes, the female hummingbird appears most indifferent.

The many acres of flowering meadows attract great numbers of hummingbirds to the mountains. The rufous is by far the most common although the calliope hummingbird can often be seen on the eastern slopes of the Cascades. This is the tiniest of all the birds to be seen in the Northwest.

Swallows are the ballerinas among the birds, for their every movement is one of ease and grace. They dart, whirl, sail, and dive over the lakes and alpine meadows. Violet-green swallows are the most common. They enjoy the presence of man, possibly because flying insects are common near human habitations. The tree swallow is so similar to the violet-green that close observation is necessary to make a positive identification. Both have pure white breasts and shiny green backs, and their beautiful soaring flight is a delight to the eye.

The northern pine siskin skillfully demonstrates the art of close-formation flying. With hundreds of birds massed so closely together that they appear to be almost wing tip to wing tip, the flock wheels and turns in the air as though governed by but one mind. With never a collision, the massed birds swirl through the air, continually changing their relative positions in the flock. Man has tried in many ways to explain this wonderful communal flight of the siskin.

It is both exciting and laughable to watch a family of ravens go through their aerial acrobatics. They play tag, follow-the-leader, and cops and robbers with as much enthusiasm as a small group of children. During July and August family groups of four and five are often seen together, the young fully as large as the parents but often still being fed by the old birds. They dive and chase and soar about the cliffs and over the canyons apparently with thought only for the enjoyment they are having.

It is deplorable that the state game departments place a price on the head of this interesting bird and encourage every man and boy with a gun to shoot him. Ravens are so few in number that they can do no appreciable harm to the game birds of the state.

The birds of the Cascades have given many happy hours to thousands of people who have visited the mountains. During the winter the Clark's nutcrackers, Oregon jays, and chickadees entertain and cheer the skiers. The pure white ptarmigan is sometimes found on the snow fields by the skier who ventures away from the well-beaten trails. Such a find is as thrilling as the long ski run down a mountain slope.

The spring and summer birds become a part of the mountains when the warm summer sun melts away the winter's accumulation of snow. The green forests, logged-over and burned-over areas, the colorful flower fields, and even the bare rocky peaks are gladdened by the cheerful song of birds. Birds are as much a part of the Cascades as are the emerald lakes, rushing rivers, and glistening glaciers. They do not quietly wait to be observed, however, but demand attention with their merry songs, bright colors, and aerial displays. The weary hiker may fail to see the beauty of the jagged rocky peak, but he seldom fails to enjoy the sweet evening song of the hermit thrush. The camper may take the giant firs for granted, failing to note the grandeur of the stately trees, yet he invariably jumps to his feet when a pileated woodpecker swoops from one tree to another. The appeal of the mountain birds is so great, indeed, that bird hikes are taken into the Cascades by many city dwellers.

The Cascades would be incomplete without the large variety of birds which find food and shelter on the mountain slopes and in the deep valleys. Without the birds, the mountains would lose a great deal of their fascination and charm.

WHERE THE DRY FLY IS QUEEN

by Herbert Lundy

On the afternoon of the third day they came down the steep trail from Long and Quinn lakes, digging in their heels and grumbling. It was a mile down to the roaring North Fork of the Willamette, and two miles up to the Taylor Burn guard station where they had left the car—twenty miles, fourteen lakes, and fifty million mosquitoes ago.

The food was gone and they were hungry. Mountain pterodactyls with turbojet engines, contemptuous of the Army's vaunted insect repellant, had raised long welts on their hands, necks, and faces. They had lost their way twice and had cut across lava beds, down canyons, up ridges, out of the pines and into the fir forest, through swamps tracked by elk.

They had rested on a high ridge, watching the trout rise on a lake a quarter-mile below, too weary to accept the challenge. They had frozen by night and cooked by day. Two of them, in their forties and office-fat, had watched the sixteen-year-old boy now fording the North Fork and romping ahead up the last—perhaps fatal—grade, wipe their eyes with a three-pounder at Rigdon Lake.

They were tired, gasping for breath, five pounds lighter,

303

sweating, dirty, hungry. They were extravagantly happy.

The back-packers had not seen a fisherman, nor anyone else, in three days. In the cool folds of their down sleeping bags were twenty rainbow, averaging a pound or thereabouts. And they had watched one evening, but hadn't caught, a great-grandfather of a trout—a yard long and almost as deep—boiling the placid surface of Lower Eddeleo.

The last two-mile climb was murder. Alternately, they condemned to eternal fire the man of questionable ancestry who had tipped them off to the marvels of this little swing around the backbone of the Cascades, and laid plans to return the following summer by helicopter—or at least by a shorter route—and catch that monster fish on a dry fly. The car looked like a heavenly chariot, despite running boards bashed by rocks on the climb up the ribs of the Cascades to Taylor Burn. They paused to tell the ranger that they had put out a smoldering fire at Wahanna Lake, and that the black bears had pulled down half the trail signs and broken them into bits—a favorite bruin sport.

On the drive out to Redmond they passed Irish Lake, Taylor Lake, Little Cultus Lake, the Lava Lakes, Elk Lake, Sparks Lake and a half-dozen others, stopping the car to watch the evening rise, wondering why in the world they hadn't fished some of these instead of half killing themselves —and knowing very well why they hadn't.

When they got back to the summer cabin on the Metolius River—that ever clear and constant stream which rushes out of the subterranean vault of Black Butte—the first thing they saw was the mess of trout in the kitchen sink. The finicky Metolius rainbow, whose indifference had urged them to the lakes, had chosen that evening to feed on the surface. The women had done almost as well as the men, and even the younger children had taken rainbow on dry flies.

The women hadn't got the feel of the wilderness—the fifty thousand square miles of it, back from the highways and forest roads—that guards the incomparable lake basins of the Snoqualmie, Deschutes, and Willamette National Forests of Washington and Oregon. But they had caught fish.

There is fishing for everyone in the great mountain range of the Pacific slope; no need, really, to tote into the high country to take rainbow, steelhead, eastern brook, European brown, cutthroat and Mackinaw trout, or the heavy, migrant Chinook fresh from the sea. Actually, the stream fishing is better in the lower, accessible reaches.

In much of this fishermen's empire, from the Canadian border to the Klamath River in California, the dry fly is queen and its subjects the most fortunate of anglers. But the purists have no monopoly, for big and little fish are caught with every kind of bait and lure produced by nature and devised by man.

Let no false impression arise. Success on Cascade lakes and streams is measured, as it always is, by the skill of the angler and the feeding whims of the trout. That is why those who like to spend a week or longer on waters they have learned to know, by chapter and verse—even though these be next to a paved highway—may catch more and bigger fish than those restless ones forever seeking strange pools and spending much of their time in travel.

It is the escape into solitude, as well as the hope of better fishing, that drives some into the wild country. There are many others who like company.

THE SULLEN, WONDERFUL DESCHUTES

In all of America there is no trout river like the Deschutes—that bleak and treacherous flow which heads in the lakes of Deschutes and Klamath counties, plunges over rims of lava and ambles glassily between broad and swampy meadows, then drives with relentless power through nearly one hundred miles of central Oregon canyons to join the Columbia River above The Dalles.

From Madras to its mouth, the Deschutes races between great painted cliffs and canyon slopes choked with barn-sized rock fragments fallen from the stratified walls. It is a sullen journey. Except for occasional rapids and the falls at Sherars Bridge, the angry, even downsurge of water rushes unbroken for miles.

The railroad to Bend and Klamath Falls clings to one embankment, crowded between the grasping river and the canyon walls, until it climbs out of the gorge to skirt Madras and slash across the central Oregon plateau. On the opposite shore is the abandoned roadbed of another line, the loser in the hell-roaring race between Hill and Harriman to lay the first rails into a rich livestock and timber country which, in 1908, had only wagon tracks through the sage to serve as roads.

Few anglers reach the river by rail. Passenger travel on parlor cars hitched to the tails of freight trains is time wasting and badly scheduled. For many miles no automobile roads descend into the canyon. The abandoned Harriman grade is choked with sage and thorn, many of its tunnels are blocked, great chunks of roadbed washed away by cloudburst torrents—but withal it is a handy pathway for fishermen, and in minor stretches it has been converted to auto travel.

The main stem of the Deschutes flows in a southerly direction out of the Lava Lakes at 4,700 feet elevation on the east slope of the Cascades, is impounded for irrigation by Crane Prairie and Wickiup reservoirs, rounds the turn through ponderosa pine forests and across bare black beds of lava to flow north through the city of Bend, where it is restrained again to form Mirror Lake in Bend's beautiful municipal park.

The irrigators have taken such toll that the Deschutes for miles below Bend is sorely depleted—but it is still a clear and powerful stream. It regains its strength and becomes a different river when it plunges into the canyon and is swelled by the clear Metolius, the rampaging, flooding Crooked River, and the Indians' Warm Springs River.

This is a harsh and forbidding canyon, burned by the midsummer sun and swept by cold winds in spring and fall. For miles the banks of the stream are lined with poison oak thickets growing taller than a fisherman's head, through which he must thrust to work the rock shores where the big fish lie. Valley quail and Hungarian partridges fly out ahead. Rattlesnakes give their timely warnings. Scorpions hide beneath the rocks and small gray lizards whisk across the brown earth. Ticks are there in hordes in the spring, but are seldom encountered after midsummer. There has not yet been a case of Rocky Mountain spotted fever traced to the Deschutes, though many—some fatal—to the Crooked River country and other streams to the east. (But wise anglers take their tick shots faithfully each spring.) The vegetation, chiefly sage sumac, and juniper, is as harsh as the land.

An angler accustomed to the forest-bordered streams of

the mountains or coast, or the gentle brooks of the flat country, will not forget his first sight of the Deschutes. Here are
few gravel bars and no mild pools, no fords, few shaded
runs. The broad, deep, growling river sweeps through rock
banks without slackening its pace.

The treacherous Deschutes has claimed many lives. Its
diabolic currents tug gently, at first, at the feet of the unwary, urging him insistently toward midstream. But out a
little from shore, his ankles may be seized with an iron grip
that pulls him relentlessly into fast and fatal waters which
sweep outward and suck downward. Some of the luckier ones
have regained the shore a quarter-mile downstream.

This is the river named by the Indians Towonehiooks,
and by Lewis and Clark, who discovered it on October 22,
1805, Clark's River. The name that stuck was put on it by
the French-Canadian voyageurs in the fur trade—Rivière
des Chutes, River of the Falls, either in reference to the falls
in the Deschutes at Sherars Bridge or because it flows into
the mighty Columbia near the Chutes, or The Dalles.

The great native trout of the Deschutes are the Pacific
steelhead and their sisters the rainbow, identical in form but
of different habits. The steelhead come up from the sea to
spawn in the protected gravel beds of the main stream and
tributaries. Unlike the Pacific salmon, most survive the
spawning ordeal and return to the sea. They are followed in
time by the fingerlings, though some may remain for their
life span in a river that is rich in food. But the vast majority
of the Deschutes River rainbow are resident, as are most of
their progeny, and some of these grow almost as great as
the silvered wanderers from the ocean.

Steelhead from six to twenty pounds are taken on wet flies,

as they are in the Rogue and Umpqua rivers, and with spinners, plugs, and bait close to the mouth of the Deschutes
and for sixty miles upstream. A record twenty-eight-pounder
was beached in 1946. But dry fly fishing for resident rainbow
is the sport that has made the Deschutes one of the most
popular trout streams of the West, despite its forbidding terrain, its snakes, ticks, and poisonous shrubs, and its moody
behavior.

There are times when the big fish rise in the Deschutes
in ravenous abandon, and unskilled anglers make fabulous
catches. These periods of intense activity usually are in afternoon or evening, though often there is a good morning
rise in the heat of summer. The Deschutes is not always pre-
dictable and has broken the hearts of fishermen who have
not learned its ways. Sometimes the best of anglers, old-
timers on the river, will not raise a fish all day, though conditions seem favorable.

The Deschutes is at its magnificent peak in years when
the snow runoff in the mountains is normal and the Crooked
River behaves itself, from early in May until the end of
June. The hellgrammites of the big salmon fly crawl out
from under their submerged stones and onto the alder and
willow branches, and, warmed by the sun, soar off in uncertain flight. Some fall into the stream in pairs. Then the rainbow lie close in to shore, under the overhang of brush and
occasional trees, sometimes in fast water so shallow that their
dorsal fins show above the surface. A smart angler will work
cagily upstream, making use of what cover is available, and
always casting first as close to the edge of the water as he
can without fouling his fly, thereafter working outward until

he has covered the run to the edge of heavy water. Often he
will see a great trout rise lazily to the surface to gulp a drift-
ing salmon fly. He will give that trout a minute or two or
longer, then duplicate the fall and drift of the natural insect
with a high-floating bucktail caddis. The strike sometimes is
casual, sometimes vicious, but always the fight is terrific, for
these rainbow of the Deschutes are heavy and as powerful
and lively as the river itself. They are great aerialists.

The common fault of fishermen not familiar with the
feeding habits of the Deschutes rainbow or the peculiar nature of the stream, is to overcast feeding trout. They clamber
down the rocky shore to the edge of the stream, driving the
fish into the depths, and cast far out on the profitless current.
No great ability as a caster is required on the Deschutes, except in the department of placing the fly gently on the water
and permitting it to drift naturally on the surface. Women
and children who know this primary principle often are as
successful as more experienced male companions.

July and August are dead months on the Deschutes for
the dry fly fisherman, though there are magnificent exceptions. September is tricky, but often the fish rise hungrily,
smashing at tiny, light-patterned flies with more power and
seeming anger than in the spring, and fighting harder and
longer. In September the rainbow are at the peak of condition. There are no spawners, those dark fish which one sometimes catches and releases early in the season. The trout
have fattened on insects in the summer and their flavor is
superior.

September, besides, is a grand month in which to fish the
canyon. There is a touch of fall in the air. The nights are
cool and the warming sun of midday is welcome. Poison oak

is less infectious, the ticks are in hibernation, and snakes are
not so commonly encountered.

Bait and spinner fishermen do well on the Deschutes when
cold weather nips the bug hatches, or Crooked River goes on
a rampage after an Ochoco forest rain and dirties the main
river. (Someone should get the government to build a mud-
control project on the pestiferous Crooked River, which has
ruined many a Deschutes trip.) Sometimes nymphs and wet
flies are effective—as in May and June of 1948, when an
unusually big runoff of snow contributed a share to the
Columbia River flood which wiped out Vanport City. But
season for season, the dry fly will take more trout and bigger
fish if reasonably well handled.

There is a stranger in the Deschutes—the brown trout of
Europe, the same that brought back angling in many an
eastern stream after the native brook trout were depleted.
The brown is not so highly regarded in Oregon and Washington as the rainbow, steelhead, and cutthroat, but nonetheless, he is a formidable opponent. His rapid rate of
growth, willingness to hit a fly—or anything else, for that
matter—and fighting heart have earned him a place in certain lakes and streams of the Cascades. The Oregon Game
Commission made a mistake, however, when it introduced
the brown to the Deschutes.

Original plantings of brown trout were in quiet waters
above Bend, but the adaptable migrant has moved downstream and up. Some persons think he will in time take over
the entire river. If his raiding habits destroy the rainbow,
Oregon will have lost an irreplaceable asset. No other stream
of the Cascades has so much natural food, nor so much water
providing trout havens which cannot be reached by fisher-

men, as the Deschutes. Fishing from boats has been banned
below Bend, but the brown trout may be as destructive as
anglers afloat.

STEELHEAD IN THE SUNSHINE

The world-wide fame of the Rogue and Umpqua rivers
of southern Oregon, as greenly inviting in their mountain
and valley borders as the Deschutes is grim and forbidding,
has been built on the steelhead. To many, this is the trout
supreme, and in those rivers he rises to the skillfully placed
wet fly with all the power and savagery acquired in his
battle for survival in the perilous Pacific.

There is never-ending campfire argument over the reason
a steelhead hits a fly, but frequent agreement that it is not
usually because of his hunger during his purposeful ascent
from the sea to the gravel beds high in the Cascades where
the spawning mission is completed. Movement of the fly and
testiness of the giant trout have something to do with it.

There are variations in technique, but the usual and most
profitable method of taking steelhead on a fly is to quarter
the cast out and downstream and to bring the fly across and
around to the near shore, and retrieve for another cast
through the same water; then to move downstream two or
three steps, and repeat. Frequently, the terrific strike will
come when the submerged fly has reached the limit of its
downstream sweep; sometimes, when the fly is dragging
across the current toward the near shore. It is wise to retrieve
in fox-trot rhythm, with adequate pauses to intrigue a wary
fish that may have followed the fly from midstream.

There are long runs on the Eel and Klamath rivers of
northern California and the Rogue and Umpqua of southern

Oregon in which a line of anglers will pace down through a run, keeping their places and moving along like so many robots. It is a kind of fishing so alien to the delicate placing of a dry fly over feeding rainbow that some sensitive souls cannot support it. But there is no greater thrill than that derived from the smashing strike of a steelhead and the strength and courage of his fight.

A reasonably experienced angler can handle Rogue and Umpqua steelhead (which range in weight from two pounds to twenty-two pounds) with a 6-ounce, 9- or 9½-foot fly rod that has plenty of backbone, rigged with a heavy double-taper or torpedo line of standard thirty yards length, plus one hundred yards of backing line, and a leader tested for four pounds and upward (depending on how clear the water may be). That is, he can handle some of them, if he remembers to give his monster plenty of the butt—making the fish fight the entire rod—and if the steelhead can be persuaded not to return to the Pacific.

Sometimes it is necessary to follow a big one downstream for hundreds of yards, if the terrain permits it, fighting to turn him at every pool. An agile angler has an advantage, and this is no sport for a man with a bad heart.

Big flies, tied on size-six and size-four hooks, in bright patterns over silver and gold bodies, are the steelhead killers. Every veteran has his favorites. Some of the best have been worked out by those who live along the steelhead rivers, or who have made a career of fishing them. Streamers and bucktails are popular, and jungle cock feathers are particularly enticing to the Pacific rainbow. The fish are partial to gray, green, and brown patterns when the May flies are hatching. At other times the Royal Coachman, Professor,

Jock Scott, and such old favorites will hold their own with
the local developments like the red-bodied, red-and-white
hair-winged Umpqua Special.

The Rogue and Umpqua, in which steelhead may be
caught roughly from July through October on artificial flies,
are easily accessible by highway, train, and plane for much
of their distances The angling pressure is severe. Some of
the best stretches have in effect been closed to general angling
by the purchase of adjoining property by wealthy sportsmen and others. But National Forest lands are open. Writers
enamored of the steelhead have been prone to grow lyri-
cal about these streams. Game Commission studies, however, reveal serious depletion of the steelhead runs, attrib-
utable to overfishing and in the Rogue to unscreened turbines
and irrigation ditches. The Oregon Game Commission now
operates its own screen manufacturing plant in Jackson
County and is making progress in stopping the waste of fish
on agricultural lands—a loss that once canceled the gains
in production from sixteen hatcheries.

Tremendous war and postwar increases in population on
the West Coast have more than doubled the angling and
hunting demands. Both the Oregon and Washington Com-
missions face a tremendous struggle, with inadequate financ-
ing from license revenues, even to maintain the present
resources in fish and game.

The West has been profligate with its wildlife, and only
recently has there been growing among the bulk of anglers
and hunters the understanding that big bags are history. The
great game fish of the Pacific, the steelhead, is a trophy not
to be killed in numbers. But the difficulty in taking one or
two of these fish, the real test of angling skill and patience,

has so enhanced the steelhead's importance among the fraternity that more and more fishermen seek his capture.

One should think of the steelhead as an individual opponent, a trophy of great worth, as a hunter thinks of a bull elk or mule deer.

The French gave the Rogue its name, "La Rivière aux Coquins," because of the nasty dispositions of the Indians who lived on its shores, and the Umpqua took its name from another Indian tribe. The forks of the Rogue rise high in the Cascades, the middle finger in Boundary Springs near the border of Crater Lake National Park. In the forks above Cascade Gorge, into which the river plunges with spectacular abandon, the resident rainbow trout are partial to the dry fly. Below the gorge and for 150 miles to the Pacific, the seagoing rainbow and cutthroat trout and the Chinook and silverside salmon make their pilgrimages. The cutthroat are not there in the numbers of old, but there are lunkers to be had when conditions are favorable. Sometimes a single egg in a deep eddy will produce surprising results. The salmon are particularly susceptible to spinner, wobbler, and plug.

A fifty-mile boat trip through the canyon wilderness of the lower Rogue, starting below Grants Pass and ending at Gold Beach or thereabouts, when the steelhead and salmon are running, is likely to set taciturn fishermen to babbling like a four-year-old with his first trout. There are no roads, no habitations to speak of. There are virgin forests and deer on the ridges. There are no lines of robot anglers, elbowing one another, hence one has leisure to fish as one wills. It is a trip many save for, and few complete. But a tip to the stranger: Be sure of your boatman.

The Umpqua, springing from the snow meadows south of fabulous Diamond Lake, traverses wilderness in its upper reaches. There are giant native rainbow for many miles in canyon pools accessible only by trails suitable to hikers and riders. The guardian cliffs enclose the river, so that a fisherman too often must climb laboriously hundreds of feet to open up another stretch of a hundred yards of rarely visited water. The Umpqua National Forest enfolds all, and the curious deer pass through camp to reach the river.

Great falls block the upward migration of the anadromous fish, and for miles below they are spent but busy at their spawning. When one comes out of this charming land by horseback at the Perry Wright ranch, above Steamboat Creek, he is back in steelhead waters, and as he passes downstream by highway the salmon fishing gets better.

Much of the attraction of the Umpqua and Rogue lies in the variety of fishing, the length of seasons, and the remarkably fine weather of summer, fall, and winter. Farther to the north, steelhead fishermen work the streams running into the Pacific from the Coast Range with gobs of salmon eggs and spinners, in rain and sleet and snow; in southern Oregon, lightly clad anglers cast for steelhead with flies in the sunshine. But the northern winter fish are heavier and stronger, on the average, and they too can be taken on a fly rod, if seldom with a fly.

A FAMILY RIVER

The greatest stream of the Oregon Cascades, and the largest river wholly within Oregon, is the Willamette. Its middle fork comes out of Summit Lake and runs down through pine timber past Oakridge, to border the Southern Pacific's main Portland–San Francisco line and the trans-Cascade highway linking Eugene and Klamath Falls.

It picks up numerous creeks and rivers, including fishable Salt and Salmon creeks, the North Fork of the Willamette which follows tortuous canyons out of Waldo Lake, the Coast Fork above Springfield, and the famed McKenzie below Springfield. In the hundred-mile flow north through the fertile Willamette Valley to a junction with the great river of the West, the Columbia, ten miles north of Portland, the Willamette is joined by other Cascade mountain rivers swelled by glacial discharges from towering Mount Jefferson, the Three Sisters, and Mount Hood: the North and South Santiam, the Clackamas, Molalla, Pudding, and their tributaries.

The Willamette is a family river, from its parent lakes to the Portland city limits where thousands of skiffs, cruisers, and yachts patrol the channels in March, April, and May, trolling for the giant spring Chinook, finest of the Pacific salmon. In its lower reaches, children and adult newcomers from the South and Middle West dangle for catfish, perch, and crappies, and cast for large-mouth bass.

Above Eugene, the rainbow take over. The Middle Fork of the Willamette, above Oakridge, is bordered by the green pines and firs of the Willamette National Forest. Forest camps, some with shelters, provide handy family camp sites. There are mountain meadows choked with wild flowers and sweet wild strawberries. The trout are heavy and active, and rise to the fly from May through September, with varying degrees of enthusiasm. At the approach of fall, big rainbow as fat as lake trout and much more lively show their interest in a stone fly, fished wet, both above and below Oakridge.

The McKenzie is another story. This is the habitat of the famous McKenzie river "redside," a compact and active rainbow particular in his feeding habits, difficult to fool, and marvelous to eat. The river is hard to fish afoot. Its best runs are protected by brush and trees. The clear water is a handicap to inexpert casters.

Fishing from boats is permitted in water almost inaccessible to wading anglers. Members of the McKenzie River Guides' Association—sponsor of a "white water parade" of boats each spring before opening of the trout season—will take the responsibility, for a fair price, of getting anglers through Martin Rapids and other tempestuous stretches of the twenty-mile run from Redsides to Leaburg Reservoir. The guides have developed a rough-water boat distinctive in the McKenzie, high prowed and high sterned, which is the safest means of transportation on that fast and rugged stream.

The McKenzie guides will not take "meat fishermen"— the users of salmon eggs and other bait—and have such a low opinion of hardware fishermen that they will consent to the use of spinners with the greatest reluctance, if at all. This is a splendid river for the dry fly, and the guides hope to keep it that way. The stream is restocked from hatcheries using native trout. A boat trip through the McKenzie rapids is an experience in itself. The fighting redsides make it so much fun that it must be sinful.

Other major streams flowing west from the Cascades to join the Willamette provide fair fishing, at intervals, but in no way compare with the McKenzie and upper Willamette. There are several reasons. One is overfishing, for they are nearer the Portland metropolitan area. Another is obstructions: the power company dams with inadequate fishways and open turbines on the Clackamas—once a great salmon, steelhead, and cutthroat stream—and the new government dams building on the North and South Santiam rivers. A third is the heavy runoff of snow water which scours the river bottoms of marine life, limiting the number of resident trout. Rainbow planted in the Clackamas go out to sea, to return, if they can hurdle the dams, as steelhead. A fourth is pollution of the lower Willamette—a desecration to be corrected by new sewage-disposal systems in Portland and other cities —which has taken as great toll as the dams of the anadromous fingerlings seeking the Pacific.

The Sandy River, a Columbia tributary at Portland's eastern doorstep, and the Cowlitz River across the Columbia in Washington, are the food meccas for dipnetters when the smelt come in from the sea on the spring freshets. Once the Sandy was a good trout and salmon stream, and progress has been made toward bringing it back. But recovery is slight, and each year more fishermen come.

FROM MOUNTAINS TO SOUND

The state of Washington, like Oregon, is blessed with tremendous angling resources in Cascade lakes and rivers. It has, besides, its vast food basket, Puget Sound, the front yard of Olympia, Tacoma, Seattle, Everett, and Bellingham, and the great seabound wilderness area of the Olympic peninsula with its superlative trout and salmon streams: the Quinault, Queets, Clearwater, Hoh, Soleduck, Bogachiel, Elwha, Hamahama and others with names equally fascinating.

The Sound itself is so great an attraction to trollers and spinning reel casters that for many years the streams which flow out of the Cascades were fished but lightly. Washington anglers turned first to the Sound or to the mighty Columbia or to the lower reaches of the tributary rivers where great schools of king salmon (the northern Chinook), silversides, steelhead, and cutthroat once fought upstream to the spawning beds. Times there have changed, too. Road builders have opened mountain streams and lakes. Trails have been improved into the wild back country. The population has spurted. And the angling pressure is on, everywhere. The white-capped Cascades beckon the fisherman into the green foothills where the native and imported trout lie in shaded pools.

At Packwood, on the Cowlitz, one can hire horses to leave the Pacific highway which borders the lower river for miles, for a trip into the solitude of its upper reaches. There, the big cutthroat idle, with resident rainbow, before returning to the sea—the orange slashes which give them their name brightened to flame, and the spots showing dark and bold. This large river flows west and south to join the Columbia at Longview. Like the Willamette, it has a run of great spring Chinook. Anglers are reported to have taken them up to seventy pounds, and the average is about twenty-five pounds. There is year-round fishing for steelhead, fall Chinooks and silvers, and big cutthroat.

Some of these Washington tributaries of the Columbia have excellent runs of summer steelhead. Among the best are the Kalama and Wind rivers. In the Kalama, paralleled upstream from the Pacific highway for seventeen miles by a good road, summer steelhead sometimes will strike a wet fly as readily as those in the Rogue, and they are bigger fish. The best fly fishing for steelhead is in July and August, and for cutthroat and rainbow trout from July to September. Boat fishing on the lower river is excellent from the end of February to June, and again in September and October.

Wind River crosses the north bank highway at Carson, fifty-five miles east of Vancouver. Fly fishing for summer steelhead starts in June and lasts through the season, when roily water does not make it necessary to resort to spinners and roe. There are rainbow, cutthroat, and eastern brook in the upper reaches and tributaries.

A road which climbs out of the Wind River canyon ten miles from Carson traverses lava beds and passes such lakes as Goose, Forlorn, Blue, and Indian Heaven. A fork of this road opens another lake basin which includes Steamboat Lake and extends to the north fork of the Lewis River, while the Guler Fork reaches the White Salmon River and returns to the north-bank highway. It is surprising and delightful country, well worth a few days of leisurely exploration.

There is similarly a good balance between the anadromous and the resident fish in the Klickitat and the Little Klickitat, the Washougal, the Lewis, and other mountain-fed streams entering the great river of the West. There is a reason for the fine runs of sea trout and salmon on the Washington shore. In 1935 the traps, seines, and fish wheels which had been indiscriminately scooping out brood trout, steelhead, and salmon since the beginnings of the commercial fishery in 1853, were banned from the Washington side of the Columbia's channel by vote of the people. Stream fishing improved, despite an increase in anglers, in the years that followed. Oregon voted out the destructive fish wheels in 1927, but not until 1948 did the people banish traps and seines. Better escapement of the spawners from the Pacific may be expected if these measures shall be followed, as conservationists insist, by careful enforcement of gill net mesh laws and seasonal restrictions.

Washington has no such river as Oregon's Willamette, flowing from south to north across half the state, to intercept the Cascade streams rushing toward the sunset. The Coast Range which forces the Willamette northward to the Columbia extends in Washington to the wilderness mountains, the Olympics. When these Cascade rivers have cut through the narrow coastal plain to the salty tidelands, Puget Sound receives them in the region between the city of Olympia and the mighty Fraser River of British Columbia.

But the Snoqualmie and Skykomish rivers, close to populous Seattle and Everett, make the most of their brief journeys from mountains to Sound, joining near Monroe, after tumultuous beginnings in many forks, to become the placid Snohomish.

These are Jekyll and Hyde rivers whose personalities change with the seasons, and in an hour's drive. There is year-round fishing from boats in the sluggish Snohomish, for sea-run cutthroats, steelhead, and salmon. Then for a strip of thirty miles, made accessible by roads and the Sunset Highway, the turbulent, tough main Snoqualmie rises. Below Snoqualmie Falls there is excellent fishing for winter steelhead in January and February, and for cutthroat and rainbow after the river clears somewhat in mid-July. Just east of the town of Snoqualmie, the main river forks to North, Middle, and South—snow-fed mountain streams in which the fly fisherman comes into his own when the cool nights of August and September check the melt. In the North Fork are many rainbow, with a few large ones taken each year; in the Middle Fork, many cutthroat and some rainbow; in the South Fork, smaller rainbow, cutthroat, and eastern brook. In these rivers one can almost name his own time, tackle, and fish.

The other leg of the Snohomish, the Skykomish, as well as its North and South Forks, are in the Snoqualmie's pattern. The South Fork and its tributary Beckler and Rapid rivers are most popular in July, August, and September. They are well stocked with rainbow, from eight to ten inches in length, and a family of fishermen will approach them equipped with flies, eggs, and spinners. A ten-inch rainbow on light tackle in a mountain stream is not to be regarded lightly.

There is a river north of Everett which has gained increasing fame of late for its steelhead. These are summer-run fish and the Washington Game Department has wisely restricted the stream to users of artificial flies. There are rivers enough where the "goofer" fisherman can operate, and few where the "purist" has elbow room. Besides, Washington saw what was happening to Oregon's Rogue and Umpqua rivers.

This river is the North Fork of the Stillaguamish, and the time to be there is between June 15 and September 15. The best fishing is below Oso. Large bucktail flies in bright patterns are the killers.

Dimming trails of the gold hunters follow the northward reaching Skagit River toward the British Columbia border. The city of Seattle has pre-empted much of the upper river for hydroelectric developments. There are long closures above Ross Dam, but one should make the trip, by City Light's railroad, if only to see the tropical forest and gardens that the late James D. Ross left blooming among the glaciers.

There remains good fishing for rainbow, cutthroat, Dolly Varden, whitefish, and summer steelhead in the main Skagit below Ross Dam, and in the Sauk and Suiattle rivers after the first few cool nights in September. A large run of winter steelhead enters the lower Skagit from January to May, and the lower Sauk is noted for steelhead at the tail ends of freshets in January and February. The glacial Suiattle usually is muddy, but it is famed for large rainbow and cutthroat, as well as runs of Chinook and silver salmon.

EASTWARD TO THE COLUMBIA

On the east side of the Washington Cascades there is a land shaped in character both by the bearded mountains and the broad Columbia, as great in opportunity for the angler as for the fruit men who have enriched its valleys and the wheat men who have burnished its plateaus. Beyond the Big Bend of the Columbia, to the north, lies Okanogan County. Okanogan means "rendezvous" in the language of the tribes that gathered for potlatch at Osoyoos Lake on the British Columbia border. Fishermen and big-game hunters rendezvous still in Okanogan and Chelan counties.

Okanogan River, splitting the county from Osoyoos Lake to the Columbia, is not highly regarded by fishermen. It is sluggish, and its principal inhabitants are the spiny rays. But west and south of the Okanogan is the Methow, a large Columbia tributary with many forks and creeks arising in the high mountains. Rainbow in the Methow average longer than ten inches, and there are big Montana spotted cutthroat and sulking Dolly Varden. Some people fish for steelhead and salmon there, but the Methow is too far from the sea for the fish to be in good condition. They should be left alone

Fishing in Mount Rainier National Park.

Rappeling off cliff on Mount Shuksan Mount Baker is seen in distant clouds

Climber protecting party below with a shoulder belay He is guarded by a piton driven into rock crack behind

to spawn. The Methow, easily accessible by road, clears after the spring runoff. The West Fork above Winthrop has several good tributaries—Wolf, Goat, Early Winters, Robinson, and Rattlesnake creeks. Chewack River (the north fork) is almost as good.

The fisherman prospecting southward enters Chelan County, and has wasted his trip if he does not take a launch through the cliff-bound scenic finger of water that thrusts for ninety miles into the heart of the Cascades—Lake Chelan.

This mile-wide, blue-stained scenic nugget, protected by mountains rising to elevations of seven or eight thousand feet, gives one an idea of the relentless power of glacial action. There are cutthroat, rainbow, and silver trout (landlocked blueback salmon) in its depths. Tumultuous Stehekin River, which plunges into the upper end of the lake, attracts many fishermen. In August and September, when the milk has cleared from the stream, there are large rainbow and cutthroat waiting in the main river, and good fishing also in Rainbow, Company, Agnes, and Bridge creeks which may be reached by forest trails. Lake Chelan and the Stehekin fortunately combine their scenic appeal with excellent fishing. There are many such places in the Cascades.

Rainbow and eastern brook in the Entiat River, and rainbow and cutthroat in the usually clear Chiwawa River, average between eight and ten inches and are not, as a rule, particular whether one offers them flies, single eggs, worms, or spinners with bait. Roads and trails lead to good tributaries and lakes.

The Little Wenatchee River forms near the summit of the range, is trapped by beaver dams, and enters Wenatchee Lake. After August 1 one can take both rainbow and cut-

throat on flies in the river. The six-mile lake harbors cutthroat, rainbow, eastern brook, and silvers (landlocked
blueback salmon). The main Wenatchee River, which heads
in the lake and flows sixty miles to enter the Columbia, is
a piscatorial laboratory stocked with cutthroat, rainbow, eastern brook, steelhead, Chinook salmon, Dolly Varden, and
even the famed Kamloops trout from the Fraser River
watershed which have grown to world's record size—thirty-
seven pounds—in Idaho's Pend Oreille Lake but have not
done so well in streams such as the Wenatchee.

Rainbow are the best fish in the Yakima and Naches
rivers, farther south, with some large ones to be expected in
the day's bag. There is a severe drain on the Yakima for
irrigation water for the thirsty orchards of the valley, and
the river is at its best toward the end of the irrigating season, when there is a decrease in the discharge from the
reservoirs. Both streams are fished heavily, since roads parallel their banks.

LAKES FOR THE FUTURE

How can one who has sold his soul to the river sprites,
who is hopelessly fascinated by the lilting ride of a dry fly
in fast water, do justice to the priceless lakes of the Cascades?

Yet these are fulfillment for thousands of anglers today,
as well as the shining promise of the future. Hundreds of
them are in primitive areas of the National Forests, to be
reached only by trail. Many of the greatest producers are
accessible by automobile, with varying degrees of ease. In
their green and blue depths no dams for power, irrigation,
and flood control obstruct the movements of the fish, and

pollution from city sewers and factories is barred forever. Food is abundant, and native rainbow, cutthroat, eastern brook, German brown, Kamloops, Mackinaw, and the lively landlocked blueback salmon, variously called the kokanee, yank, or silver trout, sulk in the depths or, while feeding, dapple the surface with a thousand concentric patterns.

The stranger scarcely can credit the information that only a few years ago most of these volcanic lakes were as barren of fish as the glaciers and snow fields that feed them from springs and rills. The origin of many lakes was so recent, geologically speaking, and outlets so obstructed, that fish life neither developed in their waters nor infiltrated from the rivers that flow to the sea. The explosions of Mount Multnomah, thought to have been a mile higher than the Three Sisters, and of Mount Mazama, together with lesser volcanic action perhaps no longer than three centuries ago, were responsible for the creation of hundreds of lakes. Water gathered in craters of extinct volcanoes, valleys blocked by lava flows, and depressions gouged by glaciers. Some of the mountain lakes have outlets which plunge over precipices too high for fish to clear. Others have no visible outlets. Some have no inlets, no spawning gravel, and are dependent on subterranean springs.

In the great lake wonderland on the eastern slope of the Cascades in Oregon, much of it accessible in summer and early fall via the famed Century Drive from Bend, a fisherman can pass scores of lakes in a day's drive, and can reach hundreds of others by trails. The comparable area in Washington is the Snoqualmie Lake country. Down the backbone of the range run the Cascade Crest Trail in Washington—

531 miles from the Canadian border, through five National Forests, to the Columbia River—and the Skyline Trail in Oregon—400 miles through five forests to the California line. Throughout their length these crest trails are fed by tributary trails from east and west, and beside them lie the lakes, cradled in fir and pine forests and black lava. How many lakes are there? Probably 1,400 at least, though forest service and state agencies seem not to agree on the number.

From a fishing standpoint, Oregon's Diamond Lake should be known as the mother of Cascade lakes, for it was one of the earliest to be stocked and for years has been a major producer of rainbow eggs from which hundreds of other lakes have been planted with the Prime Minister of Cascade trout.

Diamond Lake lies at the eastern end of Douglas County, at an elevation just under one mile, and its 3,000-acre surface extends 3½ miles on the long axis and 1½ miles across. The maximum depth is 52½ feet and the lake is generally shallow. Its outlet forms the North Umpqua River. On all sides rise majestic mountains clothed in deep forest.

The first recorded planting of rainbow fry in Diamond Lake was in 1910. Insect and marine life in abundance, the early-day difficulties of reaching the lake over poor roads, and the short fishing season between snows, encouraged the growth of trout to mammoth size. By the early 1920's Diamond's fame had spread afar. Trout of six and eight pounds were run of the mine, and there is one record of a 27½-pounder. Despite increased fishing pressure after the opening of a paved highway from the east and the improvement of the Diamond Lake extension of the Crater Lake highway from Medford, giant trout still prowl the depths in numbers. A 21¾-pound rainbow was taken by an angler in 1941.

The Oregon Game Commission has operated one of its most successful hatcheries on Diamond Lake for many years, and has maintained a fairly constant stocking policy since 1938. More than 2,000,000 trout fry have been liberated in Diamond each year, except in 1939 and 1943, and the brood trout of Diamond have contributed their offspring to many another Cascade lake. Restocking and control measures, including a five-fish daily bag, legal size limits, season regulations, and restricted areas, have not, however, prevented Diamond from declining in angling rewards and consequently in popularity.

Diamond was low in creel average among four Oregon lakes intensively watched by the Game Commission in the summer of 1948, with 24,693 anglers and 27,872 trout checked. These four lakes—Diamond, East, Paulina, and South Twin—gave up forty-five tons of trout to 67,000 anglers in the one season. In each there was a five-fish daily limit.

There are two ways to look at all this. One can stay at home and mourn the old days, when the United States Forest Service was advertising summer homesites on fifteen-year leases at $10 and $15 a year with glowing accounts of fishing, camping, and hunting: "The legal day's catch is fifty trout or thirty-five pounds." Or one can say, as does one old-timer who has not lost interest, "Things ain't what they used to be, and never was."

It helps to remember that most of the Cascade lakes were barren until stocking operations began. Many of them have no suitable spawning beds and must depend upon man's assistance for maintenance of good fish populations. For a decade or two after fish were introduced into these uninhabited lakes, they prospered marvelously. There were few fishermen and few roads. By the late 1940's the fishing demand more than doubled. But biologists of the state and federal agencies are learning a great deal about fish that was not known before. The lakes have been their finest laboratories.

Scores of lakes have been ruined by fishermen's carelessness. Live bait often is irresistible to big trout. For many years anglers carried buckets of minnows to Cascade lakes. When the day's fishing ended, they dumped the live, unused little roach, chubs, and suckers overside. The survival ability of the reprieved minnows proved greater than that of the trout for which they were intended, and lake after lake became so infested with scrap fish that the competitor trout dwindled in numbers.

South Twin Lake, 130 acres in size, was one of the worst of the scrap fish lakes until 1941 when the Game Commission poisoned all fish in its waters. Between 1941 and 1948 the Commission liberated 11,116 pounds of trout of various sizes in South Twin. Anglers took 32,200 pounds of trout in three seasons after the lake was reopened in 1945. There is no natural reproduction in South Twin, but careful management made it possible for 6,027 anglers to catch 12,525 trout weighing 8,961 pounds in the summer of 1948.

The state of Washington is experimenting with a managed lake program, costly to administer but one promising excellent results. It would involve the periodic poisoning of all fish life—trout with the scrap fish—in selected lakes; closure, restocking, and maintenance of proper fish balances.

Oregon has not gone so far, chiefly because of lack of funds, but the state has achieved some excellent results in selected lakes such as South Twin.

There are lakes hidden in the National Forests of the high Cascades in which perhaps a dozen huge, bottom-feeding rainbow or eastern brook are the sole inhabitants. They do not reproduce their kind, because of the absence of graveled inlets and running water, and they are most difficult to catch. When trout fry are introduced, the grandfather trout have a banquet. From the point of view of the public, these lakes would offer more if the few lunkers were destroyed and a new trout population introduced.

Certain shallow and accessible lakes ideally suited to angling with artificial flies have been restricted to that lure, both in Oregon and Washington. In them it is easier to control the roach by seining, or to keep trash fish out entirely after poisoning. There are so many lakes in the two states that no reasonable objection can be raised to reserving a few of them to those anglers who find their greatest enjoyment in fly fishing.

Two famous lakes in the Deschutes country of central Oregon are Paulina and East lakes, nestled in Newberry Crater east of Lapine. Thousands of limit catches are taken from these waters each season: eastern brook, rainbow, and brown trout. Trollers and still fishermen have unusually good luck, but when the big trout are feeding on the surface in the late summer there is superlative fly fishing There are giant Mackinaw trout in the depths. When Game Commission employees find them in the shallows they net them and transport them alive to the Deschutes River, for the Mackinaw raise hob with fingerlings.

Paulina and East lakes were barren until a party of central Oregon sportsmen packed in fish fry on their backs many years ago. The natural food and chemical content of the water proved to be ideal for the growth of trout of all kinds, and the state soon came to recognize the value of such a fishery. In 1939, only 1,612 anglers were checked at Paulina. In 1948, there were 14,168 anglers. If one accepts the Fish and Wildlife Service's figure of the value of trout caught—$5 a pound—the 65,700 trout taken in the summer of 1948 from Paulina and East lakes, averaging about one pound, were worth $328,500.

In the lake country of Washington's Snoqualmie National Forest, in an area encompassed largely by contiguous King, Chelan, and Kittitas counties, there are 700 fishable lakes of all sizes and shapes, some accessible by good roads from Stevens Pass and Snoqualmie Pass, others by trails.

Many of these Washington lakes, more recently stocked than central and southern Oregon waters, have been managed with care and are excellent producers. The Snoqualmie lake country extends roughly from Trout Lake in the north to Keechelus, Kachess, and Cle Elum reservoirs in the south, and for thirty miles east and west. Keechelus is typical of the larger waters. There is a run of silvers starting about May 15, with the best fishing in June and July. Cutthroat, rainbow, eastern brook, and Montana black-spotted trout offer the angler good variety in a day's bag.

Cascade lakes in the high country, far from highways and forest roads, originally were stocked from back packs or mule trains. Both Oregon and Washington have been using airplanes in recent years for some of this high lake planting. A small plane equipped with a belly tank of fingerlings dips down to an opening in the forest, skims over the lake, pulls up sharply as the release is made, and circles for altitude as the young fish pelt the surface. The survival audited by field men has been high.

These are the lakes, the rivers, the creeks of the great Cascades, protected by the National Forests and assured a limitless supply of water from the glaciers and snow fields so long as the forests themselves are protected.

The thin, far cries of coyotes defying the dawning day came from the sage lands over the eastward hills. A canyon bat, out all night and obviously in a vile mood, beat directly across the shining river and plunged into a thicket. Salmon flies stirred sluggishly on the lower branches of the willows. Smoke from the campfire drifted lazily in acrid unity with the odor of boiling coffee.

Not one of the three, gulping the hot cakes and eggs, missed the deep "kachunk" from the eddy above the camp. They stood quietly, backs to the fire in the chill dawn, and watched. The trout rose again, this time rolling on the surface. It looked like a rainbow, a sixteen-incher or better. The men turned, for this was a ritual, and each drew from his pocket a two-bit piece. Wordlessly, they matched. The head had it.

The winner tied a soaked leader on the tapered line strung the night before on the nine-foot rod, attached a fly and greased it with Mucilin. As the others watched, munching reflectively, he waded carefully into the icy water and cast upstream into the eddy.

MOUNTAINEERING

by Grant McConnell

When, in the fall of 1845, Joel Palmer arrived at The Dalles on his way westward, he found he was a latecomer. Many settlers' wagons were before him, and the little frontier community was crowded with families waiting for a chance to go down through the Columbia River Gorge. Oxen could draw their heavy loads no farther along the route of the great river. The first of the Cascade foothills rose just a short distance ahead, and beyond it there was a succession of cliffs and rockslides descending into the river. The boats, which were the only means of finishing the last tantalizing stretch of the westward journey, were too few for the needs of the caravans which were arriving in rapidly growing numbers. The boat operators were taking advantage of the situation by charging exorbitant prices for their services. The most dismaying thing to Palmer, however, was the prospect of a long wait when the season was already late.

He soon learned that another party just ahead of him had decided to break a new wagon route through the mountains and was then on its way westward around the south side of Mount Hood. Persuading a few families to follow him, Palmer set out on the tracks of this party. The route he followed was not entirely new. There were an Indian

337

trail and a stock trail in the general area. No wagons, though, had ever attempted the crossing. Within a week Palmer caught up with the advance party where it was at work cutting a road through the dense forest.

The advance party's leader, Samuel Barlow, whose story has already been told, had no real knowledge of the route he was attempting, yet he was sure there was a pass somewhere ahead. Joel Palmer and two other men therefore decided to make a scouting trip on the upper slopes of Mount Hood. Leaving the others, they went up the wide boulder-strewn canyon of the White River, a turbid glacial stream. They reached timber line and then crossed the broad southern face of the mountain. They met a group which had been sent ahead with the cattle, but as there was no indication of a route possible for wagons, Palmer and his two companions decided to go higher up the mountain for a better view.

They soon encountered snow, and the men with Palmer became discouraged and stopped. Palmer, however, was more determined and continued up the strange slope. Several times he had difficulty with deep crevasses, so it is likely that he had ventured onto the Zigzag Glacier which lies on the southwest side of the mountain. This glacier is neither very steep nor badly broken, but for a man wearing moccasins and with no experience of the high mountains, it could not have been easy to cross. Palmer by his own story went about a third of the distance from timber line to the summit. From his high point he looked down and saw the pass which he and Barlow had hoped to find. Looking up toward the peak, he reached the sound (but then not too well accepted) conclusion that it could be climbed.

Joel Palmer's reconnaissance from the side of Mount Hood was one of the most remarkable features of the establishment of the Barlow Road. It was one of the earliest trips by white men to the high regions of the Cascades. Even today when mountaineering is a popular activity, there are many people who find something fearful and mysterious about snow that lasts the year around. In Palmer's day little was known about the high mountains of America, and he, moreover, was a farmer from the flat lands of Indiana. Yet he managed to go well up the side of Mount Hood and to come away with an astonishingly accurate idea of the scale of the mountain. He estimated the distance from timber line to the summit as three miles, and the height of the topmost cliffs as several thousand feet. Both estimates were close to the truth.

PATHS TO GLORY

Although Joel Palmer did go high on the mountain, he was, after all, on a mission not an adventure. Mount Hood was for him only a view point from which to discover the pass for his wagons. By contrast, meet Thomas J. Dryer, owner and editor of the *Weekly Oregonian* and mountaineer extraordinary. An exponent of the rugged type of frontier journalism so well described by Mark Twain, he issued thundering editorials from his little office in Portland and held forth on the splendors of the region of which the big volcanoes on the horizon were conspicuous examples. In August, 1853, he set out with a party to make the conquest of Mount Saint Helens. His party succeeded in reaching the summit and he brought back this harrowing account:

"The higher we ascended the more difficult our progress.

Suffice it to say that, by constant and persevering effort, we were enabled to reach the highest pinnacle of the mountain soon after meridian. The atmosphere produced a singular affect [sic] upon all the party, each face looked pale and sallow, and all complained of a strange ringing in the ears. It appeared as if there were hundreds of fine-toned bells jingling all around us. Blood started from our noses and all of us found respiration difficult."

While Dryer's climb of Mount Saint Helens is generally accepted as a valid first ascent, the story of the climb has some interesting features. Saint Helens has nothing either on its sides or on its summit that could fairly be described as a "pinnacle." The topmost point is only a rounded area slightly above the rest of the long curving rim of the glacier-filled crater. As for the trouble in breathing, it is clear that the members of the party were bothered by a touch of mountain sickness, a common phenomenon to climbers who are either in poor condition or who try to go too fast. The usual symptoms are nausea and giddiness. The fine-toned bells which the party heard on Saint Helens were either the wind or the art of Dryer's journalistic style. The bleeding which occurred on the expedition was probably suffered more in retrospect than at the time. Early accounts of mountain exploration in the Alps are filled with stories of nosebleeds and similar sufferings. It may be that Dryer felt obliged to add this detail to make his climb convincing. Certainly Dryer was fortunate in being no more familiar with the stories of the Alps than he was, for he might have encountered cousins of the dragons which early writers found in Switzerland.

In the year following his ascent of Mount Saint Helens, Dryer climbed Mount Hood. Ignoring the easy slopes of

the mountain's south face, he went up the much steeper
ridge to the east of White River Glacier. For a long time
after Dryer's climb no one followed this route, and many
climbers believed it to be impossible. This belief, in fact, was
the basis for some of the doubt that has been thrown upon
Dryer's story. Today, however, there is an established route
up this ridge and it is used frequently. On the climb, the
rarefied air again played havoc with Dryer's party. Three
of the six climbers were compelled to stop. It was apparently
the steepness of the climb that was too much for one of them.
Dryer said that the slope had a pitch of 70.5 degrees. This
would have been a veritable cliff, since most slopes of more
than forty-five degrees appear to be vertical. A fourth member of the party, an Indian guide, was stopped at the head
of the big slope by a whiff of the fumes from the sulphur
vents there. Dryer and a companion named Wells Lake
went on to the summit.

At the top Dryer conducted observations with which he
calculated that Mount Hood was 18,361 feet high. His
figures are not available, but he did report that the data he
used included the latitude and the average thickness of snow
on volcanic peaks in different seasons at various elevations.
He invoked the name of Humboldt to certify the method.
At any rate he arrived at something other than a round
number.

Owing perhaps to the nature of his personality and the
accident of a rivalry with his business successor, Dryer has
not generally been given credit for the first ascent of Mount
Hood. Henry L. Pittock, who acquired Dryer's paper under circumstances which suggest the possibility of ill feeling,
led a party to the top in August, 1857. From the details of

Pittock's account, there can be little doubt that his group did reach the top. He noted the narrow ridge-like quality of the summit, the awesome drop on the north side, and the magnificent view of Rainier, Saint Helens, and Adams, all features which are familiar to the thousands who have since followed Pittock's route. Pittock, however, claimed to doubt that Dryer had ever reached the summit. Although Pittock deserves credit for an original climb on the mountain, he scarcely had grounds for denying Dryer's claim to the first ascent.

Mount Hood was the scene of a really horrendous adventure in this same period. A party led by a certain Belden made an assault on the mountain. This is the account of the climb: "They ascended as high as they could travel, first with snow shoes, then with *ice-hooks* and *spikes*. When they had reached some 18,000 feet high, respiration became very difficult, owing to the rarity of the atmosphere. At length, the blood began to ooze through the pores of the skin like drops of sweat, their eyes began to bleed, the blood rushed from their ears." There is nothing in all the annals of Himalayan mountaineering to compare with this gory ascent, and it is astonishing that Belden found Mount Hood to be only 19,400 feet high.

The altitude of Hood was brought down to 11,225 feet by the report of a surveying party in 1867. There may or may not be any significance in the fact that this was also the year in which the mountain was first climbed by women.

THE TOP OF THE RANGE

The fifties also saw the first mountaineering activity in other parts of the range. Mount Shasta was climbed by E.

A. Pearce in 1854, the same year that Mount Adams was first climbed. There was a serious attempt to climb Rainier during this decade. An army officer, Lieutenant A. V. Kautz, felt the challenge of the great mountain as he looked across the gravelly prairies near his post at Fort Steilacoom. In the summer of 1857 he persuaded the camp doctor to join him in a climb. Kautz apparently had some idea of the problem facing him, for he took considerable pains with his equipment:

"I made preparations after the best authorities I could find, from reading accounts of the ascent of Mont Blanc and other snowy mountains. We made for each member of the party an *alpenstock* of dry ash with iron point. We sewed upon our shoes an extra sole, through which were driven four-penny nails with the points broken off and the heads inside. We took with us a rope about fifty feet long, a hatchet, a thermometer, plenty of hard biscuit and dried beef such as the Indians prepare."

On July 8, Kautz and his party set out. They followed the valley of the Nisqually and went through miles of dense timber and luxuriant undergrowth. Frequently there were areas where the fallen timber reduced their pace to a literal crawl. The Indian guides were reluctant to approach the mountain, for in common with many primitive people they were afraid of mountains, which they thought to be peopled with spirits. However, Kautz and his companions succeeded in reaching the southwestern side of the mountain.

"Our camp was at the foot of a mountain spur several thousand feet high, and the river close at hand. The gloomy forest, the wild mountain scenery, the roaring of the river, and the dark overhanging clouds, with the peculiar melan-

choly sighing which the wind makes through a fir forest gave
to our camp at this point an awful grandeur."

There are few areas more deceptive to the inexperienced
eye than the high mountains. The scale of distance and
height, the strange landscape of snow and ice, the absence
of trees, and above all the extraordinary clarity of the air,
give false impressions of the magnitude of the big peaks.
There is a story of a tourist who was taken to a hilltop above
Paradise Valley for a view of Mount Rainier. When the
mountain suddenly came into view in all its magnificence,
the tourist glanced at it and kept on walking. His disappointed host asked where he was going. "I thought I'd go
on to that snow-covered point over there," was the answer.
His objective was the summit of Rainier itself, eight thousand feet above. Kautz made the same kind of error, for he
was certain that from his final camp near the last stunted
pines he could reach the top in three hours.

Kautz did not get to the summit, though he was himself
satisfied with his attempt. He confessed that there were
higher points above him, but from his turning point
". . . the mountain spread out comparatively flat." Certainly Kautz should be given credit for a splendid try. The
mountain was just a lot bigger than he thought.

The recognized first ascent of Mount Rainier was made
in 1870 by Hazard Stevens and P. V. Van Trump. With
them on their approach to the mountain were an Englishman, Edward T. Coleman, and a guide. The latter, a
Yakima Indian named Sluiskin, was thoroughly skeptical
about the venture. However, for the sake of the pay—and
perhaps for a good laugh—he took the climbers over the
finest obstacle course he could devise. He warned his clients

about the folly of their intention, pointing out that the mountain was the home of evil and that they could never hope to return if they went onto its slopes. However, the climbers were persistent, and Sluiskin led them in and out, up and down and around the rugged heights of the little Tatoosh Range. Coleman, the only experienced mountaineer in the party, played out under the treatment. Stevens and Van Trump at last arrived at the head of Mazama Ridge, a small spur that joins the body of the mountain. Here, at last, Sluiskin saw that they were in earnest and tried eloquently to dissuade them from throwing their lives away. Recalling Sluiskin's harangue in later years, Stevens wrote out a free translation which suggests that the climbers must have been shaken by it. However, their purpose held, and leaving the already mourning Sluiskin to wait a promised three days before reporting their deaths in the lowlands, they went onto the mountain.

The route followed by Stevens and Van Trump was one which for some perverse reason became the principal trail up the mountain during the next seven decades. It led up over simple glacial slopes to the base of the great cliff now known as Gibraltar Rock. There are many mountaineers today who can remember the passage that came next. It was on a ledge that angled across the face of the rock. The ledge was certainly wide enough for walking, but on the left there was an exhilarating drop of many hundred feet to the broken surface of the Nisqually Glacier. There was nothing difficult about the passage; you just walked along it. However, the whole of Gibraltar Rock was rotten; seldom has a feature of any mountain been so poorly named. At any moment cascades of rocks ranging from the size of a pea to that of a piano could come crashing down on the ledge, and there was no refuge anywhere along its length. Local accounts later said that the cliff was held together only by the ice that clung to its face. Natives warned newcomers to time their trip so that the descent past Gibraltar should be made before eleven in the morning, since later in the day the sun would play on the cliff and thaw the ice. Although many parties went up this way, few succeeded in getting down before morning was past. Since Gibraltar continued its bombardment day and night, the warning served only to cause some very early risings and to spoil enjoyment of the view from the summit.

At the end of the ledge there was a short ice "chimney" which gave access to the last long slopes of the upper mountain. From here on, the problem became one of endurance and persistence in threading the maze of big crevasses that seemed to circle the summit. There are crevasses in this gable part of Rainier that are as large as any in the world. Some are wide V-shaped canyons which could swallow whole villages. Others are narrow little slits in the ice; you step across them easily, but as you do so you see beneath you a great dark pit that seems to expand on either side and to be bottomless. Still others are only faintly visible shadows in a smooth snow expanse. These are the blind crevasses; new snow has covered them with a thin insubstantial carpet. They can often be detected more easily from a distance than from nearby. One of the arts of mountaineering lies in the ability to sense these blind crevasses.

Such was the route of the first ascent. The crevasses are to be encountered in any approach, but the promenade around Gibraltar was a very special hazard. Stevens and

Van Trump arrived at the summit at five o'clock in the evening. Wisely deciding not to try to go down that day, they took refuge in one of the steam-heated ice-caves of the summit crater. These caves are formed by fumaroles and have saved the lives of benighted climbers on several other occasions. On their way down the next day, Stevens and Van Trump had difficulty with the ice chimney just before Gibraltar: "At the steepest and most perilous point in descending the steep gutter where we had been forced to cut steps in the ice, we fastened one end of the rope as securely as possible to a projecting rock and lowered ourselves down by it as far as it reached and thereby passed the place with comparative safety. We were forced to abandon the rope here, having no means of unfastening it from the rock above." This primitive rappel (or roping down) underlines the wisdom of having an adequately long rope when climbing any big mountain. With more rope, the two explorers could have doubled it for their descent of the chimney, and recovered it by pulling on one end. Fortunately there was no great need of the rope on the balance of the trip.

The ledge around Gibraltar has now fallen to the surface of the lower Nisqually Glacier and the route is no longer used. This is without doubt the most fortunate change that has occurred on the mountain. Generations of climbers succeeded Stevens and Van Trump on that ledge, and almost every party had some hairbreadth escape from falling rock. Mountaineers make a distinction between danger and difficulty. There may be difficulty without danger and danger without difficulty. The Gibraltar passage was dangerous, yet it offered no challenge to skill. There is now a variety of routes up the mountain, and it is interesting that one of the most popular is approximately that taken by Kautz on his early attempt.

While the ascent of Mount Rainier was accomplished with little of the boasting that accompanied the first attempts on Mount Hood, the claim was stoutly made for a long time that Rainier was the highest point in the nation. Later, however, surveys that were indisputable put Mount Whitney in the Sierra eighty-seven feet higher. Then Mount Elbert and Mount Massive in Colorado were measured and were found to be twenty-three and ten feet higher, respectively. The National Park Service lists Rainier as fourth highest, but now even that claim must be revised since the Coloradans have entered Mount Harvard's elevation as just nine feet higher than Rainier's. Sometimes local enthusiasts simply ignore the claims of other mountains; only recently the statement was made in print that Rainier is "higher than any peak in the Rocky Mountains and the third highest in North America." In the summer of 1948, however, one group decided not only to face facts but to amend them—by building a tower on Rainier's summit that would top Whitney. To the disappointment of this party, Park rangers forbade the undertaking.

CRAFT AND TOOLS

One of the curious facts about the early period of climbing and exploration in the Cascades is that it coincided with a similar period in the Alps. During the middle of the nineteenth century the Alps were invaded by a new type of tourist. He came equipped with rope, rucksack, ice ax, and heavy nailed boots. He set forth with native chamois hunters as guides and climbed nearly all of the big peaks. The Matterhorn, last of the giants, was climbed in 1865. Slowly the superstitions of the mountain inhabitants gave way before the familiarity acquired in company with the tourists. The climbers themselves learned much: how to use the rope, how to pick a route on high peaks, when snow will avalanche, and so on. At first the objective of climbing mountains was scientific. Men wanted to know the air pressure at high altitudes, and how glaciers moved. Then gradually the scientific measurements began to be mere excuses for climbing. Mountaineering developed as an art with its own techniques and its own codes.

For the most part, the first climbs made in the Cascades were the result of an independent impulse; there was little direct contact between American mountaineers and those of Europe. Yet, whether from coincidence or some nebulous element in the cultural atmosphere, the first ventures onto the peaks of the Cascades took place during the time of the golden age of climbing in the Alps. If Lieutenant Kautz' preparatory reading is excepted, the one instance of European influence on early climbing in the Cascades was the ascent of Mount Baker. Edward T. Coleman, who later joined Stevens and Van Trump in the approach to Rainier, attempted in three different years to reach the summit of Mount Baker. He was an Englishman then living in British Columbia. When Coleman finally succeeded in 1868, he paid deference to the touchy nationalism of the Americans by unfurling the Stars and Stripes on the top of Baker.

Coleman came equipped with rope and ice ax, the two symbols of Alpine mountaineering. It is safe to guess that his ice ax was the first to appear in the Cascades. For many years the development of mountaineering in the western

United States went its own course, with climbers learning for themselves the dangers of the mountains and the ways to avoid them. The primary tool was long the alpenstock—more often than not homemade from a broken rake or shovel. Only comparatively recently have Northwest climbers taken to the ice ax, and one may still see parties going up large peaks of the range equipped with (or perhaps impeded by) alpenstocks.

From a technical standpoint, the skills of the western mountaineers lagged behind those of the Europeans. The use of the rope was poorly understood. Often it was either not used at all, or too many climbers were joined together on a short length. At least one fatal accident was the result of the latter mistake. As time went on, the mountaineering desire of many people who lived within sight of the great volcanoes of the range was met by the organization of large parties. These parties, composed of individuals of diverse capacities of endurance, would set forth in the dark hours of early morning and then would slowly and haltingly plod their way upward. Groups of a hundred became common. One on Mount Hood contained over four hundred in a single line. To lead such a mass pilgrimage required as much military as mountaineering skill. There was danger in these large parties. Each additional climber increased the danger of falling rock and ice. Moreover, the large groups went slowly, and a good pace is frequently an essential to safety in the mountains.

Despite the slow development of mountaineering techniques, the peaks continued to be climbed. Although the volcanoes for the most part are not difficult ascents, the accomplishments of the early climbers should not be underrated. Just getting to any of the big mountains was a sizable task. Few roads existed, and it took a long time to go through the jungle-like forests of the western slopes. Climbs which were daring adventures then are today simple, with the use of crampons, heavy spike-studded iron frames which are strapped to the shoes. There are many long steep ice slopes on the glaciers of the volcanic peaks. With modern equipment these slopes are sometimes easy, but often they rank with good ice climbs in the Alps. To go up them, jabbing steps with the point of an alpenstock, could not have been simple.

NEW ROUTES

By the end of the nineteenth century nearly all of the big volcanoes of the Cascades had been climbed at least once. Mount Jefferson was first climbed in 1888 and Glacier Peak in 1898. The only important volcanic peak unclimbed was the North Sister, which remained so until 1910. While Jefferson and the North Sister are more difficult than most of the volcanoes, the reason for the late climbing of all three peaks was their inaccessibility. Even today it is necessary to pack into these mountains by trail.

The advent of the mountaineering clubs brought people into the mountains in large numbers. Climbers were largely limited for many years, however, to visiting the most accessible mountain areas. The forests had few trails, and the existing roads were poor. Just to get to Paradise Valley on Rainier or to Government Camp on Hood—places reached today by hard-surface highways—necessitated something resembling an expedition.

The great prize of mountaineering is always a first ascent.

Until a difficult looking peak is climbed there are usually some doubts that it can be climbed. Though the second and third ascents may be over the same route as the first, they never seem so difficult. There is a psychological hazard in the first attempt that is not present later. Generally the later climbers also have the advantage of knowing something about the successful route. With most of the big volcanoes already climbed, there remained for the new generations of mountaineers only the achievement of taking new routes if they wished the flavor of pioneering. During the early part of the twentieth century this became the objective of leading climbers of the region. New and difficult routes were blazed to the summits of practically all of the volcanic peaks. On Rainier, it is true, an easier and more sensible route than the one past Gibraltar was found on the northeast side. However, the mountain was attacked from all sides, and routes were taken from nearly every direction. There were even climbs on the loose rock of the great Willis Wall.

One of the finest of the new climbs was that of the east face of Mount Adams. C. E. Rusk, who had grown up on a pioneer ranch at the foot of the mountain, organized a party for the attempt in 1921. The east face had always been regarded as the impossible side of the mountain, and probably for this reason, as much as for the deep impression the sight of it had made on him as a child, Rusk was determined to make the climb. The dominant feature of this side of Adams is the Castle, a towering formation of lava which rises out of the broken surface of the Rusk Glacier. The foot of the Castle is separated from the glacier by a bergschrund—a great crevasse whose upper lip overhangs its lower. With difficulty Rusk led his party along the edge of the bergschrund until he came to the rock buttress at the edge of the glacier. Then Rusk took to the steep and rotten rock.

"Telling Coursen to see that I had plenty of rope, as I had to go in a hurry when I started, I made a dash up the first point of rock. I gained some slight advantage from my momentum, and my rapid climbing lessened the danger of the handholds and footholds giving way beneath my weight. I was thus able to get far enough up to grasp the upper projections and draw myself to the top, where I clung, for a time, panting for breath . . . The intermediate steps were passed without great difficulty; but when the last one was reached, a narrow chimney was seen leading up. As there appeared to be considerable danger from loose stones, I cautioned those below to stand well to one side, sheltered as much as possible by projecting points of the cliff. As I climbed up through the chimney, I had to pass directly over the boulder which had lodged in the cleft. When I was fairly on top of it, the rock suddenly gave way. I braced myself desperately from wall to wall across the chasm. The rock went out from under me. Fortunately, it did not catch the rope, and as the rest of the party was sheltered to one side behind the bluff, it crashed harmlessly on to the ice below."

Soon the party was just under the last cliff of the Castle, but it was more than a thousand feet high and composed of loosely cemented rock. First Rusk tried to pass around the south side of the great crag. It would not "go"; the party turned back toward the north across a steep slope of ice and snow. The northern face, however, was as bad as the south. The only thing remaining was a broad chimney

about which Rusk had great misgivings. Nevertheless, the
party went up it. Fortunately the climbers were on the side
of the gully, for during their ascent they heard the clatter
of numerous rockfalls in the main chute. The gully was the
key to the Castle.

Twelve hours had been consumed in the climb of the
Castle, and the summit of Adams was far above. The climbers decided to bivouac in the high col between the Castle
and the body of the mountain. A storm came up, but the next
day was luckily fair and the summit was reached. The "impossible" climb had been made. Several parties have since
repeated it.

BASALT

Thus far most of the climbs in the Cascades had been
made on snow and ice. Volcanic rock is exceedingly poor and
untrustworthy. Solid looking projections that seem to offer
excellent handholds pull out readily, and there is a continual
fall of debris from the cliffs. Snow and ice are more reliable,
and the early climbers quickly learned the wisdom of avoiding the crumbling cliffs of the volcanoes. Where new routes
were made which required rock work, such as that of the east
face of Adams, an element of risk was always present. Thus as
skill with the ice ax and later with crampons was acquired by
the mountaineers of the Northwest, ice climbs of increasing
difficulty were made. Sunshine Trail on Mount Hood and
the eastern ice wall of Mount Jefferson, both climbs of considerable severity, became almost popular.

This was the big distinction between climbing in the Cascades and in the other ranges of the country—between ice
climbing and rock climbing. Most of the other ranges were

deficient in ice; the Cascades were seemingly deficient in good rock. In some parts of the country the new sport of rock climbing was beginning to gain popularity. In the East, climbers practiced on the Palisades along the Hudson and in the granite quarries of New England. Later the sport spread to California, where some remarkable ascents were made on the sheer walls and spires of Yosemite Valley. Paradoxically, many of these climbers came to prefer rock climbing to mountaineering. What had started as a form of training became an end in itself. In the eyes of some, it was as though a musician had come to prefer the playing of scales and finger exercises to the playing of sonatas and quartets.

Those who climbed in the Cascades developed their techniques on ice, which at any rate had the virtue of taking them into the high zones of the real mountains; but they were not immune to the contagious lure of rock climbing. In 1923 a group of boys from the town of Bend startled climbers of the region by announcing the ascents of two dangerous looking volcanic spires, Three Fingered Jack and Mount Washington. These peaks are the most spectacular features of the lake country of the central Oregon Cascades. Many people had admired their slender profiles but few had ever dreamed of trying to climb them. The rock was known to be very poor, and the probable hazard was thought unjustifiable. Nevertheless when the spires had once been climbed, other parties came to repeat the ascents and even to find new and more difficult routes. The rock was poor but not so bad as had been thought, although one experienced mountaineer had a bad fall from the top of the high chimney on Three Fingered Jack.

Along the sides of the Columbia River not many miles

from Portland there are great cliffs of basalt. Basalt is a volcanic rock of considerable hardness but it is seamed with many fine lines, and pieces of it will come out at the slightest touch. Moreover, its surfaces between the cracks are smooth and slippery. In distant geologic times a vast area near the Columbia was spread over by successive flows of this molten rock. These continued until a deposit three thousand feet deep was reached. From the banks of the river the entire depth of this basalt can be seen in cross section on the cliffs above. At several places towers of sheer rock stand out from the cliffs. Once they were connected to the walls of the cliffs but the connections have weathered away. Now and then climbers stopped to inspect these towers, but the appearance of the cliffs was forbidding and the rock proved as unpleasant as it looked. For a long time any attempt to climb on basalt was dismissed as foolhardy and out of the question.

The attempts were made, however. Ray Conway, one of the foremost mountaineers of the region, tried one of the lowest of the towers, Rooster Rock. He found a long slanting fissure in the rock of the southern face which led directly to the summit. Strangely, the slanting route did not require vertical climbing and in fact the climb was not unduly difficult. On other spires, however, convenient transverse chimneys were not available. Rooster Rock was regarded as the only tower whose summit was accessible. Wistfully, climbers looked over the different cliffs for possible routes and then gave up.

The most imposing of the basalt spires is Saint Peter's Dome near Bonneville Dam. Its riverside face rises two thousand feet, half of that height being cliff. The easily ap-

Rappel party on Nisqually Glacier, Mount Rainier

Skiing on Mount Rainier

Sunset on Mount Baker seen from Table Mountain

proached saddle on the opposite side is closer to the summit, but there the cliffs are not only sheer but overhanging. One of the bands of rock of which the tower is formed is harder than those beneath, and there is a perceptible lean outward. Repeatedly, climbers came to the foot of the Dome or to the saddle, took one despairing look, and departed. There was speculation as to what kind of an enterprise would be needed to put somebody on the top. Projects involving blimps and harpoon guns were put forward, but never seriously. One engineer did invent a sectional ladder which he proposed to bolt to the surface of the rock. On attempting it, however, he found that his drills succeeded only in tearing loose great masses of rock.

By 1940, Northwest climbers had learned something about the use of pitons—iron pins that could be driven into cracks in the rock. Pitons had been the key to the difficult Yosemite climbs. When pitons were put into the basalt cracks, however, they had the same effect as the bolts of the ladder-building engineer. Nevertheless, a small determined group of climbers decided to persevere. On four successive week ends this group camped at the saddle and worked on the exposed faces of the Dome. At first they went out onto the awesome west face. Their equipment included ". . . a great assortment of pitons of every type and description, piton hammers, extra heavy sledges for knocking out loose rock, expansion bolts, several hundred feet of rope, padded pants and shoulder protection and plenty of will to succeed." The going was very difficult but one thing was learned—a very short thin piton would stay in basalt without prying off masses of rock. On the first day an advance of forty feet was made. Two men who later served with the

Army's mountain troops, Joe Leuthold and Eldon Metzger, alternated in leading the attempt to force the passage. They came back on the following week end and returned to the west face. This time a total progress of fifteen feet was made. Metzger succeeded in advancing over an overhang to a ledge several inches wide. However the ledge merged into the cliff directly beneath a large overhang. The next week end was spent in tearing down many tons of threatening loose rock from the overhang, but there was still nothing solid to be found and the effort was useless.

Meanwhile, members of the supporting party had been studying the walls of the Dome for some new line of attack. There was one hopeful sign. Above the saddle there were indications of firm rock, though it was made inaccessible by an overhang beneath it. Hopefully, the party assembled under the overhang. Metzger climbed to the shoulders of a companion, and while others held him against the bulging wall with ropes from either side, he began to climb. Although the hour was late he managed to go thirty-five feet, putting in two parallel lines of pitons as he went.

On the fourth week end Leuthold started up via the pitons Metzger had left. He went twenty feet farther and was past the worst of the rotten rock. Occasionally a piton would not hold, but all were tested and progress was made safely. Leuthold and Metzger took turns; each advanced the line of pitons until he was exhausted and then roped down to the bottom. After a last climb of an hour and a half on the exposed face, Leuthold succeeded in reaching the top of the first basalt layer. He was on a roomy ledge fully three feet wide. He set an anchor bolt in the ledge, and the others came up readily. The ledge went around the Dome to the base of another cliff of good rock. After the first long pitch this was simple. Beyond, there was a steep grassy slope and then a group of large trees. Using the only available hand-holds, the grass, Jim Mount went up to the trees and the summit was won. It was a triumph of skill, daring, and co-operation.

THE NORTHERN PEAKS

The ideal mountain of a mountaineer possesses slopes of ice and snow as well as steep rock. Certainly it is not capped with a grove of trees, however well protected its summit by overhanging cliffs, and it is not dominated by higher slopes of parent hills alongside. Saint Peter's Dome was without doubt one of the most difficult climbs made in the Cascades, but it was scarcely a mountain. Throughout the United States there are relatively few mountains that meet the qualifications of having both good rock and ice, and climbers have tended to become specialists according to the characteristics of their vicinities. In the Cascades the specialty had been ice climbing, since most climbing was done on the volcanic peaks. All the time, however, there was a large area of unexplored and unclimbed peaks in the Cascades which possessed to a high degree the diverse qualities of the ideal mountains. These were in the tangled ranges of the northern system.

It is difficult to account for the many years of neglect of these peaks by mountaineers. Climbers from other parts of the country passed by on their way to other ranges without seeing what lay near their route. This at least was understandable. Local climbers themselves knew little of the northern system. As late as 1935 one of the climbing clubs formulated a list of "major" peaks of the Northwest. It included only one of the big mountains of the northern system, and that one not the greatest. Later a second was added but the list was still ridiculous, as perhaps any list based on such a distinction must be.

Although there is no conclusive record of the early ascents of the northern peaks, Mount Stuart was apparently one of the first to be climbed. A stick bearing the name Angus Mc-Pherson and the date 1873 is said to have been found on its summit. Stuart lies well to the side of the main chain and is rather isolated from the great constellation of the northern system. Mount Shuksan, the close neighbor and rival of Mount Baker, was climbed by Asahel Curtis and W. M. Price in 1906. For many years Stuart and Shuksan were the only popular big climbs in the northern system. New routes were found on both mountains. The Mountaineers of Seattle built a lodge at Snoqualmie Pass and from this base made innumerable climbs on the rugged peaks nearby. These peaks, though small, provided an excellent training ground for some of the later climbs made by the Mountaineers. The sharp spires above the little town of Index, a short distance from Puget Sound, attracted some attention; a cash prize was offered for the ascent of one of them. Several outings of the Mountaineers and the Mazamas were held in the heart of the northern system, but few climbs were made since too much time was spent in travel over the difficult terrain. This was very nearly the extent of climbing in the northern system until the thirties.

In the summer of 1931 Bill Degenhardt and H. V. Strandberg ventured into one of the wildest parts of the Cascades, the serrated ridges above the headwaters of the

Skagit. They encountered a serious problem as soon as they
left the valley trails. The hillsides of the region are covered
with a dense growth of brush which is almost as discourag-
ing as the cliffs above. The two climbers clawed and fought
their way to the timber-line zone. In every direction was a
bewildering number of peaks rising from expanses of glaciers. Degenhardt and Strandberg remained on the high
ridges instead of descending after each climb to the luxuries
of valley camps. They were rewarded with eight first ascents,
some on Colonial Ridge and the others in the well-named
Picket Range.

The following year saw for the first time one of the most
enthusiastic of the new pioneers in the region, Hermann F.
Ulrichs. Ulrichs, a musician and an individualist, traveled
and climbed extensively through the lonely area of the
northern system, sometimes with companions and sometimes
by himself. During the thirties he set something of a record:
twenty-one first ascents, many of them difficult. The prize
which he most sought, however, Mount Goode, eluded him.
After several attempts, including one harrowing climb
when he was pinioned to the terrible wall of the mountain,
he left the range. Ulrichs learned more of the region than
any other person and his are the best articles on the mountains of the northern system.

Through the middle thirties there was a rapid succession
of first ascents in the system. In 1936 there was a remarkable list of climbs which included Mount Agnes, Challenger,
Dome, and Goode. Each of these was technically more difficult than any of the volcanoes. The quick order in which
they were climbed is a measure of the spread of new mountaineering skills. Almost all of the difficult peaks of the

northern system were found to require pitons for safety if
not for direct aid.

Bonanza Peak, the greatest of the northern peaks, was
by an odd chance the last big mountain of the range to be
climbed. The maps of the entire northern system are seamed
with inaccuracies. Through one of the errors of the current
maps, a bench mark is shown on the summit of Bonanza.
Since few people had been to the remote points from which
the height of the mountain is visible, the climb was assumed
to be simple and to have been made by mapping parties.
However, Everett Darr, an ardent mountaineer of Portland, explored the area near the mountain and was struck
with the grandeur of the peak and with the obvious difficulty of climbing it. He later examined an early map of the
region and learned that the names of two mountains,
Bonanza and North Star, had been transposed in reprintings
of the map. The big peak had once been called North Star.
There was a bench mark, but on the mountain now bearing
the latter name. Climbers had concentrated on Mount
Goode, believing it to be the highest unclimbed summit of
the Cascades, while the greater peak a few miles to the south
was still untried.

Darr spent a total of several months during different
years in examining the sides of Bonanza. He found it a
mountain with defenses almost unparalleled in the range. On
the west side gentle slopes led fairly high on the mountain,
but from there on a vertical tower barred the way, and even
with this tower won (as it eventually was) there remained a
long distance of jagged ridge. On the northeast side a large
broken glacier seemed to offer access to several points on the
summit ridge, but these points were a long way from the

top, and again the ridge could not be traversed. The situation seemed the same on the other sides.

In 1937 a strong party camped at Holden Lake beneath the Mary Green Glacier. In between bursts of a June blizzard the route up the northeast glacier was attempted. After a long hard climb the party reached the summit ridge, with the top in sight but impossibly remote across a deep chasm. The route was abandoned. There remained a direct attack of the face above the Mary Green Glacier. Starting at two o'clock in the morning, Curtis Ijames, Joe Leuthold, and Barrie James headed toward the forbidding wall. Leuthold led up the steep rock. The face was so smooth that belays were often a hundred feet apart with no fissures available for pitons. These was an unpleasant element of danger, too, in that the cliff was swept by avalanches. Three times the climbers narrowly missed being hit. There seemed to be no hope of reaching the summit, but under the steady leadership of Leuthold the rope went slowly upward. Eight and one-half hours were spent on the cliff, and finally the party was at the summit ridge. Ijames has compared this ridge to a comb with loose teeth. Leuthold crossed it, knocking out as much of the loose rock as he could, and then stopped. The others asked why he did not go on and learned that he was on the summit. The descent lasted well into the night, and camp was not found until twenty-three hours after the start of the climb.

There are still unclimbed mountains in the Cascades' northern system. Some will prove to be easy, some difficult. Whether a first ascent is made or not, a far greater experience awaits the newcomer—discovery for himself of a land of innumerable glaciers, serrated ridges, and great mountains.

SKIS ON THE CASCADES

by *Charles D. Hessey, Jr.*

"The time will come when more people will go to Mount Hood in winter for sport than now go in summer."

The astute outdoorsman responsible for that statement wrote the words in 1903. Today Mount Hood ranks first in point of attendance of any ski area in North America, and it is doubtful if even perfect conviction could ever properly have prepared the prophet for current reality. For in 1903 the Pacific Northwest was raw and sparsely populated. Fewer people then set foot upon the mountain in an entire season than now ski there in one day. The prophecy contains no mention of speeding ropes, notes no clanking line of mechanical chairs lifting bundled skiers a mile above the timber line. Neither, apparently, did the vision encompass the snow-crawler which carries skiers higher still.

Given a bird's-eye preview of the actuality forty-five years after his prediction, our prophet would surely have exclaimed, "Every skier in the West is here today!" Then in the interests of accuracy we could reply, "Far from it, friend. Mount Hood draws only a small percentage of skiing Westerners; in fact, only a small part of those who utilize the Cascade Range for their winter sport attend

367

Mount Hood. From fiery Lassen Peak to icy Mount Baker the Cascade peaks have their centers where thousands ski. What you foresaw for Mount Hood has happened everywhere."

To assign any special merit to the Cascade Range merely because of the terrific mushrooming of the ski sport on its slopes in the past several years would be to fail in objectivity. Skiing has exploded all over the land. Given snow and an incline, people will ski. To the great majority of them it makes small difference whether the snow be on a cultivated hillside, on a sagebrush slope, or on a glacier-cloaked giant. Chair-lift, T-bar, or rope tow—give them uphill transportation and the public will ski in a pasture.

Nevertheless, as it is almost impossible to ski in the Cascades remote from the influence of at least one majestic mountain, even the packed-slope skier who rarely wanders off the rutted runs has come to see himself as blessed with respect to scenery and terrain. The big volcanoes jut into the Arctic-Alpine zone for thousands of feet, and so are timber free. On their open slopes fall such quantities of snow that summer's sharp ridges melt into winter's flowing contours.

"Where else," asks our skier who has suddenly discovered the range, "can you drive to your skiing in October and in July?" Then his face lights with this further realization as he adds, "Where else in the U.S.A. can you ski within short walking distance of your car the full twelve months?" If there are such places he does not know of them, and he is happy in the knowledge that the Cascades offer numerous such places, even if he, Mr. Average Skier, has never taken advantage of the fact.

NOT SO LONG AGO

In reading the small amount of literature available on the activities of the region's first skiers-for-sport, it becomes embarrassingly evident that he, Mr. Average Skier, has little in common with the hardy gentlemen who first dared the heights in their big snow season. Today he must have the best of hickory skis, the finest in handmade boots, the most rigid type of binding. Clothing must be light, roomy, yet warm, and tailored to the tolerance of the Society Editor's camera. A continual ululation, mournful and demanding, rises from the centers for more and longer uphill devices, preferably the type most likely to put a shine on the seat of "Pro-model" downhill pants. Better accommodations and food at lower prices, better snow clearance, more accurate weather forecasting, lighted slopes for night skiing, conveniently located hospital paraphernalia to minimize the penalties of folly—these are but a few of the things which today's skier considers necessary to the proper enjoyment of his sport. Contrast all this with the equipment available at the turn of the century, when skis were hand-hewn from a fir log, bindings made of rawhide were anything but rigid, and the entire personal wardrobe was summer's outdoor costume converted to winter use by multiplication. It seems that everything was inferior then; everything, that is, but spirit. The mountains flung down their challenge. A few men heard, and accepted.

The earliest mention of skiing in Mazama records (the Mazama Club is Portland's oldest climbing organization) was in February, 1897. At that time a party of three men made its way to Cloud Cap Inn on the northeastern side of

Mount Hood. Each man used one long pole for balance, progress, and brake. The progress was achieved by "climbing" the pole, braking by riding it hard. How crude their system seems when compared to today's perfected techniques! And yet before we crawl too far out on the thin and brittle limb of condescension, let us review the facts: in mid-winter of 1897 these men successfully completed a trip to Cloud Cap Inn at timber line on Mount Hood. At the time, it was many, many miles, and many thousands of feet in elevation from the nearest snow-free road. Even today, with all the vast increase in the skiing brotherhood, and with all the wonderful improvement in winter outdoor equipment, there are only a handful of persons sufficiently ardent to make trips of comparable difficulty.

It was only natural that by far the greater number of pioneer skiers were new Americans from the Scandinavian countries. They had found, particularly in the Pacific Northwest, a landscape and a climate similar to that of the European homeland. It was also natural that the first magnets to draw them were the volcanic giants, one or more of which dominated the horizon from all the centers of population. And yet it was not until 1914 that we find skiing mentioned in the publications of the Seattle Mountaineers. Norwegians were testing Cascade snows. Their enthusiasm was so contagious that within two short years the Mountaineers' winter outing at Paradise Valley on Mount Rainier was an annual event. Not all who attended were skiers, it is true, and the few who used the long awkward boards on that initial trip carried them clumsily across the body while climbing the trail on snowshoes. As ducks take to water, though, so do folk who love the mountains take to skiing; it is, indeed, the key which opens for them the full year's treasure of their favorite landscape. The winter outings at Paradise were continued until 1930, and since that date the Club has maintained facilities for its members at several of the skiing centers.

Improvements in technique and equipment stimulated imagination, and the years 1927 and 1928 saw the first attempts to scale Mount Rainier on ski. The route chosen was the only one feasible for skiers; early one April morning the party left Starbo Camp and started climbing Interglacier in six inches of fresh powder snow. At 9,500 feet, still a vertical mile below the summit, the lack of sufficient time became obvious and the four climbers turned their tips downward to enjoy the long descent under ideal conditions.

A second effort was made in May. This failed because of a great wind which assailed the climbers at 13,000 feet. Skiers can find a comfort in failure which summer climbers lack. The reward in this instance was 7,000 vertical feet of beautiful running.

Sigurd Hall, who later lost his life racing on another side of this same mountain, made the first successful ski ascent. The first night was spent at Steamboat Prow, where the Emmons and Winthrop Glaciers part company at 9,700 feet. In the morning the peak was sheathed in glare ice. He persevered, often forced to stamp several times until steel edges had enough purchase on the glazed surface. On the descent, skiing above 12,000 feet was out of the question, and skis had to be carried until that level was reached. There the snow had softened sufficiently to allow control, and progress thereafter was achieved in a manner more in harmony with the basic purpose of arduous ski climbs.

Here and there throughout the area, local museums display crude boards scarcely recognizable by modern standards as skis, which were used in delivering mail in the early days. With a pedestrian history such as that, it is difficult to disagree with those who know the Cascades well when they say that, insofar as skiing is concerned, its most exciting history lies ahead.

THE LAY OF THE LAND

That typical bit of western optimism is standing on two strong legs. One of those legs is the rapidly increasing population, the other is the available terrain. Any Cascades skier who gets around in his mountains will look you right in the eye and tell you that no mountains in the world offer finer terrain for skiing than do the Cascades.

"There is no argument," he avers with supreme self-confidence. "What, for instance, does a skier want in slopes? Well, that depends upon how good he is, or upon what he is used to skiing. Most skiers prefer long timber-free runs when they can get them. Just as an example, take a look at Mount Shasta. Massive, and 6,000 feet above timber line.*

"Let's say he has a taste for the bizarre along with fine terrain—and who hasn't? At Mount Lassen he can ski on fifteen feet of snow alongside boiling mud and sulphur springs. Or at Crater Lake he can run the slopes above the bluest lake on earth, on a mountain that fell in upon itself.

"Does he prefer open-woods running? The eastern slope of the Cascades with its brush-free yellow pine forests is

---

* "Timber line" is a term used freely by Mr Hessey. He refers to the limit of free skiing. To the botanist the timber line is the last tree, at about 9,500 feet, on the north side of Mount Shasta (Editor.)

made to order for him. Or, at higher elevations, the scattered alpines in the parks near timber line make picturesque and exciting natural slaloms.

"Perhaps he's from the East, and feels lost outside the confines of a trail slashed through thick forest. Where is there a more luxuriant growth of big evergreens than on the ocean side of the Cascades? He will find trails cut to his liking at Stevens Pass, Snoqualmie Pass, and at Mount Hood.

"He likes the excitement of glacier skiing? Let him come and climb Mount Baker.

"Finally, if he's a hickory-shod Daniel Boone, and wants to pioneer, there are scores of exciting peaks and skiable glaciers up to three miles long which have never known those distinctive parallel grooves."

The volcanic origin of much of the range is responsible for the type of country which most skiers know best. The penetration of the towering cones into arctic climatic conditions and their ready accessibility to heavily populated areas have made them the logical focal points of winter sports activity. Ancient volcanism also has been generous to the skier in supplanting heavy forest with barren lava beds in certain sections. Throughout the Cascades the distinguishing characteristic is the lofty peak, white with snow, suspended above a blue haze covering miles of surrounding forest. That is the classical representation of the range. In fact, the word volcano is so often associated with the Cascade mountains that even today it surprises many Westerners to learn that the range also contains, in a granite wilderness in north-central Washington, what the Forest Service calls "the most rugged ranger district in the United States." The skier blesses the volcanoes, for in their solitary immensity they provide him with runs which are among the world's finest. Nevertheless, he is glad to hear that his range also includes the other kind of peak, massed in chaotic profusion, frothed with living ice, and not lacking in that superior angularity of sculpture which distinguishes granite forms. These are the North Cascades. They extend from the crags of the Stuart Range, in mid-state, north to the Canadian boundary. No simple chain is this, but a complex of ranges one hundred miles wide, much of which is only now being thoroughly mapped.

Figures on the number of glacier-bearing peaks cannot be accurate until the maps are published, yet it is safe to say that well over one hundred such summits gleam in that wilderness of forest, stream, and rock. This is significant to the skier in denoting heavy snowfall, great walled cirques far above timber line, and a mountain landscape as exciting in its potentialities as any in America. Everywhere the main valley floors are low, well under 2,000 feet in elevation, yet even there the snowfall is heavy. The peaks average about 8,000 feet, with many reaching more than 1,000 feet higher, so runs of impressive length and fall are to be found. While much of the country is far too rugged to attack on ski, there is much more than enough superlative terrain to last out the winters of a man's life.

Perhaps the finest midwinter sport is obtained on the eastern slopes. Along the main axis of the range, absolute timber line occurs at lower elevations as one travels north. For example, at Mount Shasta it is found at about 9,500 feet, while at Mount Rainier only a few isolated alpines grow near the 7,000-foot contour. This trend is reversed as one goes east in the mountains. Alpine larch and white-bark pine find foothold above 8,000 feet in the eastern section of the North Cascades. Since the clouds have been raked by the peaks to the west, snowfall is lighter, the air is drier and colder, and the occurrence of forests at high elevations provides shelter in the zone of deepest snow and consistently freezing temperatures. To anyone who has groped his way downhill through a typical Cascade snowstorm, the advantages of midwinter skiing in the eastern section are obvious.

FORECAST: SNOW

Everyone who has listened to conversations among big-game hunters knows that there are only three sizes of bear: a cub, a yearling cub, and "the biggest bear I ever saw in my life!" Man's natural propensity for exaggeration also operates fully when describing snow depth, the standard estimates being: a trace, six inches, three feet, and "at least twenty feet of snow!" Undoubtedly the greatest snowfall in the United States occurs on Mount Olympus in the Olympic Mountains, where most of the approximate annual two hundred and fifty inches of moisture falls in crystal form. The Cascades, too, are abundantly blessed, the common criticism leveled against them by skiers being, "Too much snow." It would be difficult, in the average year, for an honest advocate to plead innocent to that charge. Men interested financially in ski resorts might advertise "Twenty-foot snow depths, and lots of winter sunshine," but skiers know how often and how hard the storms must strike to build up snow packs of such dimensions.

Mild in temperature, severe in storm—that is Cascade weather in capsule form. From Lassen to Baker, in those few places where precipitation records are kept in the deep-snow country, the fabulous twenty-foot depth is a common occurrence. Owing to the activities of snow-survey crews and easier access to areas of heaviest precipitation, information on relative snowfall at different elevations is most nearly complete in the southern portion of the range. The snows of Lassen Peak provide water for power and irrigation. Government agencies, planning ahead, measure snow for water content each spring, and the snow is sampled as high as 8,500 feet. The deepest snow at Lassen has been found near 8,000 feet in the Lake Helen basin. At the Sulphur Works, less than 2,000 feet lower, snow depth has measured at times almost ten feet less.

At 8,000 feet on Mount Shasta, the snow stick near Shasta Alpine Lodge has registered over 330 inches of snow. This, too, is considerably in excess of depths recorded at lower elevations on the same mountain. Measurements taken at the rim of Crater Lake, over 8,000 feet above sea level, again demonstrate increasing snow depth up to that elevation.

While there are no statistics available in the northern portion of the range to prove whether the same is true in that region, confirmatory evidence exists. The development of the glaciers between 8,000 feet and 10,000 feet on Mount Rainier and other lofty summits is marked. Measurements taken at Rainier at two places on the same side of the mountain offer an interesting comparison. At Longmire, 2,761 feet, annual precipitation is about 75 inches, while at Paradise Valley, 5,550 feet, it is 100 inches. An average of 600 inches of snow is measured annually at the latter spot. The greatest amount noted was in the winter of 1916-17 when, although the record was begun after the snow season was under way, 790 inches of snow were recorded. Unhappily, during the winter of 1945-46, heaviest snowfall year on record in some sections of Oregon and Washington, no one was stationed at Paradise Valley.

One wonders most about snow depth on Mount Baker. In April, 1946, twenty-five feet of snow covered the Lodge area. The Lodge is situated at only 4,200 feet, and is, moreover, located at least partially in Mount Baker's "storm shadow." The peak lies well to the west. With such depths at so low an elevation, and with increasing depths to 8,000 feet fairly well established, it seems that the annual accumulation of snow on the flanks of Mount Baker itself must be prodigious. Indeed, its well-developed glaciers indicate that this is so. Snow surveys are not made here, as virtually no irrigating is done, and power dams across Baker's streams can depend on melting ice if snow should fail.

Temperatures throughout the range are moderate, tempered by storms moving in from the Pacific. Average winter readings at all the ski areas range above 20 degrees. An occasional cold wave coming from the north or east may push the mercury below zero, but such waves are usually of short duration and serve to remind the skier, tenderly thawing the white spot on his nose with the palm of his hand, how lucky he is that his mountains seldom punish him in this way. And if the frequency of storm has its disadvantages, there are words to say for it, too. Seldom does a skier in the Cascades use yesterday's surface for his swinging, and the art of deep-snow skiing is still practiced.

The phenomenon which meteorologists call an "inversion" is one of those things that the Far-Western skier hopes will occur, if it must occur, in the middle of the week rather than on Saturday, when the friend from Denver is here to try out Cascade snows. The type of inversion which brings a thawing blanket of air to the high passes, it must be noted, will probably not happen more than three times during the season, and almost certainly not at all after mid-January. The friend from Denver would understand a chinook wind, a breeze which warms as it descends from the mountains, melting all the snow at lower elevations. But what would he say if, after skiing all day in sunshine at an ideal 24 degrees, nightfall should find the thermometer registering 33 degrees, as warm air from the western slope poured over the divide with a breath as soft as spring? Strangely enough, there is a remedy for this apparently hopeless situation. Ordinarily, to find better snow a skier climbs higher; but in the case of the inversion he clamps his skis to the carrier and in the morning drives down into the valleys of the eastern slope. Soon frost is forming on the car windows. Trees are still laden with snow, and frost feathers glisten in the little glades. The cold air lies in the valley bottoms like a lake of lesser density. The inversion is usually of short duration, rarely lasting over two days, but during this time the east-side skier has the better conditions.

What is the best time of year for skiing in the Cascades? There will be arguments over this, but if I had a month's vacation and wanted to spend it skiing somewhere in these mountains I would choose mid-March to mid-April. During that period the snow has reached its greatest depth, days are longer, morning sunshine is common, and the morning surface is quite likely to be from two to six inches of fluffy snow on a firm base—the skier's fondest hope. Restricted to a seven-day choice, I would select the first week in April. Seven winters spent in mountain cabins above 4,500 feet taught me that this week provides, for the skier who doesn't mind early rising, the most uniformly excellent conditions of the year.

These dates and conditions, I repeat, are for those who do not mind early rising—skiers who like to cruise around. If the vacationist wishes to visit one of the centers and to ski beside the lifts, it makes small difference what time of year he chooses, unless he is a camera fan. If he is, he'll take my dates. The chances of powder snow plus sunshine are better then.

THE CENTERS, NOW AND TO BE

So fast is the sport of skiing outgrowing present facilities, and so insistent is the demand for more developments, that any description of ski areas must in all wisdom be kept general. Nevertheless, major omissions in this survey are not likely. For years to come, further developments probably will take place adjacent to areas now in use. Much of the ideal terrain along the main crest, as in the Goat Rocks area of Washington, is held by the Forest Service under Primitive Area designation and cannot be developed. Also in Washington are the great North Cascade Primitive Area and the Glacier Peaks Recreation Area, both closed to commercialization. Much blame has been heaped upon the National Park Service for its attitude toward the modern trend to mechanized skiing; in Washington, at least, the Forest Service is withholding even more terrain from exploitation, and between the two departments a very sizable section of the most exciting mountain country in the nation has been removed from possible resort development.

The skier sees this as good or bad, depending largely upon

just what phase of his complex sport most appeals to him. In all fairness, however, and as a note of caution to those who thoughtlessly advocate discarding the National Park idea in favor of building a huge skiing "plant," it must be stated that no thorough survey of potential ski areas has been made, and that every center along the range has a wealth of excellent mountain country to choose from, exclusive of National Parks and Primitive Areas. A few such spots are widely known; a few are famous locally. As we begin this tour of Cascade skiing centers, present and "perhaps," I promise to introduce to you some of those little-known places. Wax up, everybody!

We are going to start at Lassen Peak, 10,453 feet, near the southern terminus of the Cascade Range, and work our way north to the Canadian border. Lassen Peak is a long journey south from Mount Baker, but gliding silently among alpine hemlock en route to the Lake Helen basin on a February morning the skier might not guess it. An average depth of twenty-four feet of snow has been measured in this area, and depths of eighteen feet are not at all uncommon. At the Sulphur Works, 6,700 feet, an area is kept open and operated by the National Park Service throughout the winter, with tows, restaurant, and warming hut available. This is the usual starting point for winter touring parties, but when the Park highways are open in late spring it is possible to drive to 8,500 feet between snowbanks more than twice the height of your car. The climb of Lassen itself is safer and more pleasant then, with a good probability of fine corn snow for your descent. Lassen Volcanic National Park is rich in contrasts, with deep snows and boiling springs, and summer snow fields shining above valleys of subtropical warmth. As in so many areas of superlative terrain in the Cascades, the absence of large population centers nearby is merely postponing the day when Lassen Peak is as famous for its skiing as for its recent volcanism.

The ski fields of Mount Shasta, 14,161 feet, are on a scale that is difficult to comprehend fully. The mountain is one of the giants of the range, and its tremendous bulk towers high above its base. There is rumor of a big development here, with a funicular all the way to the summit. This seems likely to materialize.

Winter climbers of the white massif have enjoyed downhill runs approaching 10,000 feet in vertical distance. The center of skiing activity, however, has been in the vicinity of the Sierra Club's lodge at 8,000 feet, above which the slopes rise in unbroken ermine fields to the summit rocks. Absolute timber line is somewhere over 9,000 feet, but most of the matted storm-twisted growth at that elevation is buried under the phenomenal winter snows, and skiers at the lodge level consider themselves at timber line. The summit climb, of course, is not for everyone. However, when the day comes that mechanical means for reaching the upper slopes are available, Mount Shasta skiers will be blessed, for skiing is done on the north side of this peak, a fact which pays dividends in snow quality.

From two lovely California peaks, each with a personality all its own, we now move into Oregon to a spot distinctly different. Crater Lake is the basis for one of our National Parks, and "the bluest water in the world" loses none of its exciting beauty in a winter setting. There are no winter facilities here, and most skiing is done close to the rim. The opportunities for touring, however, are superla-

tive, with enchanting views of that incredibly colored water
the reward for keeping high. To the graduate skier, the one
who has learned that there is far more to skiing than merely
sliding repetitiously down a grooved run, a winter tour in
this region will be a bright memory long after the mind has
lost the flavor of any one day of skiing with crowds on a lift.

Central in Oregon's Cascades, and just west of Bend and
south of McKenzie Pass, is a fine group of volcanic peaks
over 10,000 feet high called the Three Sisters. The North
Sister does not attract as a skiing mountain, but the South
Sister looks made to order. Perhaps the Collier Glacier on
the Middle Sister will best reward the spring skier. One
morning late in May I found myself up there without skis,
and have been regretting the oversight ever since. At that
time of year the glacier is a smooth ribbon of perfect corn
snow, not steep enough except near the summit to be cre-
vassed to a dangerous extent. It is one of those runs which
allow perfect relaxation. The skier just stands on his skis
and lets the ground unroll, or, if he chooses, he may sway in
lazy rhythm as he links his sweeping swings.

There is a wealth of excellent terrain on both sides of the
McKenzie River Highway at McKenzie Pass. In summer
the lava flows look like black glaciers; few trees have gained
foothold, so most of the area is open slope. The Sisters and
Mount Washington provide the striking scenic background
which Westerners take for granted with their skiing.

While there is no development for skiers at McKenzie
Pass, a popular area has recently come into being to the
north near Santiam Pass. The Hoodoo Bowl boasts excellent
open slopes, ski tows, and shelter, just forty-three miles
from Bend. While the Bowl itself is situated on a butte un-

pretentious in dimension or form, the area borrows grandeur
from nearby Three Fingered Jack, a solitary soaring spire
surrounded by treeless and semi-open country.

There are comforts provided at Hoodoo Bowl, but to
reach 10,495-foot Mount Jefferson, twenty miles to the
north, the skier must make serve what his back will support.
Many consider the Mount Jefferson area Oregon's finest
scenery. The mountain itself is a very steep cone, less perfectly adapted to mass skiing than Hood, yet offering the
adventurous a wealth of exciting slopes. To the few who
have done it, the tour from Mount Hood south along the
Oregon Skyline Trail to Mount Jefferson stands out as the
skiing experience of a lifetime.

To give statistics on the number of skiers who use the
Mount Hood region is useless, for each succeeding year
finds increasing thousands availing themselves of this, the
largest development on the Pacific Coast. There are chair-
lifts, rope tows, lodgings to suit each purse, places to eat,
and places in which to purchase or rent complete skiing outfits. The slopes rising above Timberline Lodge are immense
and are well suited to skiers of every ability; when storm
takes over the mountain the numerous trails through timber
provide sheltered running. On nearby Multorpor Mountain there is a jump and plenty of practice terrain. Tom,
Dick, and Harry Bowl is a cleared north slope ideally
adapted to slalom racing.

It is said that an average of fifteen hundred people climb
Mount Hood each year. Those who do it on ski are rewarded with one of the classic runs of the West, with a loss
in altitude of some 7,000 feet in a distance of about seven
miles.

Around on the northeast side of the mountain, Cloud Cap Inn overlooks the Eliot Glacier, where summer skiers keep residual snows patterned into August. Perhaps someday the residents of the Hood River Valley will have their own development here, where 11,225-foot Mount Hood shows its loveliest profile.

North of Hood the first big break in the Cascades occurs where the Columbia River rushes through to the Pacific. This marks the Oregon-Washington boundary, but, political demarcations aside, it also denotes a modification in the character of the range. Look south from the air over the Columbia. The snow peaks of Oregon extend in a straight line, each one riding the crest of the chain. Now do an about-face. In Washington two glacier-garbed giants stand guard on the same east-west plane and about twenty-five miles apart. The one to the west, the "sport," is Mount Saint Helens, 9,671 feet, the most symmetrical of all the volcanic cones. In addition to its perfection of form there are other good reasons why this spot will someday take its place with the major skiing centers. Its only access road touches mirroring Spirit Lake at the northern base of the peak, therefore, as at Mount Shasta, skiing here is done on north slopes. Timber line on Saint Helens is very low, at about 4,000 feet. This leaves over a vertical mile of timber-free skiing, which compares favorably with that of much loftier summits. Most of the mountain clubs of the Pacific Northwest plan annual climbs of this peak for May or June, and take their skis along. The sides of the cone are steep, and the descent calls for full utilization of ankles, knees, shoulders, and head. It must be skied. The full distance to Spirit Lake, involving a drop of 6,400 feet, is made on ski well into May.

When the Fourth of July rolls around, most Westerners think of fishing, swimming, rodeos, or some other seasonal pastime. You and I, though, being skiers, will think of Mount Adams and the 6,500-foot drop right back to our car which the mountain offers us while other people are popping firecrackers. This 12,307-foot peak is a massive pile of igneous rock which in winter and spring offers wonderful timber-line skiing on all sides—to anyone who is willing to make the long trek in. On only the south side may the summit be reached on ski, its glaciers having eaten so deeply into the rest of the peak that skiing is out of the question. In the average year the road is open to Coldsprings Camp by July 1. The climb takes about seven hours from Coldsprings; but when you have seen the sun incarnadine Mount Hood with its first fiery rays, and then ignite Saint Helens with the morning flame, when you have watched Mount Adams' own dawn-shadow race over miles of rolling forest, then you must count those climbing hours well spent. The run itself will find you shouting for joy.

Halfway between Mount Adams and Mount Rainier lie Goat Rocks, a designated Primitive Area of striking beauty. Several small glaciers still exist on the flanks of Curtiss Gilbert Peak, 8,201 feet, Ives Peak, and Old Snowy Mountain. I know of no finer area for high touring than this region which offers extensive reaches of alpine parks and vast sheltered timber-free basins. A strong pair of legs is needed to attain summer skiing here; but I cannot say enough in praise of Old Snowy's Tieton Glacier.

Mount Rainier, 14,408 feet, largest and most often pictured of the Cascade peaks, needs no introduction. Tens of thousands use it for winter sport, and this despite the fact that only one small section (Paradise Valley) is accessible during the eight-month "winter" season. There are tows and overnight accommodations at Paradise. The run back to the valley from 10,000-foot Camp Muir is one of those beautiful roller-coaster rides, gift of the glaciers which sculptured it.

Perfect terrain greets the ski mountaineer on every side of the giant peak. Probably dearest to his heart is the run of Interglacier on its northeast slope—a favorite in June. Skiing in the vicinity of the Park is by no means confined to the mountain itself. Although closed through the winter, Chinook Pass, 5,440 feet, on U.S. Highway 410, draws skiers for October and July skiing. Just outside the eastern boundary of the Park in the valley of Morse Creek lies the Gold Hill area, home to a group of Yakima skiers. The popular answer to the weekly question, "Where shall we ski tomorrow?" is, "Let's take a trip." The favorite tour is a seven-mile circle to "Crystal Bowl," a spacious cirque on Crystal Mountain. The view from the summit encompasses all the volcanoes from Hood to Baker, with Mount Rainier close enough to touch. Slopes are open and sheltered. Most Yakima skiers, however, use the American River Ski Bowl, a cleared north slope which, because of its low elevation, has a short season of about ten weeks. It offers overnight accommodations and tow service on week ends.

Snoqualmie Pass, 3,010 feet, is probably the most used area in the state, because of its proximity to Seattle. The many runs are largely the result of clearing operations, as the Cascades at that elevation are heavily forested.

The fastest growing center in Washington is at Stevens Pass, where trails and open slopes are served by several rope

tows and at least one long T-bar lift. Snow of good quality
is the rule here, where the ferocity of frequent winter storms
is tempered by a wise selection of skiing area. Thinking in
terms of winter wind, the Barrier Ridge is well named.

Miles to the west of the main divide lies the most north-
erly of the old volcanoes in this country, and the most pho-
togenic popular ski area in the United States. Mount Baker,
the graceful glacier-robed cone, and Mount Shuksan, burly
ice-fractured granite massif, cradle between them some of
the most enchanting alpine terrain to be found anywhere.
While the accessible runs are magnificent, and the scenic
background is of such an order as to make anyone an artist
with a camera, improvements have not kept pace. Shelter
and food are available, but the tows serve none of the long
runs. Even so, skiing in such a setting is highly satisfying,
and thousands avail themselves of it. Snow-crawling vehi-
cles are used to help those who care less for the tows to
reach the long untracked runs.

TOURING COUNTRY

Stand at the top of a ski lift and ask the first rider to
escape it this question, "What is a ski mountaineer?" If,
after a minute of pondering, your answer comes, "It has
two legs," you will have heard the truth, but, praise be, not
all the truth. The ski mountaineer also is the poet of the
skiing world. There are two of him. One is he whose ritual-
istic insistence on reaching the topmost pinnacle brings somber overtones to every outing; the other is one whose chief
delight is simply to be in the company of noble peaks. Both
look upon Mr. Average Skier—that man who rides the lift
all winter and is content—as a voluntarily caged bird whose

wings do him small good. Both are astonished at the modern
trend in skiing, with all the emphasis upon racing. To them
skiing is an esthetic activity; to admit into it the element of
Time is as though the Metropolitan were to choose its oper-
atic stars on the basis of vocal speed in place of tonal quality.

"But isn't travel among high mountains in winter dangerous?" people want to know. Like every sort of endeavor,
risky or routine, the activities of a ski mountaineer are accomplished one step at a time, and the danger to himself is
proportionate to the careful application of his judgment. It
is a man's carelessness with too familiar things that leads to
most accidents, as in the home and in cars. The danger lurk-
ing in a snow-covered glacier is just as real as that of the
family bathtub, but its very strangeness calls forth the ut-
most in skill and judgment; and this, in a sense, makes it
safer.

There is not the space, nor is this the place, to dwell upon
techniques and equipment, to recite the many do's and dont's
of this very comprehensive sport. One of the most stressed
and important of the dont's—that against skiing alone—I
have violated many times in hundreds of miles of high-
country skiing. To share your trip is always best, both in
joy and safety, but the schedules which rule men's lives are
not always flexible enough to grant concurrent freedom to
skiing friends. I take along my well-developed bump of caution, a prayer, and some experience, and these have stood
me in good stead. The risk—that factor which can never
accurately be calculated—is paid for in the sense of un-
bounded freedom which the untracked snows above timber
line beget.

For this is the country in the Cascades, as in other ranges, that woos the touring skier most persuasively. If tranquillity is the charm of the forest, excitement is the motif at timber line. The skiers trudging up from deep valleys under heavy packs feel a fine quickening of the pulse, a delicious lightening of the load, as they near the snow fields, immaculate and immeasurable, of the high country. They feel that this high world is more of heaven than of earth. Its beauty is the expansive beauty of the morning sky, its brilliance that of the sun at noon; as pure and frosty as the stars of night are the winds that move across it.

Disappointment and reward are the treasures of a ski mountaineer. It is impossible to call a high mountain tour a failure. If the objective is not gained, there still will be gain. The touring skier starts out, hoping for the best and prepared for the worst, and the worst was my allotment in the spring of '48. You will recall this as the year of the Pacific Northwest's tragic floods. For twenty-seven days I lived under the conditions which made those floods inevitable. In the following brief account of one skier's trip into one small section of the Cascade Range, I will try to indicate what that section has to offer, and to produce some intimations as to why, despite the multiplied frustrations, I have not considered the trip a failure.

Five of us, intending to repeat the previous year's spring outing, had supplies taken by pack horse to the Lyman Lake cabin in September. This is in the Lake Chelan watershed in north-central Washington. For reasons business or domestic, all four of my companions were forced to cancel their plans. Two projects decided me on going. One was to complete a Kodachrome record of the Lyman Lake area, the other to put skis for the first time on the Chickamin Glacier.

The Lake Chelan launch received me on April 24, sped me up the winding waterway between towering ranges, and let me off at the mouth of Railroad Creek, where the Holden passenger bus was waiting. At Holden, a mining camp, shortly after my arrival, light rain turned to snow with flakes nearly the size of dollar bills. This began accumulating on the two feet of old snow that lay about. During the night, snug in the Holden Boy Scout cabin, I was awakened by the manifold voices of a stiff blow, and found myself cabin-bound all the next day by a booming blizzard. The following morning under perfect skies I started out, pack laden, toward the walls of massive Bonanza Peak and the velvet ski fields of North Star Mountain.

As weather is unpredictable in any mountain country, a high cabin for a touring base is desirable if not essential. Lyman Lake is ideal because it combines perfect ski slopes, unexcelled scenery, and a sturdy log cabin. From the afternoon of April 26 until the morning of May 17 I was the sole occupant of that shelter, and on twenty-one of those twenty-two days, snow fell. At a time of year when normally the fourteen-foot snow pack would have settled at least four feet, the depth was maintained throughout my stay. Of course, my photographic project suffered. Three fair mornings, only one of which was right for color pictures, fell to me. On the finest of these I climbed the swells of North Star Park, crossed the buttressing southwest ridge beneath the west peak, then made long zigzag tracks to the middle summit, accomplishing the last hundred feet without skis along a rock-studded wind-swept ridge patterned with ptarmigan tracks. Many factors contribute to make the view from North Star a memorable one, contrast being the greatest. Eastward the black and rust-daubed towers of Bonanza provide a dramatic backdrop for the flawless expanse of the North Star slope. Slightly to the west of south is Chiwawa Mountain with its Lyman Glacier, backed by the snow-plastered wall of Fortress Mountain, continually grumbling with avalanche thunder. This is a granite landscape; but eleven miles to the southwest, rearing in purity and grace from an ice field eight miles wide, is the lovely volcanic peak called Glacier. The deep trench of the Agnes leads north-ward, and in that direction, too, the peaks extend in multiple form like waves of a turbulent sea. The blue-white massif of Dome, upon whose beautiful Chickamin Glacier I had de-signs, fixed my attention. This was May, yet with a mid-winter landscape; it was difficult to realize that in the We-natchee Valley people were celebrating an apple-blossom festival.

Daily I skied on new powder snow during the corn snow season, and every day I thought, "Surely the weather will break tomorrow." On May 17, unable to postpone my de-parture longer, I left in fog and a light snowfall, crossing 6,500-foot Cloudy Pass to start my long journey down the Agnes.

There are several sharp memories in connection with those miles. Uncertain of the trail, I made cautious progress. It was work. In the heavy forest below 4,000 feet the snow was deeply hollowed and littered with wind-scattered debris from the trees. I remember the bear I frightened in Agnes Meadows, and the first trillium blooming under trees beside seven feet of snow. I remember standing in an avalanche track at the base of Needle Peak, my attention caught by the

rushing sound of running snow. In a twisting corridor below
the sharp summit high above me I watched the avalanche
race, running its serpentine channel in at least eight distinct
waves, each wave crashing across a blocking wedge of rock
in thunderous spray and coming to rest on a slope of moderate degree at a safe distance above me.

Pitched over a soft bed of boughs on the snow, my mountain tent that night was a palace in the wilderness. Morning
welcomed me with perfect skies which clouded over soon
after noon. At the junction of the two forks of the Agnes
I was delighted to find large patches of bare ground under
the big trees, and one of these I made my permanent camp,
loving the scent of moist earth after three weeks of snow.
At nightfall the skies were clearing again, and occasional
peeks through the tent opening during the night revealed
an unblemished field of stars. At 3:30 A.M. I was preparing
breakfast under the blue-black canopy, my hopes high for
the day's adventure; at 4:00 A.M. the sky was cloudy once
more.

Unwilling to consider the day a total loss, I decided to
scout my trail. One of the big problems of wilderness skiing
is the streams. A log four feet in diameter bridged the South
Fork, but my hope for the West Fork was based upon an
avalanche bridge which, I had decided, must exist at the
foot of Agnes Peak. I therefore crossed the log and started
up the valley of the West Fork, at the head of which, about
eight miles distant, lay the Chickamin and Dana Glaciers.

Every mountain range has sections which make one feel,
"This is the very heart of the range." This attribute attaches
in strong degree to the headwaters of the West Fork of the

Agnes. Only a very few have ever seen it, and it is probable that fewer than six men have ever stood at the foot of the Chickamin. In summer the way is barred by two wearisome miles of brush. This would be no problem to me, as I could ski across it. In shortly over an hour I was approaching the northern base of Agnes Peak and had verified the existence of my bridging avalanche snow, which I crossed as though treading on eggs; it would easily have supported a loaded truck. This put me in the Meadows. Two miles westward shimmered the West Fork falls, portal to the ice-hung valley I intended visiting. Surging above my snow bridge in one tremendous aspiration of 5,500 feet, the lovely Agnes Peak now wore a filmy veil of falling snow. The way before me looked perfectly open, the only possible difficulty being potential slide danger at the falls.

A light rain began just as I retired that night, and continued intermittently until midmorning, following which the sun came out. It grew very hot, and thunder growled from the cloud-bundled peaks. The streams started rising and were off-color; but as soon as Agnes Peak's afternoon shadow fell across me there was a sudden chill, and I thought, "This will check the runoff; I needn't worry."

It was a beautiful night and a perfect morning. The snow was crisp. My heart sang as I packed camera and film and food for lunch and breakfast, which I would eat on the trail to save time. Shouldering my skis, I walked the few yards to the stream and to my log. There I stood and stared. In the middle of the stream the log was lightly awash, but worse yet, I could no longer even reach the log. This was the beginning of the flood, and the crowning frustration for me. I returned to camp, assembled my pack, and continued down the Agnes on ski until, on this twenty-first day of May, at a point under 2,000 feet in elevation, I finally ran out of snow.

And so, as I write this, the Chickamin Glacier is still a virgin ski field. Several miles northward the large Inspiration Glacier on Eldorado Peak also is awaiting its first ski tracks. Perhaps these two will be the most rewarding to those who finally reach them, yet there are many others of nearly equal grandeur, nor are the beautiful untried runs limited to the large glaciers. Scores of summits devoid of ice offer timber-free running in settings of harmonious majesty.

There is avalanche danger, of course. The forested slopes of every valley are scarred with the tracks of great slides, and the distant booming of crashing snow is common daytime music in winter and spring. The great timber-crushing slides are the exception, however. One experience in a heavy January snowstorm near Cascade Pass taught me why. The mountains are so steep that the snow starts running as soon as a few inches accumulate, and during a heavy snowfall the thunder of slides is a steady roar, a symphony of storm— background music for the ballet of swirling flakes. And if terror sweeps along on the big slides, beauty can ride with the small ones. In the high valley of Park Creek, on a spring day when the east face of Booker Mountain was very active, a sudden rocket of snow as white as an egret's feather plummeted 1,500 feet into space. Gone in an instant, the sudden breath-taking spectacle left an indelible impression.

These, then, are the gifts of the Cascade Range to the adventurer-on-ski: mountain scenery unsurpassed, and the chance to pioneer. Both attributes are priceless to the people of a nation with a heritage such as ours, and that more American skiers will turn to our range, to the ever-white section of this ever-green land, is the friendly wish of all of us who ski the high Cascades.

APPENDIX

by Weldon F. Heald

1

The following is a list of named Cascade Peaks over 9,000 feet in elevation arranged in order from the south end of the range to the north. There are several hundred summits from 7,000 to 9,000 feet high. Numbers in parentheses indicate the eleven great, snow-capped fire-mountains.

NORTHERN CALIFORNIA

Brokeoff Mountain	9,232 feet	Mount Shasta (1)	14,161 feet
Mount Diller	9,086	(Shastina)	12,433
Lassen Peak	10,453		

OREGON

Mount McLoughlin	9,493 feet	Middle Sister (3)	10,039 feet
Mount Thielsen	9,178	North Sister (4)	10,094
Bachelor Butte	9,060	Mount Jefferson (5)	10,495
Broken Top	9,165	Mount Hood (6)	11,225
South Sister (2)	10,352		

WASHINGTON

Mount Saint Helens (7)	9,671 feet	Bonanza Peak	9,500 feet
Mount Adams (8)	12,307	Mount Buckner	9,090
Mount Rainier (9)	14,408	Mount Goode	9,300
(Little Tahoma)	11,117	Mount Logan	9,080
Mount Stuart	9,470	Jack Mountain	9,070
Glacier Peak (10)	10,436	Mount Baker (11)	10,750
Mount Maude	9,110	Mount Shuksan	9,030
Mount Fernow	9,100	Mount Redoubt	9,055

399

II

The twelve National Forests of the Cascade Range, with location of Forest Supervisor's headquarters, are from south to north:

NORTHERN CALIFORNIA

Lassen .... Susanville   Shasta......... Mount Shasta City

OREGON

Rogue River .... Medford   Willamette .... Eugene
Deschutes .... Bend   Mount Hood .... Portland
Umpqua ... ... Roseburg

WASHINGTON

Columbia .... Vancouver, Wn.   Chelan .... Okanogan
Snoqualmie .... Seattle   Mount Baker   ... ... Bellingham
Wenatchee .... Wenatchee

Information about these National Forests can be obtained from United States Forest Service Regional Headquarters, 630 Sansome Street, San Francisco 11, for the California section; and Box 4137, Post Office Building, Portland 8, for Oregon and Washington. Maps and folders descriptive of the individual Forests can also be secured from the supervisor's headquarters in the above listed towns.

III

The nine Forest Service Primitive Areas * with acreage and the National Forests in which they are located are:

Caribou Peak	Lassen N. F, California	14,443 acres
Thousand Lakes Valley	Lassen N. F., California	16,335
Mountain Lakes	Rogue River N. F., Oregon	23,071
Three Sisters	Willamette-Deschutes, Oregon	246,728
Mount Jefferson	Willamette-Deschutes-Mount Hood, Oregon	86,700
Mount Hood	Mount Hood N. F., Oregon	14,800

* See footnote, page 112.

Mount Adams   Columbia N. F., Washington   42,411
Goat Rocks   Columbia-Snoqualmie, Washington   82,600
North Cascade   Mount Baker-Chelan, Washington   801,000

IV

The mountain clubs of the Pacific Northwest which center most of their activities in the Cascade Range are listed below. There are several others, not included, with interests in the Olympic Mountains, Coast Range, and mountains of the interior. The two California clubs are primarily Sierra Nevada organizations, but are listed since their interests are state wide and cover the Lassen and Shasta regions.

CALIFORNIA

California Alpine Club, 917 Pacific Building, San Francisco
Sierra Club, 1050 Mills Tower, 220 Bush Street, San Francisco

OREGON

Chemeketans, 1180 North Winter Street, Salem
Crag Rats, Hood River
Mazamas, 520 S W. Yamhill Street, Portland
Obsidians, 2181 Washington Street, Eugene
Pathfinders, 534 N. E. Prescott Street, Portland
Skyliners, Bend
Trails Club of Oregon, P O. Box 243, Portland
Wy'east Climbers, 8823 N. Willamette Boulevard, Portland
Y.M.C.A. Mountaineers, 831 S. W. 6th Avenue, Portland

WASHINGTON

Cascadians, P O Box 123, Yakima
Mountaineers, Inc, P O. Box 122, Seattle (chapters also in Tacoma and
    Everett)
Mount Baker Club, P.O. Box 73, Bellingham
Mount Saint Helens Club, P.O. Box 843, Longview
Wanderers, 414 Capitol Way, Olympia
Washington Alpine Club, P.O. Box 353, Seattle

INDEX

Printed in the USA
CPSIA information can be obtained
at www.ICGtesting.com
LVHW051941160923
758204LV00033B/194